PLANT A NEW SEED
REVISED

SONNY FISHBACK
Aka Black Gold

I don't know why, I just thought I was suppose to do that. You see, it started a long time ago, when I was a slave. As soon as I would see you, I would just put my hands in my pocket on my knife. As a matter of fact, every time I would see a black face something would rise up inside of me and say, **"call him something ornery, do something to him, he ain't nothing! Call him a nigger like the slave master trained us to do long time ago."** Do you know why we do it? Read the story, **"THE SOLUTION"**

Trafford
PUBLISHING

www.trafford.com

North America & international
toll-free: 1 888 232 4444 (USA & Canada)
phone: 250 383 6864 ♦ fax: 250 383 6804
email: info@trafford.com

The United Kingdom & Europe
phone: +44 (0)1865 722 113 ♦ local rate: 0845 230 9601
facsimile: +44 (0)1865 722 868 ♦ email: info.uk@trafford.com

Over two hundred years ago obedient soldiers for the devil like Willy Lynch and Jim Crow did something that was so terrifying, ornery, hateful, and heartless until it's effect is still felt today. They instilled fear, which was designed to result into permanent insecurity in black slave's hearts. And this implantation became basically hereditary.

They made blacks beat blacks, kill blacks, insult blacks, and brainwash blacks, under the threat of being beat, hanged, or killed themselves if they didn't do it. He stated that this action would destroy black's confidence and dignity forever.

His most effective tool was the words and labels he insisted they wear. Words!... words like nigger, shiftless, lazy, ignorant, no-good, dog, coon, ho, bitch... all titles... Titles that we black people carry on still today... Daily'... Even in jest to each other!

Willy's whole theory was based around getting black people to accept certain words and attitudes. He felt, if these people would only accept these negative words as being truth about themselves, spoken long enough and violent enough to each other, they would naturally hate each other on sight and eventually destroy each other forever. Never gaining respect from other cultures on a massive level or respect themselves.

What Willy Lynch did back then was indeed a terrible thing, installing hatred, fear, and disgust in black people's heart against each other. But that is not nearly the problem after all of these years. Oh there is no question who planted the seed, but it is US! US! US!... that keeps watering it!! We keep watering it! You keep watering it we keep watering it, so it has to continue to grow! Isn't that pitiful?

You see Willy knew The Holy Scriptures were true. He knew that if you create this character of nigger mentality, it would have to bring about four or five other characters with it. Then each one of those characters would eventually bring a foul character with them, each one with a name filled with hate, murder, robbery dis-trust, paranoia, lying, stealing, ignorance and other negative characteristics, all Sin... they were all design to become Sin some day, just as soon as they becomes full grown.

Willy and his co-workers knew that The Scripture had long ago proclaimed that after Sin has become full grown it has to bring Death! ..According to The Creator of The Universe.

James 1:15
and sin when it is fully matured, brings forth death

INDEX
PLANT A NEW SEED

ROOTS

If you have ever seen or just heard about a movie or book called "ROOTS" then you can not honestly afford NOT! To read this book. Especially if you were moved or awakened in any way.

"ROOTS" was a powerful historical examination in early American customs and culture. Yet however moving and touching it may have been, it probably fell short of offering the solution needed to correct such a degraded existence. That is why where ROOTS! Left off this book scripturely begins

INTRODUCTION

PLANT A NEW SEED

Presents

Dear-------------------------

I did not know that when I said words like NIGGER, DOG,BITCH, M.F. that I was stirring up strife and helping the devil to promote his evil spirit! I thought this were the way all black people were supposed to talk. I did not know that one day down through the generations, this language could help promote and produce a nuclear explosion. No one ever told me this language was forced upon my ancestors purposely, over two hundred years ago, then taught to me, by the devil's spirit, to try an keep me ignorant. It would inevitably one day make me unconsciously be able to help add to the destroying of myself, then the whole world! Wow!...I did not know that I had been ordained to be great, but had been tricked! Through bad language training.

But, now I know that every one of those people, who forced those poison words on my ancestors are all dead now. Not even one of them are alive today, yet I still carry on their teaching in my nature. This language had already been identified in the Holy Scripture, whether we knew it or not. It is EVIL! CORRUPT COMMUNICATION that ruins my good character. 1Cor. 15: 33

I also know now that I had never really been conscience or aware until here lately that my ancestors had been brought to America by force, in chains, and given this negative language. And this whole character that resulted in me from those poison words that I have been displaying innocently, was basically repulsive to the intelligent world. Those poison words identified me to the rest of the world as one shiftless, slothful and un-trust worthy and disrespectful. And, they cut off all my chances to any real or lasting success

I had no idea that only about 5% of black people or less had run off from the slave master to the north and escaped this kind of mentality called, Nigger!

In any event, given this kind of serious issue and emergency to bring peace and stability to nations at this time of life, would you please lend us your ear for a moment? We have a message here that we believe is from above, just for these last days of man on earth. It is about the **SOLUTION** to this long ago planted seed. And THE **SOLUTION** now starts with, and depends on, what African America does or don't do, today! The ball is now in our court more than any other time in history.

We are asking in this introduction message, would you take maybe less than a half of an hour of your time and review this message in this book and video? It is the only **SOLUTION** that we have been given today, that would lead to peace and stability to the world. This message will show and prove to African Americans, where we honestly are today in this equation, how we got into this present condition, and most of all, how to get out safely!

We realize that you are very busy so we have cut through the fat so that you could make a clear and easy decision of whether or not you think this message is valuable and needed to you and America! This could turn out to be one of the greatest decisions you make this decade

We have chosen two insert from the book for your review, one is called, "THE SOLUTION "the other one is called "BE CAREFUL WHAT

YOU ASK FOR". And of course the preface will give you an overall view

IT IS ALL ABOUT THE RIGHT CHARACTER NOW. …Let us quit kidding ourselves America. We alone have to do it. We must and we can. When African Americans become aware and fully awaken to a certain truth, then face something that is really a holdback to our race and a negative that we control. But when we do correct it, African Americans are going to become like a valuable welcome beautiful hidden treasure to America. Then the world! And all this story needs is, telling!

This new teaching and new approach will result into a new attitude in African Americans. And along with the teaching of forgiveness and uniting together in righteousness, the status quo America as a whole will begin to feel safe again, trusting and united and much less guilty for something every one realizes their ancestors did long before this present generation was even born. Would you please listen and help restore America and African American dignity?

America will start to feel forgiven, then there will be no more need felt for no more jails built, no more police added, no more paranoia between the races and fighting's ,or none of the above. Even the enemies of America will become much less confidence that they could win and much more reluctant to attack us, when they see we are united

Let's be honest , no one is saying it openly, but the truth is every body is afraid of which decision black America will make as this war that we are now in heats up. The world is just not sure. They do know though, that we, as a whole black nation, could tilt the scales one way or the other. But no one is positive we would be friend or foe, when the chips are down. We definitely need to be trusted that we would stand up in dignity, fairness and honesty with America, whatever! Especially at this time of life.

And, we have got to be honest and admit here, that because of our past record and certain events that has occurred in history, justified or unjustified, neither side is sure of us , black America, one way or the other. Yet, every body knows that we are the last people and the only people that could make all the difference in the world

However, I am happy to report, that we do have now! A new approach and solution that will remedy the situation. Actually, all that was ever needed, and is desperately needed today for African Americans to become solidly united with America, mainly African American youth, who holds the future, is a **CONSCIENCE AWAKENING.** By simply presenting them with the truth, and the whole truth concerning a particular event of history that has never been honestly addressed properly and satisfactory about America and themselves! But trust me, when it does, African American youth will become, united, solid and corrective

War, crime drugs and poverty, plus diseases that we see at this level today are the inevitable results of the lack of the proper character education. And all of these things combined are now in a position to get ready to destroy America. Let us face it; we left the laws of Moshe (Moses). It is as simple as that!

WE MUST BE HONEST ALSO ABOUT WHERE WE REALLY ARE TODAY

It is mandatory America that at this time we must **plant a new seed** with African Americans talking to African Americans first, but in complete honesty, truthfulness, and realness. Not about how bad things were, but how good things could be now. If we plant a new seed in righteousness, with new language

America as a whole today is ready and would accept and welcome at this time, new and fresh leadership, and change, even under a minority control, but under only one condition. That is, if America could believe that they were not going to be threatened, punished or accused and challenged for something that this generation in reality is not guilty of or responsible for in the first place. The new attitude in this generation must in no way have a hint of "when we get in power we are going to get even with ya'll"

The new attitude should be and will be, with the proper teaching, "when we get in power we are going to join with America in unity and prosperity"

Deep down in the real conscience of America, that is the real hope of basic America today. And we believe because of your position and excellent character that you may have been selected for us, by the creator of the universe, for these last days on earth to introduce this unique helpful solution to peace. We do know with out a doubt that this is part of **THE SOLUTION** for the last day's peace.

You may could for one, prevent black America from joining America's enemies. Once today's generation have viewed themselves honestly and where they are at divisively, in this equation, there will be a re thinking and positive change, possibly avoiding a nuclear war.

I will give you right now, before you even start reading or viewing the book or video, the only SOLUTION that would bring peace to America and the world. According to the scripture, and history.

1. The temple of Soloman must be built again in Jerusalem, soon!

2. African Americans must be told and taught this most important "Plant **a new seed** "message, and first, by African America.

No other solution has worked or will work. No matter how big our Armies are, or how many bombs the world can produce, they cannot and will not bring peace. The Creator says:

And this message of the kingdom will be preached to all
The world, by the one who bears witness to all nations; and then
The end will come.   Matt. 24:14

What message?

The message that will bring peace. The message about His kingdom. The message about returning to the Savior.

As we teach here, you can see with your own eye all the things that must take place, and is taking place right now, right before The Savior comes and set up His new kingdom. The thing that must happen first is all in Matt.24th chapter and Luke 21st chapter.

You really do not have to be all of that spiritually discerned to see that the Savior had already prophesied these things for the last days. If you would study the Bible just a little bit, you should become a believer after seeing these prophecies being fulfilled today! And African Americans have a major roll to play in this end time. For those who are seeking peace on earth, and eternal life.

This site was prophesied to be built in our generation just like Ezekiel said in his 40th chapter

PREFACE

THE REPAIRER OF THE BREACH THE RESTORER OF STREETS TO DWELL IN

To all seriously concerned people on the earth, about the future of America, and the entire world for that matter. But please, this time you must listen with your ears and your heart, especially African American youth.

According to the past events in our American history and the Holy Scripture combined, African American youth basically, holds the key to the solution today of whether or not America survives this Iraq war and the world wars that will follow, or go into complete division and chaos and drown.

This time period for these fights prophesied in the holy scripture was for today's generation. It was prophesied to be during these controversies over Israel and the start of the wars and divisions of the world, from there on out. As any TV and news program will show you today, we are almost equally divided in America over war.

That statement of saying African American youth holds the key, may have indeed sounded like a strong and vain statement to make on the surface, however it is absolutely true.

Let's face the true fact, this last day government on earth of man by man started a serious turn around and decline around mid morning Sept 13 1993 when the famous seven {7} year peace plan agreement, that had been prophesied in the scripture to take place, was finally signed into agreement and effect. It was signed by Bill Clinton, Arofat, and Rabin. Did you know this was prophesied to happen in the scripture? {Daniel 9:27}

This was no co-incident. This was the beginning of the end. Just like it was prophesied to do, to the very day ,this peace plan agreement was interrupted after three and one half years {3 ½} exactly, and then shut down for seven {7}years, right in the middle of this agreement. Or you could say ,half way through it, just like the scripture said it was to do. Isn't that interesting? Notice ,that war and sin escalated to a level never seen before in America on 9/11/2001. Remember?

This peace plan agreement that was prophesied in Dan. 9:27 to start, stop ,and start back up again, did exactly that. April 13/2004, it was signed back into agreement by President George Bush and Prime minister Ariel Shron, the very day it was suppose to according to the scripture. Now today we are actually in the last half of that prophesied time of man's government by man, and by the people on earth. I would urge you to check this out scripturally for yourself. To understand this complete prophecy, this also comes line upon line, precept upon precept, here a little there a little. {Isaiah28:10}

This truth and information has been vastly and sometimes purposely over looked in the scriptures for a variety of reasons and for many years. But is now to be made manifest world wide in these last few very important days of man on earth. You can count on it.

And this message of the kingdom will be preached to all the World, by the one who bears witness to all nations; and then the end will come Matt.24:14

I believe that all it would take for any serious fact finder or believer or even scholar to receive, understand and believe this very important urgent end time prophecy and revelation concerning a special gentile nation is just a serious canvassing of the Holy Scriptures.

Of course you must study the beginning of this prophecy, then simply follow history and just see for yourself if they are not true. You will also see that the creator of heaven and earth has most definitely been calling and calling and waiting patiently for this special gentile nation to get it's act together in noble character. Yes, African Americans are part of this prophecy. The Savior wants desperately for this particular gentile nation to join with His saints and just come on in.

Romans 11:25
Blindness in part has come upon Israel until the full number of gentiles has come in

Then He can close this whole chapter and dispensation. After which He has promised to set up a brand new heaven and brand new earth, for all of those who will just come on in { Rev.21:1}

It is important to know just who the Savior is talking to and about in the scripture in certain instances. However if you will follow along you will plainly see that these messages are not for Israel alone. Most of the time they are two told messages that will perfectly tie into the scripture for special gentile nations, like this one in **Hebrews 12th chapter**

12. **Therefore strengthen the hands that hang down and the feeble knees**
13. **And follow the straight path made for your feet, so that the lame may not be turned out of the way , but rather be healed**

The Creator of the world has sent a personal message to a special gentile nation, and a warning, but with love though, as you will see. The message is planted for the most part in the book of Hebrews to in-slaved people in general. The savior has revealed to us, that no matter what the slave master may have done to you or your ancestors that may have even lamed you, over two hundred years ago, be strong and courageous. Because, He would redeem the entire gentile nation, if we let Him.

Proverbs 22:23
Their redeemer will spoil the souls of those that spoiled them

We absolutely do have the solution

The very first thing America as a nation must settle as best they can, and soon!.. If America will even have a chance to stay afloat as a free nation now. And that is, black America must become convinced that they are a equal and valuable partner in the future of America again. Especially from here on out. Time is running out for America.

That may appear initially to sound like a vain and threatening statement on the surface. But please read on or listen and you will more than likely end up in agreement that this statement represents the whole unique situation America has found itself in today. And it is the actual total core of this much needed emergency solution. Do you watch the world news or know anything about the holy scriptures?.

This entire oration and explanation should be taken as a blessing from the creator of the entire world to America and not a threat or blackmail attempt, but rather a kind loving revelation from above.

Not only is America on the verge of dividing and erupting into the worse chaos ever know to man kind, but the enemies of America are right now, waiting in the wings ,knowing this same information that will be revealed here ready to put the finishing touch on what ever we don't do to each other, then take over America.

If that sounds ludicrous or paranoid to you, then you may not know history or the Holy Scriptures. Plus you probably do not watch the news regularly or keep up with today's world events.

Of course it is the devil's spirit fanning these flames in this war we see on TV today. All of this was prophesied in the holy scripture to take place in the end time. The devil will come with power but delusions and deception in it.

America will survive and is prophesied to survive according to the scripture. It is only a matter of how many will survive and what shape it will be left in after this fast approaching, lewd event is all said and done. The saddest commentary of this whole ordeal is that we do hold the key that could prevent it all. But we may or may not use it. America! Sad isn't it?

Isaiah 24:6
Because of this the curse has devoured the earth and they that dwell therein are desolate; therefore the inhabitants of the earth are burned and few men left

Although we cannot stop prophecy and we cannot control every event from all over the world. Because certain things just have to happen. They were prophesied to happen. But there is a way that We! America could get out of this coming up would be tragedy, that is bound to present itself soon! at a minimum lost. If we would listen to the Savior's instructions.

Listen right here, I feel it necessary that I play the devil's advocate for a minute or two by giving you a hypothetical scenario right here. It is necessary. After which ,I believe I will have your undivided attention concerning a possible avoidable crisis that no one knows the exact day or hour that this thing is going to break out or erupt, but everybody does know it is going to happen. .

Listen to this little scenario; when Bin Ladin or Ahmadinajad ,some one like these or, one of those other terror promoting guys that hates American white men, and that has dark skin, something like me. When one of them explodes a bomb over here, or when some of them get over here and are fighting America, then one of them say to me:

Look man, we are brothers, help us!...that American white man is the devil!, remember he put ya'll in slavery? You see what he thinks about ya'll , look how he treats you. We want treat you that way when we take over, help us!.....just give us those guns and things ya'll got , and don't tell nobody we are over here.

Then I have got to choose a side, don't I? I have got to make a choice whether to tell the authorities that Bin Ladin and them are hiding over here, or just join Bin Ladin and them

Do you know what? Do you know what a large number of African American's answer may be? It will be:

Man I don't know if I can tell the American authorities where Bin Ladin and them are hiding out at or not. And that they are over here with guns and bombs trying to blow up something

Why? Because I don't trust that old white man!...he is the one that hung my great grand daddy!...He is the one that put me in jail. He is the one that is keeping me down right now! How do I know he won't just shoot me and Bin Ladin?....I don't know man...I don't trust that man.

Guess what?.....he don't trust you either. That is exactly the way the general consciences feels concerning African Americans. Especially our youth. That old white man feels double the same way about you. He do not trust you no further than he can see you. He is just not sure that you would tell him the truth about Bin Ladin in the first place . you may be trying to set him up. That is why he keeps one hand on his pistol all the while he is talking to you

That is a problem right there, isn't it? Well, that is exactly where America is
Ligitimately at today. Or heading soon! .

Now couple that little story and mistrust and paranoia on both sides with maybe a recent local race up rising somewhere that just happened. Suppose it just happened in the same period of time while Bin Ladin or his followers may have been trying to recruit , telling Americans to join him and be delivered from this old American white devil. Interesting ,huh?
Now we can try and deny this reality and avoid facing it all we want to. We could just pretend that this is just another one of those imagined scenarios that just could not happen. But the solid truth according to history and the prophesied scriptures combined, is America is on the verge of

a total eruption that could destroy it.

America at this point has been duped and out witted by the devil, using the very thing that America say they believe in. The holy scriptures. The true scriptures principals are guaranteed to work. They have worked and are working right now as we speak. But for the enemy! How?... By using first, the simple principal given to all man kind that has to work, in Mark's 3rd chapter. Keeping us in America divided. The scripture promise us:

Mark 3:
24. **If a kingdom is divided against itself, that kingdom cannot stand**
25. **if a house is divided against itself that house cannot stand**
26. **so if satan has risen against herself, she is divided and cannot stand -she has come to her end**

It is really as simple as that. According to the Savior. We can all complicate it though. If we choose. The solution and only solution given to us by the Savior to this fast approaching chaos in America soon is simple.

However,I would warn us all to keep this in mind. The solution will not be what some geniuses would probably prescribe as the answer. That is, more violence on it's citizens and minorities, to beat them back into order. And more jail space to confine them and keep them under control until this thing blows over. No! that would be at this juncture, the right recipe for total destruction of this entire nation. Then ,the world ,maybe.

Truthfully, at this point in history, there would not be enough jail space to just lock up blacks again and keep them quiet and out of the way. There would not be enough guns again to dominate black communities until this all blows over. There would not be enough killings of African Americans to scare them back in their place again or none of the past thought to be remedies. Only blood baths and possibly total annihilation of this society may occur.

This truthful assessment and researched analysis of this crucial situation has been compiled using as foundation, history, the holy scriptures, common sense and just the obvious plain to see every day news account of this situation. We should be able to confirm these truths with just our natural eyes, even if we knew nothing about the scripture or prophecy. .

In these present threatening coming up events ,which are guaranteed to present itself, maybe erupt! In America! And soon! The truthful reality is, African American citizens of all levels, do hold the key to the solution and the future for peace in America. And the total out come will be determined, not by rich or middle class people, but by basically the common every day people. In reality ghetto life, if you will. Interesting….isn't it?

There is just no way around it, so let us face it. This country cannot survive from here on out after 9/11 except it unite in righteousness. It is almost embarrassing to say, but the creator of the universe gave the solution to these problems to us! The people in America. But the enemy has took them and is using it against us! And as we continue to explain and demonstrate , you will see that African Americans do hold the last key in this dispensation that will determine the out come

I wish I could apologize, but I did purposely create that whole hopefully eye opening scenario concerning Bin ladin or some of America's enemies that could become a reality. It was to hopefully, get the attention of somebody. Preferably everybody. Plus somebody who is in a media position. It was also to try and place some immediatecy on a problem that just cannot wait, be dragged out or procrastinated on any longer, waiting to find the best approach or time to handle it. Because this scenario is not ,just a possibility any more, but rather a probability now. More than likely now.

This could even be an emergency situation. And the exact position we could find ourselves in, in the morning! At the very least, this scenario most definitely do merit America's immediate concern and action. That is the bad news.

The good news is, there is a **SOLUTION,** that could lighten this inevitable would be burden. It was given to US! America! By the creator of the world, just for such a time as this. And there are men who has wrote these instructions down in a book, researched them for their authenticity, put the entire revelation in a book and video and is ready willing and able to start teaching and preaching these life changing and saving revelations. And ,to the ones they must preach it to first. African Americans. **PLANT A NEW SEED** The only question is, are you willing to help save America?

You and I for one as concerned, informed African Americans should be teaching and preaching this **SOLUTION** to our own brothers with conviction and passion. And we can. After anyone start preaching and teaching this **Solution** that has been given us by The Holy Father, the whole world will eventually get on the band wagon of teaching this character change. That is exactly what it is going to take to save the world today. Character change.

ORNERY BUT CORRECTABLE. WISDOM CALLS OUT TO ALL MAN-KIND The only corrective and lasting solution now for America's division is, blacks, Hispanic and all other minorities, must feel convinced somehow now that this is their country too. And that they have a big stake in it's survival and a lot to lose in it's defeat. American blacks especially must be now educated and honestly, and by their own people first ,as to certain matters that pertain to basically them alone. Although we are aware that people in general normally do not like to hear about their exclusive part in responsibilities, yet it still must happen!

In launching this new honest repetitious teaching America's status quo will also have to make a decision that we believe they will be willing to get past. They must be willing to at least face the truth that a long, long time ago that America did seriously error in a couple of areas that they are now willing to face ,admit correct it and change. We will then be able to get on with the **SOLUTION.** Which is the only thing important today! **The SOLUTION!**

With this honest humble beginning ,all of America will start to listen first, then evaluate this character change message, but trust me, all of America will eventually join in it's progression. Because all intelligent people know that we all must change some of the old thinking in America if we are to survive.

As strange as it may seem to some, nevertheless this unifying message to America must start first at the most under rated and forgotten level of America, the so called ghettos. If the ghettos do not feel they have a stake or a chance for partnership with America, at this juncture, they could become influenced by every evil revenge seeking, lying America hater there is. What happens in the ghettos as quiet as it is kept, does effect the safety and well being of the whole world! It spreads. Believe it or not. .

So called ghetto people are thought to be clannish, yet can be convinced to help save America or help destroy America. History has over, and over, proved this. Granted though, a lot will depend on just who is preaching and teaching this "**Let's save America** " message. It should come from the ghetto.

In any event, as painful and embarrassing as it might be, America have just got to face the fact that slavery did create this whole coming up chaotic divisive possible calamity. But now it must be willing to help educate and abandon some of those long ago made standard policies that resulted into crippling the very people that are needed today to help defend and unite America. They could become friends or enemies. America must at this cross road ,offer every American a fresh start.

Let just all face it, a bad seed was forced planted a long time ago in African America purposely, that became basically hereditary. That seed has now manifested itself into what it had to develop into one day, according to the scripture and law of sowing and reaping. A divided people a hopeless people and a un-decided people. The facts is, that seed that was planted in African Americans as a whole was defiled and bad when it was planted, it is still bad today and it will never get any better, it can only get worse! So it has to be replaced. There is no other honest way to say it or get around it, other than replace it!

However, black America is intelligent enough to realize that all of the people responsible for that lewd act of planting division and separatism in the hearts of blacks people are all dead today. Not a single one of them are alive today. That is one of the reasons why African America today, is ready and willing to abandon the destructive pattern that was forced upon them unaware, by the slave trainers.

Nevertheless, every one realize that America may have to still reap some of the
percussions produced by such a ornery teaching and seed. And correct it. America can admit it, correct it, and move on to success. Or it can continue and deny this situation ever even existed and become ultimately even more divided and possibly destroyed. There is now just no other way except unite. We have now been given a real workable **SOLUTION** by the creator of heaven and earth that is done only by one way. The Savior of the world's rules. And it starts *by teaching and preaching PLANT A NEW SEED for black America.*

This whole **new seed planting** message, with repetition, must start with blacks preaching to blacks in honest truth initially. Teaching blacks about where they are seriously at with America at this time in this equation. Which will prove to be eye opening, And maybe even embarrassing to a degree. Yet we must of course still teach and preach truth about how we got into such a degraded mentality of a called nigger character, which was through a purposely thought out plan of slavery.

Then we must prove from the Savior's point of view, but to our satisfaction, what should our now, present part and participation be with America today! Even after all that has been said and done. Yes, we do have to get past revenge, what ever!

Then finally ,where we are all guaranteed to go, or the catastrophic results we will receive, right along with America. If we do not get wise and unite in righteousness and reverse an old bitter root that was planted in us with out our permission, yet still effects our character. And it effects the attitude, trust and the peace of the whole world. African Americans can reverse the whole tide.

We have some work to do America . One may even say, we have some-what of a bitter pills to swallow. Never the less they will heal all of America of what ever happened over two hundred tears ago, if swallowed The heavenly Father that created us all has admonished us that there is nothing cute, honorable, or holy about being an outcast ,ignorant, un-patriotic or disrespectful to yourself and your neighbor, no matter how you acquired the nature.

However, that is how we were trained to be from the first entrance into this country. And we were trained with whips, ropes and guns to be what we now know to be ignorant and divisive. It was on purpose. Actually ,we were never suppose to learn how to organize in righteousness and support righteous causes or support each other. Now, America is afraid, afraid of what it created. We were trained to say and act like niggers. Negative!

This process was called "Divide and Conquer" A process that works. It was prophesied in the scripture to work. The early slave masters knew it would work. They went by the scripture's principals. It is now days, being used on white America , Democrats v. Republicans. We must be honest about the whole picture.

Here is the good part though, once this truth has been told and realized, basically by African Americans that this whole character planting in us was a terrible handicap and mistake, this whole nation will begin to change and unite with America. And it may seem like over night.

For the first time in history, I can see black youth being proud to be knowledgeable, respectful, of themselves and their brothers, plus patriotic as opposed to what we now call, HOOD! Soon they will no longer follow vanity. Some youngsters have been duped into believing that school is square, and to be disrespectful, and vain and so called HOOD!....is somehow a good black quality. But in our teaching ,history and the scripture will identify and prove this thinking to be an illusion.

Plus contrary to what may be a majority's opinion on this subject ,that with this kind of straight forward awareness and too honest teaching, black people will become insulted, embarrassed then become more divided against America, Just the opposite will happen, trust that. After hearing and seeing this **PLANT A NEW SEED** message and revelation in books and videos, black America as a whole will begin to seriously realize for the first time in history in America ,their unique yet vulnerable position . Which at this point ,is also threatening to America truthfully. .

In any event, black people are sensitive and intuitive, they will automatically become conscience of this handicap that was forced fed them through a purposed plan in slavery, given the total truth of the entire situation. They will then start a successful surge in righteous character. It is already starting. It is now starting to become a shame to be thought of as ignorant any more in black America. No longer, after hearing these message will it be fashionable to be Hoody! Plus soon , you will probably never hear a black call another African American a nigger again! Can you see this solution emerging?

Again, that all was mostly bad news. Wasn't it? But the fact were all supported by history and the holy scriptures. And just common sense by observation. But the good news is, we can change and avoid all of the would be catastrophes if we would do just one thing right here. **PLANT A NEW SEED** and it will also grow.

Honestly, the only thing that America and the rest of the world should be focused on for the most part, at this late date in history is, survival!... What ever happened in the past has happened now, good bad or different. Our only concern now should be, do we have a **SOLUTION?**.... a **SOLUTION!** ......And I am happy to report, we do have one. Just listen for a minute to these lyrics in this George Benson song will you? And see if you agree, this is the solution. It says:

I believe the children are our future, teach them well and let them lead the way, show them all the beauty they possess Inside. Give them a chance to love, and make it easier

A GRUESOME HISTORY: In the early 20th century, an average of two Blacks were lynched each week for nearly 30 years.

ACKNOWLEDGEMENTS

F.S.O. [for superstars only] is an organization that has purposely elected this title for its existence. It is mainly because it is truly filled with superstars in heart on its rooster.

F.S.O. would like to thank at this point one of the super stars of help mates, Miss Phyllis Artman for being such a helper and super believer in a cause that is sure to help change the lives for the better of an entire nation of people and of countless youngsters of all nationalities.

So we simply just want to say in clear words "THANK You" to Phyllis for believing in me and this worth while universal project with your encouragement your patience, and all of your extremely valuable contributions that was so necessary to make this seemingly impossible project a reality. You are truly the epitemy of a super star

Speaking of super stars, there is one in this outfit that without his video technical ability none of this would be even possible, Michael Bell, Michael who was a valuable member of the pentagon team in Wash, .D.C. has spent long hours away from his own business M.B.S. Technological Solutions assisting F.S.O. in this worth while project to upgrade his Afro-American brothers and sister. Thank you Mr. Bell.

Sonny & Phyllis   *Micheal Bell*

A LITTLE BIT ABOUT THE AUTHOR

SONNY FISHBACK is a singer, actor, composer, screenplay writer, and author of the books *"Plant a New Seed" and "King of the Game"*

Sonny was born in Nashville, Tennessee and raised in Louisville, Kentucky. Sonny lived in New York City for over twenty-five years. He was in the music industry as a singer, composer of music & lyrics for James Brown and many more famous artists. He currently lives in Louisville, Kentucky and is in the process of filming his new movie called, *"Plant A New Seed"*.

Plant a New Seed was conceived and written by Sonny during his incarceration where The Creator of the entire Universe gave him a mission to plant a new seed in a special people in America.

People all over the world believes as this author believes, concerning Afro-Americans and their most valuable roll that they will most certainly have to play in the next few years. This roll concerns the future of America, and finally the future of the entire world. This roll was prophesied in the Holy Scripture for the latter days. Now these last days are fast approaching and just about upon us.

This will be a great responsibility on Afro-Americans to help make peace and save America from the adversary, which is trying to destroy the earth, and according to The Creator of the universe, Black people will have the final decision deciding this fate. The problem is, how many will listen to HIM and be counted righteous. For only through righteousness could one make the right decision that will save America. However, there is a solution and this author believes that Afro-Americans will unite and rise to the occasion once they are truthfully informed.

This author has attended many of meetings with dignitaries and heads of states who also knows the importance of all black people's help and uniting at this crucial time in history. And together they are all basically trying to find a way to bridge a serious gap in race relation that has lingered on and on, un-necessarily through out America's existence.

Below are just a few of the people who were guest in the home of a concerned patriot The honorable Michael Wildes, the newly appointed mayor of Englewood NJ {Dec. 2003}

This gathering was also for another very important cause called "Boys town." These kinds of events and others like it have inspired this author to seek out and promote this important solution for Afro Americans called, "PLANT A NEW SEED".

1. Debra Jones – Founder of Mothers of All Colors
2. Pastor Lester Taylor Jr. – Pastor of Community Baptist, Englewood, NJ
3. Sonny Fishback – Author Plant a New Seed.

1. *Sonny Fishback*
2. *Mayor Dinkins – Former Mayor of New York City*
3. *Debra Jones*

1. *Sonny Fishback*
2. *Stanley Lokko – Chief of Ghana*

1. *Mayor Dinkins*
2. *Uri Lupoleanski – Mayor of Jerusalem*
3. *Michael Wildes – Mayor of Englewood New Jersey*

1. *Fat Joe—Superstar Rapper*
2. *Debra Jones*
3. *Friend*

Mah'Gee Foster & Company. She is proud to be associated with the book and film ***Plant A New Seed.*** While typing the book (manuscript) I found it to be an interesting account of one man's journey into the truth of The Word. Mah'Gee has been associated with theatre and the entertainment field for over twenty-five years. She spent a year in St. Louis, MO at the St. Louis Black Reperatory Company as an Administrative Intern in Press Relations.

Sonny Fishback

PLANT A NEW SEED

The Doer

Be ye doers of the word and not hearers only...

I was amazed and so saddened and probably more embarrassed than anything else, one un-forgettable evening. I was sitting watching the six o'clock news casters announce that The Local Grand jury had refused to indict a local white policeman after he had admitted to shooting a black male over nine times to death. The man was in their custody, with handcuffs on, cuffed behind his back. Neither would they acknowledge even that the officer had really done anything wrong. To this group of mindsets, this guy seemed only to have got what he deserved.

My amazement really didn't come from just that though. Nor did it come from even the fact that during this break, the local politicians and the Mayor of the city appeared on TV and commenced to explain and justify this extremely lewd act. But with a justification, and un-conscious and seemingly disregard for any reasonable intelligence, that should make one have to throw up, claiming how the decision by the Grand jury and the police was justified. Although that was amazing, that is not what amazed me the most either.

My first amazement and frustrations I must say came from how some of my black brothers and sisters seemed sort of numb to this kind of event and seem so willing to just listen and accept these explanations and rationalizations of this carefully explained justification

Although just for anybody to have to merely listen to someone force justification like that down your throat, plus even expect some people to just accept it, was just as painful, insulting and evil as the crime itself. In reality, it was just so difficult for me to understand how any human being would think that they could just shoot another human being down with handcuffs on behind his back and it be all right, even justify it...

So right there probably started the most informative and important revelation of my life. It suddenly dawned on my conscience a disturbing revealing yet necessary question. This thought asked, "Is it possible that WE! Black people have allowed a mind set this vicious and inconsiderate of human life to mature to this degree?"

Although I realized that this was not a good time for Black people to be feeling any worse, especially about themselves, But, could this be a devastating wake up call in some very important areas that WE! have been missing for so long?

I could not seem to keep from questioning myself as to, "could this be the inevitable results of something WE! did or didn't do? Is it possible that WE! Black people ourselves have convinced a lot of people with this evil mind set, that WE! Black people deserve and will except this humiliation and genocide of our race at no cost to them? And could it be maybe because of our lack of the right kind of retaliation or corrective measures in the past?" That was a sobering thought that will not seem to go away.

The decision for some police officers to shoot a black person with no real thought or fear of retribution, or to lock up a black person for any little minor offense they feel like, should not be of any real amazement or surprise to anyone living in this country today. Especially certain parts. Or if it is, I would have to ask you, where have you been for any part of the past two hundred years or so?

Nor should it be bewildering to anyone to discover that the system for the most part just by tradition has sometimes defended, protected, and justified those who would claim that they were just trying to do what they were paid to do in the first place. This is not to say that every police officer that puts on a gun goes out purposely, just to hunt down and kill a black person. But in reality, none of this attitude by some people is new. So that didn't amaze me either.

My true amazement and frustrations really came from the true fact that WE! US! ME! or my black brothers and sisters, are still even at this late date, just continuing to ask the same questions over and over again, plus following the same pattern over and over and over every time these things occur. Or maybe I should say whenever some of these evil events, that really happen daily, are somehow forced out into the open view for every one to see.

As I sat there sadly, almost in a state of depression, I somehow recalled my past again and how awful, I use to feel when I was a young man, and heard about one of my black brothers being lynched or shot down, sometimes for just being black! or heard about some of these same kind of events, even back then. Then I started to feel that much more helpless and guilty for some reason, as some voice from within kept reminding me, "This should have been dealt with by now!"

So I did ask myself, " have we! Black people just learned to live with this disregard for our life by some people, and do we have any respect for ourselves left? Aren't we still saying the same old things over and over? Things like, "oh why did they kill that man like that?" Or, " oh, isn't that a shame?" or even, "What are THEY going to do about them killing that man like that? That's wrong!" …no kidding!

What are THEY! going to do? What are THEY! …going to do? Now I do not want this to come as a big shock and surprise to you, my seemingly blind, forgetful and forgiving brothers and sisters, but what THEY! are going to do is, the same thing that THEY! have been doing!…. Surprised?

The question should cease to be by now, what are THEY going to do, but what are YOU! going to do? What are you! and I! going to do to stop it! What are WE! going to do new? WE! keep saying it's wrong, WE! seem to understand that perfectly. But what are WE! going to do to change things?

Here is another truth, my people that WE! best understand before it is too late. If WE! don't change our projection and their perception of what WE! will accept, and what WE! will do, then THEY! are going to just continue delivering US what THEY! think WE! are satisfied with or allow. I kept thinking to myself, "Wow! that was a ridiculous useless question to ask, ' what are THEY going to do?' its picture clear, what THEY! are going to do."

To be honest, THEY! have proved over and over and over again, exactly what THEY are going to do. That particular mind set is very consistent in their actions. And very united. THEY! are in no way hiding it.

It is sad but, WE! are also very consistent in our actions of no counter solutions or at least no real concrete corrective measures, actions. And that part is not hid either. As a matter of fact, THEY! sort of, expect and depend on US! having OUR! same reactions or attitudes WE have always had in the past, in response to this mindset's historical un-hid actions.

THEY! are dependent on getting certain responses from us like they have always got, and THEY are judging them as no real unified objections, no real undeniable solutions or actions, no real opposing unified commitment. Which the lack of these actions has proved over and over to result in no meaningful lasting resolution.

That is the thing that amazed and saddened me the most. I thought to myself after later receiving this revelation, "Oh, how I, and my people have missed the boat."

Then I pondered, "Just how much longer can a people or a race exist, like this?" Oh sure, we can easily point out or at the oppressor's faults. That's not hard. That's crystal clear. Or WE! can always say "THEY! are wrong to keep doing us like that!"… Anybody with half a brain or heart can see the cruelty in a mind set that would look to oppress like that. So what else is new?

What are you going to do about all of this? What are you and I going to do about it? That should be the only honest question asked. What are WE! going to do NEW! If WE! think it's wrong, WE did say THEY! Or THEM! was wrong didn't WE?

Keep this in mind, when WE! say THEY or THEM! In this oration, this THEM! Or THEY! Is not a color, it is, and always have been, a particular mind set. Spiritually and physically. That is what makes THEM! So powerful and united. THEY all feel the same way, about YOU black people.

You need to understand though, just because one has a white face, does not mean by no means that he has this same nasty narrow selfish dangerous mind set as THEM! Make no mistake about that. THEY or this spirit is in a category all by THEM! Self.

As a matter of fact WE! may as well get ready and face the fact that WE! have some with BLACK faces with this same particular narrow mind set as THEM! Which is a much deeper problem? However, there is still an answer and a forever-lasting corrective solution.

You may be amazed, terribly saddened, and surprised yourself at this point my brothers and sisters, but the answer to your question of "What would make a mind set think that it could cold bloodedly and un-con-

4

sciously just shoot down this people to death and get away with it, even if they were helpless and with hand cuffs on?" The painful reality is, You told him he could. Yes, you and me said:

"It's alright, ya'll can do this, and it is justified, he ain't"
nothing but a nigger"

Now you should not be able to stop reading or listening right here. Any conscience or caring or even reasonably intelligent person should be offended or at the very least curios about the justification of such a profound accusation like that. I know I was when I first received the implication of such a statement. I gave the permission for genocide of my people? You got to be kidding!

I needed desperately to know just who this YOU! was that gave permission to kill my people or me. And I needed to know why? And how it was given. And when? What about you? Wouldn't you have to have this proved or disproved about yourself if someone accused you of stuff like that? Do you even care?

In any event, let me continue in what led me to this very important revelation, that could deliver my people or help keep them in bondage.

Suddenly, as I gazed around the room that I was sitting in watching TV with the other guys of what seemed to be the finishing off of my people, I discovered sitting right next to me was a guy name Frank.

Frank was a white fellow. Yet he seemed to be quite destroyed by this breaking news, just as much as I was. And I must say we had become sort of friends here lately, at least friends enough to express to each other what we both were obviously feeling right now, concerning any person, being shot to death, numerous times cowardly and viciously, by a policeman, while having hand cuffs on. And yes, let me admit, I was incarcerated at the time, for a traffic offense, and just waiting to go back to court. We were all being held in a minimum security holding facility, just waiting for the judge to make a decision concerning bail.

As it turned out, this white man was in a sort of uncommon situation himself. Although he was in no way torn between what he thought was right or wrong, he definitely knew right from wrong, with out a doubt I found out. But he was a little perplexed about how to approach me about this solution he thought was best for this problem.

_____

I found out that he had already been actually looking for someone who he could talk to about situations like this. Some black person, someone whose conscience was may be stirred up. Some one who wanted to start to present a different picture of Black people to the police, or for that matter, to the world?

It was somewhere in the middle of tear, frustration, and bitter anger during the course of our very sensitive carefully thought out conversation and sort of grieving session that I learned a very important truth about my people and myself. Frank and I did sit there together playing chess and listening to this horrible newsbreak. And listening to the politicians seemingly trying to justify this tragedy over and over. I found out that this Caucasian's basic concern stemmed from the fact that, he himself was married once to an Afro-American woman and has some mixed blood, mulatto, children of which one he seemed to absolutely worship, so to speak.

Finally, after listening a while to this horror story on TV he obviously couldn't manage to hold his true feelings in any longer, witnessing this awful brutality, so he abruptly interrupted the TV, turned to me and said, "Man, why do your brothers keep letting them think that they can do that to them and get away with it? That is so sick! Don't you care?"

I was just about to lose my cool at that point and respond very impulsively and I must admit now, ignorantly! I was just about to yell out, "Honky! You got to be kidding! Do I care? Those are my people! Are you asking me if I care if the cops just shoot them down, like animals?" But it was a good thing I didn't. Because little did I know I was about to be led to a revelation that could be the solution to the way people look, and think of me, and a solution to all problem in all race relations. Somehow, I was able to restrain my impulse and answer somewhat intelligently.

I responded calmly to this obviously troubled man and said, "My friend, you just don't know how much I do care, I've lived with this kind of butchering of my brothers and sisters every since I can remember. But what can I do? I am powerless against this sort of thing. I cannot stop these animals from shooting us down like that. I wish I could".

He responded, probably the way I should have, and said, "But you are not powerless man! That's what I am talking about, you can do something! THEY think that same thing! That you won't do anything! THEY are confident that your people will just let it die without doing anything that will make sure it will never happen again…if I was black, I bet you I would do something!"

"Do what?" I responded.

This gentleman turned to me, seeing that I was getting a little bit aggravated, but yet interested, and began to try and reach me with out offense. He said, "Look man, could I talk to you about this sensitive subject without you punching me out?"

I answered again, "I don't know man, I don't know if you understand my people, you might need to be black to understand what I am feeling right now pal"

He replied again, "I'm not sure if I understand your people either, but I do understand my people, and why they do what they do…look man, I want to tell you something right here, and you could help us both if you wanted to, if you cared."

"There you go with that, if I cared stuff again! What is up with you man? Hold on!.. don't you see those are my people being done like this?" I screamed!

He responded back just as serious, "No you hold on! I've got some of your people in my household, in my family!"

After that little defense mode, this Caucasian calmed down and said, "Look, I'm married to a beautiful black chick, and I have a beautiful son. He may not have black skin, but his mother is still an Afro-American person.…he is a smart talented little guy man, I mean this guy has unbelievable talent man, for sports, for making music, and that is not all he can do. He can really pick up on just about everything. If he wants to. He has just natural intuition about stuff that even amazes me. My son is great man! But do you know what my son does to himself every single day? Why he makes sure that he puts himself down, every day. Him and his friends get together and call themselves some names that you wouldn't believe"

I wanted to be perfectly clear as to what this strange man was saying, so I replied, "names? What kind of names?"

He didn't hesitate, he made it plain "Hate names, they absolutely hate each other. Yet, they will go out of their way to find each other; just so they can put each other down. Man I want my son to stop hating himself like that…why that will destroy him! And his friends, someday! See I give him everything I can think of to let him see that not only do I love him, but also that he is worth something!"

I immediately became interested because I felt something there from him of sincerity. He sounded confused but honest and serious. So I replied, "What makes you think he hates himself, or hates his friends?"

"My goodness man," he responded, "weren't you listening at all? Look what he calls them...every day! And look what they call him! All-day! He even calls himself that! Nigger! Nigger! Nigger! Nigger! All day man...as soon as they see each other they start the insults up, 'Yo! My nigger, my nigger, my nigger! My dog! My dog! My dog!"... They even call each other hoes and bitches! That is so evil man. I can't make him see that he is a handsome intelligent young guy, not a nigger!"

"So how will that destroy him? They are just joking! I mean, it seems he is only trying to be sociable, and communicate with his friends...how will that get him destroyed?" I asked

He replied rather angrily this time, like I certainly would have too, in the past sometimes. If I had only known what I know now. He replied again, "My goodness guy, do you know what those words mean? Those are hater's words man! Don't you know those words are saying, "I am nothing, I am a fool, I am ignorant, and helpless and need killing?"

I had to interrupt him right there, "Hold it man! Hold it! What are you saying?"

Now I was offended. I sat straight up and started to get super ignorant this time. Again good sense prevailed somehow. I restrained my impulse to first just ask him a question before clocking. I asked, "What do you mean, by deserve killing dude?"

At that point, I think he saw the need to calm himself down, and calm me down too! I think he sensed I might not know the true origin or the cruel implication of some of these foul words that are spoken daily by some people, and that I may be getting a little offended myself.

So he was a pretty smart cookie, he changed his whole tone and went directly to, "My brother,...maybe you don't know....I hate that it happened, but didn't you know that those words were given to your great ancestors , by my great, great grand parents, a long time ago to oppress you?"

" To oppress me! ...why is that?" I asked

"Just to keep your ancestors, then finally you! in a slave mentality, so they would have to keep working his land for him?...did you?...my son is not going to be nobody's slave, my son is as good or better, as any body else...you didn't know this though?" He replied.

I tried not to let him see it, but truthfully, I was furious about that comment. But there was something in that comment of deserved killing, and slave mentality that made me more curious. But I made sure that I calm myself again so that I could just ask a few questions, before clocking.

Again, good thing I did, because the conversation turned out to be really necessary and interesting, and factual. And as hard as I tried, I could not for the life of me seem to find one single fault or opportunity to charge him with trying to insult me or put me down, so I could clock.

As I was still paused and sort of lost for words, probably looking baffled, I think he felt an obligation at that point to explain his profound accusation of "Need killing" to me, but calmly and carefully though.

I looked over at this guy, tears were flowing down this poor fellow's cheek now, and he seemed to be struggling to try to explain something to me. Hoping all the while that he wasn't making things worse, and that I would somehow understand the depth of this matter, he would now and then, apologize with seemingly over whelming guilt for his ancestors.

In any event, since I was kind of paused he just continued, "Look man, I'm terribly sorry than this whole slavery thing happened, but it did, I can't change that, but my great ancestors were great believers in the Bible. They knew that the scripture were true. They knew if you apply anything according to the way The Creator of mankind said it would work, it would work with out a flaw...oh don't worry, some of them will have to give an account one day for doing what they did, but they still used the strongest thing there is to capture and enslave your people. And the method they used was one that had to work because it was God's principal for all creation in action. The principal of sowing and reaping."

I replied, "Sowing and reaping? God's principal?"....

He said, "Yes man, sowing and reaping! It will work on anybody, no matter if they are black or white, rich or poor it doesn't matter. It will work for an evil man or a righteous man, whoever uses it, and they knew this."

I asked him, "What did they do man?"

He replied, "They brought your ancestors over here to America, by force, then forced some words on them, and planted them in their vocabulary and in their hearts...so deep, until they started to believe them...

didn't any body ever tell you about that man?"

"Oh yeah." I explained, "I know my great ancestors were kidnapped and brought over here and made slaves for that old white man. But all of this about them admitting that they needed killing and was stupid. I have never heard that! That is ridiculous for anybody to do. That is stupid."

"No! Not stupid, ignorant would be more like it" He continued to explain to me "You see, ignorant only means, anything that you just don't know about yet, you are just not aware of something yet that's all. That's a lot different from being just stupid, you see. You could become aware of your mistake, then you will no longer be ignorant to it, you could definitely become aware of what you were doing or saying wrong some day. That would means at some point you now know, understand? But your ancestors had no idea of what they were saying, and the inevitable results of what they were saying and doing until it was too late. They didn't even know that this was God's principal at work. Working in reverse of what HE would have. How could they? They couldn't read or write this English language that they were being made to digest daily."

"How could some body make you digest something man?" was my question. So he answered again,

"Sometimes it was under the threat of being hung or something else worse, if they didn't repeat certain words over and over every day. Then sometimes my people still might just pull a few of your people out of the crowd, in plain view of the rest of your people and beat them so un-merciful with a whip or something until most of the time they would die. Just because one of them didn't say these defiled words given to them, convincingly enough for my forefathers. So they would make them an example for the rest."

"Convincing enough?" I asked

"Yes, convincing!" he said, "you see my forefathers wanted your people to say these poisonous words like they meant them, and say them until they believed them. Or face another beating or hanging"

"Hold it man, hold it, hold it man!...are you saying that God hates all black people, and wanted white people to be in charge of us and treat us like that?....what are saying man, This is God's principal?"

He answered back again, but slowly this time, "You are going to miss the whole point man, I can see that right now, you are going to miss the entire point if you don't start listening right...this has nothing to do with whether you are black or white. Or how God feels about it. This principal still has to work for who ever use it! And who ever they use it on. It will work on a dog, a cat, a woman or a man, a black man or white man. It will work for a flower if it was used. This was a principle from The Creator of the Universe for all mankind and all Creation. And it had the same power in it that HE used when HE created the universe, and the same principal it takes to make a baby. You plant a seed, and then water it, and it will automatically grow. That is all there is to it…and even God can't change it. Because that is the same principle, HE put in place for every thing and everybody. Even for making the world."

He paused then continued saying, "My forefathers just used it on your people for his own selfish benefit, that's all."

"Oh your ancestor were smarter than anybody else, they were in direct touch with God, huh?" I must have sounded a little sarcastic to him so he calmly replied,

"The instructions for its success were written down in the Holy Bible for every body to see. Whether God liked what was happening or not, HE would still have to honor his principal and allow it to work, because HE is the one that set this principle in motion. HE set it up. Oh a person may wind up having to pay dearly for using this power if he uses it for evil purposes, but that won't stop God's principal from still working, for any body."

I don't think this guy could stop himself now; he seemed quite emotional especially about God. Sometimes he seemed almost apologetic for God's awesome power. Never the less, I think he felt he just had to make me understand something. So he continued.

"You've got to understand something man, my people knew the scripture, and your people couldn't even read or write the language. My people knew that words alone had power. They knew that if they could plant these negative words in your ancestor's heart, they would heritically; unconsciously have to plant the same things in their children's heart. And on and on and on."

"Now why would anybody want to plant some negative stuff in anybody?" I asked

Frank answered "This would eventually become a hard root, which is nothing but a nature, or you could say a characteristic, or just a belief in something, or better yet, a beginning of something. That's all a root is, a beginning. Then after a few generations of this constant watering of this root, or the constant watering or training of this implantation, or this nature, it will become just natural to grow like that. You'll just start saying certain words automatically, and believe them. You see the foundation has been established. You will also finally start acting like you talk because you believe it."

I could see this man was working up a way to explain something. He wanted desperately to talk about something. But he did check himself first. He stopped and said to me, "I believe I can speak honestly to you man without you getting offended, you seem intelligent, may I?"

I did have sort of mixed emotions right here, but I was definitely interested. This man had made some profound accusations and statements to me! I definitely need to hear more. I'm not sure that I could stop him now no way. So I just agreed and said, "Go ahead, be my guest."

So he happily continued saying, "Well the words my people planted in your people were the words that meant just what my people needed your people to think. They created some words just for your people. They needed your people to think this, that they had to work for my folks, they were supposed to be inferior to my folks, and that they were helpless and lost without white folks. The words created had to also mean, 'I KNOW THAT I AM NOT AS WORTHY AS YOU WHITE FOLKS, BECAUSE YOU ARE SMART AND I AM IGNORANT, AND I DEPEND ON YA'LL.'...That was all engulfed in the spirit of some words that my people created for your people to use."

"Wait a minute" I interrupted… "are you saying some of the words WE black people use today were created just for US? Poison words?"

"Exactly!" he said, "That's why my ancestors so carefully chose words to force down into your peoples spirit. Words like, shiftless, fool, lazy nigger, coons, useless and poor, no good, bitch, monkey acting, ignorant and stupid, and even worse words. And they would call your people this everyday. Then make your people agree with it, and then repeat them back."

"Repeat them back? For what?" I asked

At that point he carefully tried to explain, "This was the beginning of implanting a thought in somebody, and forcing them to believe it. And if you train that thought and train that thought and train that thought, especially applied by brutal force, it will grow in your heart. And if you ever allow yourself to believe that you were any one of those things, weak, guilty, and ignorant, you will even learn to accept punishment without fighting back. You will think that you deserve it, and are helpless"

At that point I was beginning to feel angry and insulted, and I guess he seen it. As I just commented, "Whoa man, this sounds ornery!"...but it still didn't stop him from explaining this very valuable thing he thought was important.

He just continued, "See man I told you that I hated that this whole slavery thing happened. It was ornery, but it did happen. But I believe if your people had known that God set down this principal, and what they were accepting was destroying them, some of your people would have probably died before they would have submitted to this implantation in their spirit. Even if it meant getting beat to death. Which some of them did, that wouldn't accept this seed."

"You mean that wouldn't admit that they were worthless, a nigger!" I asked

He then admitted, "Yes, that is all it was, a seed planted. You see the principal that God has set up, is forever. It says, whatever you plant is the same thing you have to receive back from that implantation forever"

I wanted to make sure I understood him clearly , so I replied "Just because some body said that they were worthless like the word nigger means, is that what you are saying, right?"

"Yes, In other words God is saying, if that is the root or characteristic you plant in something, if the ground accepts it, and you water it, that is the same thing that will grow. Nothing else but that! .forever, until it dies. You see, a word is also a seed....Look, do you mind if I show you something?....Look, it's right here, in the Bible, here....just let me show it to you, the scriptures are true. Look what it says here in **Proverbs 22:6...**It says

Train a child up in the way it should go... (THE WAY YOU WANT IT TO GO IS WHAT HE IS SAYING) ...and when he is old he will not depart"

Now my ancestors used this principle like this, because they knew it had to work. God is the one that said this principle had to work. So they just said, let us:

Train a slave up in the way we want it to go, and when he gets old he will always stay a slave, still. {HE WILL NOT DEPART FROM THE SLAVE TRAINING.}

You see? …My people are smart man! Because they knew all the scriptures were true, and had to come true. They knew that God can't lie. They were smart like that. They knew that this had been tried and confirmed by other scriptures. They knew that whatever you plant is the same thing you will have to get back, if you train it that way."

I thought I had him just where I wanted him so that I could clock on him, So I replied quickly replied "You mean, if you beat it into them?"

He replied back just as quickly "Or just train them to just say certain words over and over…but yes, your people were trained daily, with brutal force. You see, all my people really depended on originally was the scriptures principals. Plus they had a promise from God that said, Look at this a minute will you?" He took his bible again an began reading

GAL. 6:7
Be not deceived, God is not mocked, what so ever a man soweth THAT! Shall he reap!

That was the first pause he took in a while, but it didn't last very long. He began all over again with: "Do you kind of get the picture? Do you see what they were really depending on to build this country up into a strong prosperous nation? The scripture man, the scripture!….what ever God said would work….and yes, they thought the scriptures were only for them, white folks! The people in America. Most of them had never seen anything else but white folks. They weren't concerned at that point about no black folks, red people, yellow people, or no other people. They were only concerned at that point about making this country strong and rich. They really didn't know a lot about any other people at first. In fact, when they finally did see some other people, people who didn't look like them, or talk like them…most of them didn't even believe that this was a people. Some of them thought that this was some kind of animal or something"

"what!"

"yes, It couldn't talk like them, sometimes it didn't walk like them… It didn't eat what they ate sometimes. So they really didn't understand about other cultures originally. So, they would just go look and find that scripture that said, "This is what will make it grow", and they would just believe it and do it. This is the principal that makes it grow, so this is the principle that they used, that's all."

"my goodness, what was on your people's mind?'

"What they concentrated on most was working the land. They needed something or someone to plant crops to grow on the land. Therefore, they concentrated mostly on the fundamental principles of GOD of sowing and reaping. In other words, if we do this what will we get, if we do that what will we get? See?

"What about other people man?

"They weren't interested at that point, in any race relations, there weren't any races. Or no politics, there wasn't any politics, no voting bills, or things like that. They were only interested in growing, planting, and building stuff so that they could make this country strong."

Frank sit back in his chair , seeing that he had my un-divided attention and said "Just listen to this principle, and they got it from the BIBLE. So they knew it would work...I'm telling you man, your people were up against powerful stuff. This was not just some little weak battle going on here against some other man; this was GOD'S principals at work. This was all the power there is in the universe in action. Listen to the principal that was used here...Look

Proverbs 24:27
Prepare thy work without, and make it fit for thyself in the field: afterwards build thine house

What did GOD just tell them to do? What principal did he say use and it would work? Prepare thy work!. Didn't He? They took that literally. It doesn't make any difference that it was going to be used for selfish or evil purpose or not, all they know is God said, "If you prepare it the way you want it, you can build on it ..Make it fit for yourself....Your ancestors were their work, as far as they were concerned. They prepared your ancestors and made them fit for my ancestors self. His purpose. Then my forefathers could build something; build their houses, .do you see it yet? Now how did they prepare your ancestors?"

I had to answer right there "With un-merciful brutal force, it looks like to me"

Frank agreed again "In the beginning it was with whips and chains and ropes, but finally with just words, words are powerful seeds man, do you see it? Do you see it yet?"

I replied, "Uh, I'm seeing something here, but I don't know if I particularly like it though".

"You shouldn't " he said "It was cruel physical training in the beginning…but mostly with words! Just words, don't forget the same principle of sowing and reaping is still at work here, with just words…words are seeds……It 's like this, My forefathers actually wanted, and thought your people to have little understanding, even fools….and would train them as if that was the case. They didn't even consider them most of the time to be people. As far as my forefathers were concerned, this was just their work, that they were preparing. So they used The rod, and Words in their daily training…They thought the slaves to have very little understanding, and the scripture did say…look at this:

A rod is for the back of him that is void of understanding
Proverbs 10:13

I had to interrupt right there. He had certainly got his point across here "Hold up a minute man! Hold it!…I don't like what I am hearing and seeing at all! I see a character formation being formed and bred here. Something that is repulsive! I see something forming that can never be respected, nor respect themselves…I see a character being formed here to self destruct, even if no one else was trying to destroy it!…Oh man!…. I see a character that is being trained to fail, Wow! .That was so cruel of your people man."

"Yep!"….He replied, "Generation after generation after generation, my people would always get back the same thing from the implantation. Just as long as that plant kept getting watered or trained the way, they wanted it to go…get the picture?

My reply was, "I think so, the only difference here is, they weren't just training up flowers, your ancestors were training up a people to always talk and think like a slave….weak and helpless and worthless, and thinking they had to keep always depending on your old great grand daddies. Man that is sickenning"….

He interrupted me this time and said, "And it is still working, yes sir. It is still working today....I'm sorry man, but it is still working....God's principals is still working today!....that was definitely ornery of my fore-fathers but God's principals still works....you see my brother, all that it is...is God principle at work"

There was a great silence there between me and this old Caucasian for I guess maybe a few seconds. I knew about some of this as being definitely true. Everybody was familiar with at least some of this horror story about slavery from just history books. And then there was the movie, "Roots" that not only informed us more, but made most of us cry with disgust.

Still I kept wondering, why does this man keep telling me about all of these horror stories that have happened to my people then say, God's principal is still working? Hum!....Does God hate us black people too?

Truthfully, I was just about sick of this man, yet for some reason I just could not pull myself away from listening to this man's reasoning over the matter. Plus he kept calling the Creator of Heaven and earth God.

I knew what he meant. He may not know the Heavenly Father does have a name. And would feel more honored if we would take time and learn his one and only original name that HE told to the children of Israel, YAHWEH. But at least he still had his principals and power right. Plus the subject about this awesome power and principles was just too impor-tant to stop and go into any religious argument right now. His heart did seem pure, and he did have the scripture's principals in tact.

I didn't know whether to be sad, cry, laugh or just get up and get stu-pid. Something inside was trying to suggest to me that maybe I should just get mad at all white folks for doing my people like that. I wanted to say, "Man what are you trying to do get me crazy in here?" Plus, I thought "Maybe I should be mad at God too."

In any event, there was another thought that intervened and said, "Hold on a minute, this is a white folk here! And he may be trying to make you aware of something! .don't let him think that you are getting ready to get stupid too!"

The more I sat and listened the more it sounds like he don't like what happened either. So I finally convinced myself to just stay cool and try and see what I could do about all of this now....now is what counts.

So I decided to just drop my ego and foolish pride and try to deal with this thing productively, but it seemed I just had to make one more foolish comment.. I replied, "Man that was so ornery! I never realized just how ornery and low down your old grand daddies were until now...man you done told me enough stuff to make me want to get up and just act stupid in here. Is that what you are trying to get me to do, get stupid in here?"

Frank replied, "Nope, I would suggest get smart...but"...

"Dam man, no wonder some of your ancestors' off springs will just take a pistol out and just shoot some of us down cold bloodedly!...without even thinking about it...or hesitating!...they think WE are nothing...not even human beings...they don't even think it's wrong!....To them, we are nothing!" I interrupted angrily.

Frank replied again, "Well, why don't you do something about it?... You keep telling him you are nothing!...your people keep saying they are just niggers ,Why don't you do something about it!....Those are your brothers aren't they?....So why don't you do something about it, that will stop it?....If I was black, I would sure as hell do something about it. They would have to quit thinking I was an animal...yes buddies!...and to think that it is justified to treat me anyway they want to ?...no way pal!...even kill me?...no way, no way would I continue to let them keep doing that to me!. Or my brothers! I would certainly try to change that"

I was furious about now; I may have even lost my cool right there. I stood up this time and asked him in a tone that may have even frightened him. ... "Do what? Man! Do What? What can I do about an animal like that? I sure as hell don't like it...It's been happening to my people every since I can remember, but what can I do?"

This poor guy sat back in his chair rather calmly. But for some reason it seemed to me this man was sort of enjoying seeing me being bent out of shape so to speak. I think he even had a little smirk on his face as he answered me and said, "Think about it man, I don't know,...but I do know one thing for sure, it's still working, yes God's principals are still working. And I know I sure as hell wouldn't want anybody to think that they could just shoot me or my son down if they felt like it.....Yes, I would do something...God's principle still works, doesn't it?. ..See brother, I just could not let anybody continue to think that they had to build another jail for my son and me, or just shoot me because nobody could use me in their affairs That is the way society at large thinks about some black youth, you know that don't you?...Look, let me be honest though...there are some words that your people use, especially youngsters, that has formed a spirit character in them from just tradition, and God has identified them as being filthy, this scares society…look at this generation from the scriptures will you?…It reads right here

Proverbs 30:
[11] There is a generation that curses their father and does not bless their mother. [12] There is a generation that is pure in their own eyes, but is not washed from their filthiness. [13] There is a generation whose teeth are like swords, and whose jaws are like knives, to devour the poor from the earth and the needy from among men."

This guy seems to know that he had my attention now, so he just calmly kept speaking about God's principles working. But he did pause before asking me the next question. He said, "And you know what else I have to be honest about? Do you know what my son and his friends continue to tell the police and everybody they come in contact with everyday? They even say it to themselves everyday! They keep saying, they know they are dumb, ignorant and savage and proud of it"

I became seriously interested and asked Frank to explain, "when do they do this?'"

Frank explained, "Every where they go…at home, in school, in church, in a club or anywhere a gang of them get together…why my son says the same things about himself as the slaves said with their mouth and attitude about themselves. The slaves use to admit with their mouth, that they knew they were worthless!"

I replied, "Worthless! How are they saying they are worthless?"

He replied quickly this time again, "By using words that mean worthless! or the repulsive spirit it has in it. My son and his friends will even make a CD and get on TV in front of the police and everybody and be proud to say things about themselves and each other, that confess' the same things Like, 'I'm worthless' That is the same thing the slaves thought"

"But those are just words man"

"Look man, maybe you don't know how dangerous and meaningful it is. But here is what they say, 'I'm a nigger! I'm a nigger! I'm a real nigger!' Which only means, I am ignorant and unworthy of any respect as a human being, and I know it? Plus they'll even say, 'I want to shoot that nigger with my 45 that nigger brother, don't deserve to even be alive, because he ain't nothing either!…' man!"

He paused, then said, "Man I don't even believe my son is conscience of what he is even saying when he uses those ugly words, but I can't stop him, he just will not let that old slave training die! That frightens my people"

He paused again and looked at me with one of the most sincere looks that I have ever seen and said, "I was sort of hoping that maybe you could talk to my boy for me, about all of this for me. You see, I'm a white man, he won't listen to me…but you are a Afro-American man, you could talk to him, he may understand then…Don't you care man, that everybody thinks your brother is useless?. Basically, Just because he is unaware of his vocabulary? My boy could be great man, and I love that kid. But most of my side of the family thinks I'm crazy when I say he is not stupid or an animal!"

I believe it may have been at that point, when I probably realized, this man did have a method to his madness! He was purposely trying to stir me up with all of these horrible, humiliating yet truthfully facts. And I have to admit, as horrifying as these truths were, I had to respect him for his motive. He must have felt so helpless and desperate to go so far to make me understand. This man must love that boy .So I felt I had to just let him continue talking about his kid.

He said in a frustrated tone "My family says, when ever they see a crowd of my son's friends or even my son somewhere usually they have to leave their presence."

" why ?"

Frank: explained, "They say his language is so bad, even when he is alone, that it is repulsive to them and they feel like throwing up. They just feel embarrassed hearing him talk and putting himself down with those poison words, because he usually soon start to acting out the spirit of those words. They say they have often wanted to sit down with him, put him in business with them, and just try and treat him like family, but he has such a perverse tongue they can't stomach it. They say they guess they will just have to accept the root is just planted too deep in him and he'll never be worth much."

This Caucasian was getting a little sloppy now and tears had begun to stream down his cheeks again, so I couldn't dare interrupt. This guy seemed to be feeling the same pain as I was. I could only ask, " Frank are you going to be alright man?"

He said, "Yes, I'll be fine, but let me tell you something, look man, I'm in here on a traffic violation, I'll be out in a few days…I own my own business, a construction co. Yeah I got a little loaded and had a traffic accident. I make well over a million dollars a year, and have two degrees, one I don't even use. But do you know my friends still think I'm nuts for believing there is still hope for my son and his friends?"

"Why is that man?" I asked

He continued "Well you see, when ever some of my kid's friends come around, my people usually get paranoid and just leave. .Even most of my judge and lawyer friends usually say things about my boy. Things like , "Why don't we just lock them all up and forget about them Frank? You see they are all savages, just listen to them talk! Look, why don't you just give up on that boy man, these people are all the same he will never change, they are all worthless. They even admit it!"

He paused right there shook his head then said, "I hate the way they treat my kid, but I can't stop him from talking like he does, and putting himself down. Those words of his scares people."

I replied, "Scares people? Why do you keep saying WE scare people… how can words scare anybody?"

He looked at me as if I had committed murder or something. He seem definitely surprised when he asked, "Man don't you know that words are the key to identifying everything? Your words will form you, and identify you! They will tell whether you are evil or not. And they could tell all about you sometimes right away…Oh, man! You see the words that one use will tell what is in their heart…Didn't you know that your words will tell if you are evil or any good? They will tell if a man is smart or stupid, they will tell if a man is a winner or a loser. They will even tell if a man is an enemy and a hater. I'm sure you know by now, as long as a people will willingly hate themselves, no one else feel they should respect them either. They think that person is retarded."

"You mean that's the way people judge people sometimes?" I asked

Frank replied quickly, " That is how my ancestors and forefathers could always identify a person whether or not they could ever be trusted or not…you see they would look in the scripture and see what God had to say about it. Then just believe that. Like this man,…Look"….He opened up his Bible that he already had sitting next to him and began showing me another fundamental scripture that also could not be denied, it read:

Matthews 12

33 A good man out of the good treasure of the heart bringeth forth good things: and an evil man out of the evil treasure bringeth forth evil things….

That is what God said. Do you see it?"

"Hold it man", I interrupted him, "Let me see that!"…so I read it again. And that is exactly what the scriptures said…so I commented, "So God is saying here, that if you are evil you will speak evil out of your mouth?"

He seemed delighted that I seemed to be hearing the scripture correctly and answered, "Yes man, God said it, he even goes further, and look what he says up here in this verse

34 Oh generation of vipers, how can ye being evil speak good things? For out of the abundance of the heart the mouth speaks.

You see it man? Do you see it? God even goes further in this oration by saying words could eventually hurt you because the 37th verse says:

37 For by your words you will be justified, and by your words you shall be condemned."

I heard that perfectly and responded, "Huh! By what you say can condemn you, or free you?"

He responded quickly "Yes man, yes! either way….God set this principal up like that so that everybody can tell what they are dealing with…you don't have to guess, all you really need to do is, just listen a little while to what comes out of a person's mouth the most…that is really what is now in the abundance of their heart. According to God…Look

34 For out of the abundance of the heart the mouth speaks

Do you see now? Do you see how my great forefathers would think that these slaves, even though made slaves, were evil? They would continue to identifying themselves with their mouth!. An evil and wicked person cannot speak good things ..they just will not consistently speak good words...God even said, one that would consistently speak evil words like that,... is now, the same as a viper! Just read what it says for yourself man. He calls people that regularly use evil words vipers! They have a viper's heart, and just do it naturally. Everywhere they go. Oh, man God is steamed about that. Just listen to him identify this character. He calls them:

> *34 Oh generation of vipers, how can you being evil speak good things...*

He's saying evil people can't even speak good things now...consistently. Why? For out of the abundance of the heart the mouth speaks.. That is what is in there, what they speak EVIL! Do you see it?"

That verse almost crushed me right there because that is the way some of my brothers speak to each other daily....evil!....It convicted me and convinced me that this problem of people speaking evil words was something that just could not continue to be ignored. This was a principal identifying a natural obvious nature. And if the scriptures are true, God had identified it as being evil.

"Oh wow! Do you mean that is really, what is in some people's heart, a viper's nature? And they may not know it?" I asked

My Caucasian friend seemed almost elated; he jumped up and began to almost scream, "Yes! Yes! Yes! You are getting it! You are getting it! You see? You see? You are getting it my friend!...Look, my friend, that is what my forefathers planted in some people's heart a viper's nature, and when they see it, it scares them....It scares them to death man..... And that's why some people may act toward your people like they do, even shoot them. They think they are evil! And they can tell that nature by what comes out of one's mouth. You see? The words identify what is in that people. They are the one's that gave them those evil words and trained them. Don't forget they go by the Bible, what God said...Oh man, you are getting it now!"

He calmed down again and said, "I am so glad we can talk man.... you see, my forefathers chose Ornery words man...words that were ugly man…words that meant you were evil, and they planted these words in your ancestors vocabulary…finally into their hearts. And trained this vocabulary and trained and trained and trained them until this people received them in their spirits, and believed them in them hearts…so finally they started acting just like the words they were using meant, evil!"

"Man your people was Ornery, how could they do that?" I asked.

He explained, "My forefathers did this so that where ever this people go, they would be marked, and everybody would always know who they were, just by the words they would use. Then they would have to stay ignorant and destroyed and always work for him. In the fields. Their words kept them in captivity.

They knew your people would have to use these words they were taught if they didn't learn about any other way to communicate…so you see how they would always be identified as vipers? That scares people."

"That was a cruel thing to do to anybody man!" I said sadly

"Sure it was" he answered "but you see my people knew if a man said he was a viper, or if he said he was ignorant long enough he would eventually start acting that way . They knew this because the scripture had told them so. They also knew every word has to produce a spirit after it's own kind according to Gen.1:11. Don't forget my forefathers were very religious; they went by what ever the Bible would say about any situation. The scripture pointed these things out…God's principal works! Can you see it? God even warned this:

Eat thou not the bread of him that has an evil eye neither desire thou his dainty meats, FOR AS HE THINKETH IN HIS HEART, SO IS HE! **Prov. 23:6-7**

I could not go any further listening with out asking this man an important question, "Man, what are some of those words, that your great, great dads , gave my great, great dads, that meant, you were a viper! Or you were ignorant, or you were just plum no good? What are some of them man?"

He seemed surprised again and replied, "You don't know?….Man the word nigger was made up from all the worse negative things they could think up, and designed to mean, I am ignorant, inferior, lazy and all of those negative qualities combine in definition says, 'I am worthless!' And that word is potent!. man`...my people created this word just for that reason....They also made words like, scumbag, dog, bitch, hoe, piece of crap, knowing that if they were used long enough, they will make you feel and act like that....Do you get it?...Do you see it now?"

At this point I believe that there was no doubt in frank's mind that he had me thinking seriously about finding a solution to this horrible condition. I must have been looking seriously troubled.

So he must have decided to just make it plain. He even said it, "Look man, let me just make it plain, so there will be no mistake about it....my forefather would purposely say things like this to your people if one would ever make him mad,.... "Why you black ugly monkey looking devil, I ought to hang you, you act just like a monkey you are plum stupid! Now go and fetch that other monkey brother of yours and the two of you come clean this mess up!...Go get him now! And tell him exactly what I said, get going nigger! You ugly devil!"

"You saying my people would just do anything he said!"

"Now remember, your ancestors were trained to all ways apologize to Mr. Charlie for making him angry before they left. And by now, this generation had already been trained to never talk back or disagree with a white man, or any other white person. No sir! They had already seen enough of their people being hung or just beat to death for just thinking about doing that."

"hung? ...just for not doing what your old grand daddy said?"

"They had witnessed this done to their fathers, their brothers, their grand daddies, great grand daddies...for years and years. So no slave was about to talk back, or say I'm not going to do it...or even hesitate to no white man, or even look a white man in the eye, Without permission. So they would just naturally apologize for making the slightest little error, and say, 'I'm sorry master, I'm sorry I dropped it, I'm just a poor stupid nigger...but I'll run get some of the other niggers, just like you said, we'll clean it up for you boss...Oh you are right boss, I'm so stupid...I'll go right now!"

Frank paused right there , then continued to explain this ugly story to me .... "Well, he would go and find his brothers quick and say exactly what Mr. Charlie had trained him to say, 'Come on stupid niggers, come on! bring ya'll black ugly monkey looking ass on...Ya'll know we can't keep no white folk's waiting...come on, we got work to do, come on niggers before I tell Mr. Charlie to hangs your ugly ass!'

Your ancestors had heard this black ugly monkey looking devil so long, from Mr. Charlie and each other, until they actually started to believe that they were "Monkey looking devils". It became just common for slaves to say to each other, 'Oh nigger, you know you are nothing!. Quit fronting, you are nothing but a black ugly monkey looking devil, and you know it…so quit acting like you are something. You know that's for white folk!"

"man I can see clearly now, a ugly character was molded in my people, wow!" I had to admit

Frank must have known that I was getting the picture he obviously wanted me to see. So he happily continued. " You haven't heard nothing yet….the best part of the training of slaves for Mr. Charlie and the part that had the most effect came from just words, and was the entertainment. However, it was the most intensive training."

"The entertainment?" I asked

"Yes, ..you see, he would gather them all up, usually in the evening, and they would have to imitate some animal or the other. Mr. Charlie would usually choose the monkey or the gorilla. The one that could imitate the monkey or the gorilla most convincingly to everybody would usually be chose as his pet. Pet monkey or porch monkey. They would receive some special privileges though…they may get a chance to drive Mr. Charlie to town, or get a chance to serve dinner, or cook something up in the big house for Mr. Charlie and his guests or family. So every slave would try desperately to win that prize.

They became so good at this imitating until sometime you could hardly tell a monkey from a slave, or a gorilla."

"now, explain to me how that could be possible?" I asked.

"They would try to talk like a monkey, walk like monkeys even eat the monkey's food like him. Anything to win the favor of the slave master. Besides that, they knew if you didn't compete and imitate the monkey or gorilla effective enough, you may get beat with the whip almost to death for wasting the slave masters time. So the word nigger was also created to represent and identify the monkey and the slave. And after a while, and much practicing or training, as far as everyone could tell, they were the same thing. They talk a like, they act a like, and sometimes, did look alike. They practiced even looking like a monkey.

After generation and generations of this planting and watering of the word nigger, the slaves just believed that they were descendants from monkeys, or just Niggers!...they started believing monkeys were their brothers. The crazier the monkey acted, the prouder they became to just imitate him. This would win them the favor of the slave's owner. They were happy when acting like monkeys. Who ever could act the most like a monkey was considered by Mr. Charlie and the rest of the slaves to be the best nigger...because he could imitate the characteristics of this monkey better than anybody else. Some of them even became crueler than the monkey after much practice. They felt they had to survive the other slaves that was always after his position"

"What position" I asked.

Frank seemed happy to continue explaining , " Well, in the evening after all the fields had been planted, he would make all the slaves come out and get in a circle and compete for who was the strongest monkey. So you would have to fight each other. It didn't matter if Mr. Charlie would even pick somebody in your own immediate family. Sometimes with knives sometimes with sticks, whatever the slave owner would pick for that day. But it was always competition going on in the slave's camp for who was the strongest and best monkey, or Nigger. However, who ever would survive would be rewarded. He would be considered the strongest, and the most dependable obedient monkey. And that would earn him the right to come and work up in the big house. He could sit on the porch of the big house, and run errands and stuff for Mr. Charlie. He was now considered proudly to be the porch monkey, or the house nigger."

"So the porch monkey had it made with the slave master!"

"Oh, but porch monkeys would still have to practice being strong and monkey like too, because there was always another slave that wanted his position, up in the big house, where if you were trust worthy to be obedient to your position for Mr. Charlie, He would let you keep the rest of them in line. Even hang some of them for him."

"my goodness !"

"But you would eat well, as long as you never tried to step out of your place as a monkey, or try and encourage another monkey to learn to read or write or something. You would always have to remember to say out of your mouth you knew you were just a Nigger. Plus each group of slaves would always gather around when ever there was a fight or entertainment going on and pull for their side, or their group. It just became natural for each group to divide up and cheer and yell, 'Kill that nigger! Kill that Nigger! Kill him! Kill that black monkey ass Nigger! He ain't nothing ! He ought to be dead! Kill him!'

That just became natural, for the monkey or nigger to live like that, trying to destroy each other. Mr. Charlie told them to do that. Then after each fight, the winner would always rush to his owner, Mr. Charlie for his normal pat on the back and ask, 'How did I do boss? Didn't I destroy that nigger for you? was I a good nigger?...didn't I kill him for you quick enough?...let me work up here with you boss, I'll be a good nigger, for you!'...You see it now?"

"So, that's how that whole attitude got started? Dam!" I replied.

That was all I could basically say....I was almost destroyed by these revelations. But I had to admit that is still basically the way we treat each other. "Dam! we have got to change."

I guess Frank felt sure he was getting through to me now, just like he wanted, so he poured it on a little bit more. He said, "you see after generations of this kind of training, of one's self, the slave masters knew he would have very little trouble controlling this bunch in the future with that thinking. They just thought they were suppose to act like that with each other by habit, that is called, slave mentality....God's principal of sowing and reaping is still in effect...what they practiced was what Mr. Charlie knew would always grow, that's what he would always receive.... Forever **Gal. 6:7**

So when ever a new slave baby was born , they would just let Mr. Charlie know and say. 'Here is a new nigger for you Mr. Charlie...what do you want us to do with it?' ...Naturally, he would just put some porch monkey in charge, one that he could trust and say, 'Train him up to be a good, obedient nigger, you know the way he should go! (Prov.22:6)

Sometimes Mr. Charlie would let it come up to the big house and be raised, but most time he would just say, ' keep him down in the fields with the rest of the niggers, we got enough niggers up here....train him up the way it ought to go, and when he is old, he'll still stay the same way. He'll train his to be that same way.' God's principal will always work my friend, just as long as you keep watering it...or rather training it"

I guess it was because of my honest questions, that made this guy feel like I was seriously interested, and beginning to receive the revelation of

God's principal at work, that he wanted me to see.

I did believe The Bible was true, and that The Creator did give these instructions to holy men as they were moved by Him. (II Peter 1:16-21) so I had no trouble believing that these principals would work for who ever uses them. I guess that is why he felt comfortable now, enough to tell me this personal story about his son and his first cousin. I think he felt he had me just about, where he wanted me.

He paused, so I commented, "Man that's enough to make somebody sick at the stomach."

He continued, "Yep, it should be....It certainly should be...Listen to this personal story of mine my friend. My first cousin owns a restaurant and bar, downtown. And it usually stays full of a lot of wealthy people, who would just normally party in there, all night, and most of the day. But when ever my son goes down to that restaurant with two or three of his friends, the place usually empty out kind of fast.

So my son asked me one day, 'Pop can I ask you a question? Is Uncle Jack and Aunt Marie ashamed of me because my mother is black?'

I told my son, 'No! Son, don't ever think that. They Love you, and they Love your mother, why would you think that?"

He answered me and said, "I don't know, it's just that whenever I go down there to the restaurant lately, since I grew up a little, they don't seem too friendly anymore. They don't seem to want to come over and sit down and eat and talk with us, or be real friendly with me anymore.'

I asked him, "They don't speak to you?"

"Oh yeah," he said, They always give me a big hug when I first come in. And say I love you.., but then they just take off....I always bring some friends with me, that they can see have money....My friends are always dressed in new clothes, and expensive shoes and gold chains...New Mercedes Benz and new sports cars, all of them. Plus my friends will all try to spend a lot of money in there too. So they know these are not guys who are broke, pop. But for some reason, after a while when we look around the place is usually almost empty. Sometimes Uncle Jack leaves early too."

I had to ask "what was that all about?"

Frank said, "Well, I told my kid not to worry about all of that, Jack just probably had somewhere to go, you know he is a very busy man, so don't worry yourself about that kind of stuff, it'll be alright ,I Know they love you...But you know something my friend,....I just said that to my son so he wouldn't feel hurt, but it will never be alright…you see, I already knew about that problem…I had already had this same conversation with my first cousin Jack who owns the restaurant, just lately. He told me, he didn't know what to do either…poor guy, I feel sorry for him too…he don't know what to do. He said he loves my boy it is his nephew, but when ever him or his friends come around he always feels like he is going to get sick or throw up, or something. He says, he knows that they all got money, but he would rather do without it. Because their language and vocabulary is usually so foul and loud and evil, it runs his business away. He says they destroy his business by running his customers away. He told me that their talk reminds his customers of the old slavery days and the racial problems of long ago, and it just makes most of them feel ill, and uncomfortable."

I interrupted there, "You know what…I have got to agree with him right there, that foul language will make you feel ill sometimes. It even does me that way…"

Frank did seem happy about that comment from me, he jumped right back in though, and said , "Jack told me that some of his customers said that they are not prejudice against the color black, and I know they all are not. Some of them are married to black people. But they told him, that they try to stay there and just ignore these guys when they come in, but these guys would get so loud and call each other such foul names like 'My Nigger, My dog! Bitch' , and even worse words …and they would be so loud and foul until it was impossible to just even ignore these guys. He said, it's just disgusting to them and just ruin their evening. These guys act so unruly, until they wouldn't even let the people ignore them…

So rather, than complain to Jack, the other customers would normally just try and slip out of the restaurant somehow. Then maybe come back another time when these guys weren't there….Jack said he would have to do the same thing sometimes himself, or hurt my son's feelings, he felt. He said it is just something about that foul word, Nigger, that destroys the atmosphere, and he can't take it. Because they usually start acting like the word"

I had to agree again, right there…. "Oh, boy, you know I do understand that whole picture right there, sometimes I don't even know how to solve that,…that can be quite complex…as a matter of fact, it is insulting and embarrassing for one to call me a dog or a Nigger!"

I believe this Caucasian was feeling quite comfortable now, revealing his frustrations. He said, "You got to understand something, man. Most of these people know the story of what their ancestors did to your people, and most of them try to forget it. See they know all about these ugly words, good! They know what they were created for and given to your great ancestors. And they know what they can do. So when they hear these repulsive phrases, it makes them feel sick. It embarrasses them for the most part, and then starts to make them feel guilty and paranoid for something that happened before they were born. Knowing they couldn't even explain it all to your people themselves So they just rather not be around all of that....Oh it's a mess man...those words are poison...poison...they were designed to be poisonous. God's principal, works every time...It's still working"

Then once again, we were both silent for a few seconds...this guy seemed to have gone into sort of seclusion...as neither one of us said a word. I knew he was right about those negative words categorizing people, and how they can repulse people also...I just did not have the exact solution right then to answer this man. At least I didn't think I did.

He paused a second, looked at me, and said, "Well...now how do you feel about all of this?"

I replied. "Terrible man.....Terrible"

He looked at me again sitting there quiet and completely destroyed without saying a word, but there was something in his facial look that said,... "Well what are you going to do about it?"

But he didn't say another word about it. Frank just got up from his chair, and held his hand out to me to shake. He said, "I'm sorry, I'm sorry for bothering you like this. I guess this is my problem. It is my son. Don't worry I'll find a solution...I will do something about my son's life...I'm not going to let nobody continue to think that my son is worthless and they can just shoot him down with hand cuffs on if they feel like it...I will do something!....I do care and God's principal still works."

Frank turned and started to walk quietly and slowly toward the men's room, but he stopped suddenly. Frank turned around to me and said, "Oh by the way...all of those people that gave your people those ugly words, long time ago, they are all dead! All of them! They are all dead, not a one of them is alive today. ..But God's principal still works....it's still working, yes sir,...it will still work...A man could plant a new seed."

REVELATIONS

I don't know how long I sit there staring at the TV screen...shocked and amazed as well as baffled. All I know is when I looked around I was alone. My informative Caucasian friend was gone. I had never felt so empty and helpless and sad before in my life. I did want to do something to change the way people felt about US! And how we basically feel about our selves, which is most important. But what? What could I do? I did accept though from the scripture stand point, me and my black brothers and sisters seemed in serious trouble. Even with the Creator of Heaven and Earth. What a problem! But what can I do? This has been going on forever!

So I just finally got up from my chair, and slowly strolled back to my room thinking all the time, what can I do about all of that today? Knowing this was a deep-rooted problem. And for the most part, most of my people are not even aware of the trouble they are really in.

However, I did notice something though. My old Caucasian friend had left his Bible in the chair, right next to me. So I just picked it up and took it to my room with me.

As I sat in my room, I felt more and more anger building up inside of me for somebody. I was furious inside. I was mad at all white people. The newsmen had just finished showing me what looked like just the cold-blooded assassination of my people. It felt like they were killing me! The politicians seemed as if they were justifying it, like it was really not a big deal. This Caucasian seemed to be telling me that his forefathers had trained his off spring to just continue doing this killing without regret. Like it was natural, suppose to happen.

Plus God himself knew it was happening and had at least allowed it to continue. That was this Caucasians theme song… "God's principle is still working"

I was furious with somebody. I didn't know exactly who to be mad at. Maybe my people for not taking up arms and fighting back a long time ago. No! Maybe they couldn't help themselves then…is it this white man's fault?….No, it's not his fault either. He wasn't even born. It's God's fault! I even thought once. Maybe it's my fault!

No, it's not! That thought didn't last long at all, how could it possibly be my responsibility? I didn't know who to blame. All I knew was that this was an ugly problem. Are me and my people giving some people the authority to treat us like this? Even kill us? Hum!

In any event, this "Viper's Nature", thing really, had me puzzled!.. Even though I had seen it in the scripture, "O' generation of Vipers, how can you being evil speak good things?"

The savior himself was saying this….I still couldn't accept it in my spirit as being something that my ancestors or me could have possibly agreed to be…at least not voluntarily, surely not. A nature that makes people basically afraid of you? Can't trust you? Even wants you dead? No way. Surely, my ancestors wouldn't say that they were Vipers!! Over and over and over and over? And accept that in their spirit? At least not knowingly anyway. But it seems that is what foul words will do in your spirit. Eventually, make you act ugly, and Ornery like a Viper. If I was to be honest about it.

Nevertheless, I couldn't seem to rest until I looked up the definition of a viper and see what kind of nature it really has. What are the characteristics like? Just how do they act? Even the savior of mankind says some people have that nature….could I possibly have any of that in me?

The one thing I did know was, words do all have a characteristic and carry a spirit, and every word has its own spirit. Accordingly to the scripture. What exactly, kind of spirit is this? I had to know.

Webster's dictionary identified this word Viper for me as a snake. Then gave me a few more characteristics to consider. I read through some of these meanings almost dumb founded now. But I have to say, it did register. Webster's definitions said:

SNAKE

1. Any of various scaly, legless, cocas venomous reptiles of the suborder serpentines, having long tapering cylindrical body.
2. To drag or pull with a rope or chain
3. A malicious or treacherous person
4. A disorderly chaotic place. A mental institution
5. Pertaining to or characteristic of a snake
6. Poisoning resulting from the bite of a snake
7. Worthless preparation fraudulently peddled as a cure for any and all ills
8. A process of persons who join hands and move forward in a zig-zag line.

Wow! Listen to those negative characteristics! Surely, my ancestors did not accept a nature that would have to make them inevitably a reproach to even the Creator of the universe! Then pass it on to me? O' I have got to investigate how and what would make any one do that. Surely, they did not! What could make any people accept a nature like that? Suddenly I heard in my spirit:

WORDS!

Words?..... Little did I know that I was just getting ready for some devastating truths....but I did here, in my spirit...**WORDS!**

At that point, I didn't know whether I was supposed to be happy, sad, or just be mad at somebody. But I do know from somewhere I was hearing something say. ......WORDS!

I picked my Bible back up and began to try to sort this whole thing out. But for some reason I could not get this Caucasian's face out of my mind. All I kept hearing him saying was, "What are you going to do about it? What are you going to do about all this?"

I sit there thinking "What can I do about such a complex and foul situation? People think we have a Viper's nature and hate ourselves and each other. Most of them are probably afraid of us because we hate ourselves. This is absolutely ludicrous. But I do see some things similar to a Viper's nature in some of my people's actions that need to be changed, if I'm going to be honest about this thing. And I have to admit, we did inherit it. I do basically the same things my father did, and he did basically the same things his father did"

Then I cried out, "Father up in Heaven, how could you let all of this happened? How did we get trapped like that?"

This might have been the beginning of my restoration....if I was going to ever accept restoration. Because I certainly heard from somewhere:

Thou art trapped by the words of your mouth
Thou art taken with the words of your mouth
Proverbs 6:2

For by your words thou shall be justified
And by your words thou shall be condemned
Matthews 12:37

What? I was taken by the words of my mouth? I thought we were taken by that old white man? I thought we were tapped because they had guns and we didn't? I thought that is what kept us in trouble....but the scripture is saying here that, I was trapped by the words of my mouth! Hum!

In any event, since I was pretty sure now, that this was the spirit that comes from above, the spirit of love, trying to communicate or lead me some where, I was sort of grateful for that, nevertheless I still asked The Heavenly Father, "Father, how could you let those people enslave my People like that, forcing those ugly words on us to keep us poor and helpless so long? Now we barely have a life, and No power, and now it looks like they are trying to destroy us! For good."

I heard in return, again, "You are not helpless! If you don't want to be, the power is in the tongue."

I looked up, then turned around, just to see if anybody heard me ask that question....but, I was still all alone in this room... "did I just hear I can solve my problem with my tongue?"

It turned out as I looked down into this book of instructions that I had obviously opened called the Holy Bible, there it was, opened to **Proverbs 18:21** it said as plain as day:

Death or life are in the power of the tongue and
a man must eat the fruit his tongue chooses
{The book of Yahweh}

Somehow, someway. I believe I had contacted The Creator of Heaven and Earth. Or some representatives. Somehow, someway I had made communication with the Father of Light....I asked him an important question! And he gave me an important answer....I could not stop from listening right there, No Sir! I was sure; this was the Power, from above.

However, I needed to know more. I needed to know, how does this Power work that's in the tongue? I believed that it was Him that answered but I still needed more instructions on how this power works. And I must have in my spirit, finally asked him. Because he most certainly did start talking.

I couldn't leave this room now. I just sit there quietly alone, with this Bible open reading these scriptures over and over, hoping to see or hear something else. I knew I heard in my spirit something important, but I also had the sense enough somehow to know I needed more. It just wasn't clear yet.

So I sit meditating, then asking questions to myself. I was just too close to something very important to just quit. And I knew it. But I could not put it all together exactly what all this meant yet.

Besides that, I believe the devil got busy trying to seriously interrupt me every time he could too. I believe he also knew that I was getting close to something with delivering power in it. Because just as soon as he seen that The Creator of the Universe was trying to point me somewhere in the scriptures, the prison guard would yell COUNT!...COUNT TIME!

No real problem though, I was determined this time to stay focused on what ever the scriptures were trying to tell me. I was determined to just stay with it. I would stand up, or walk outside the door of this little room and get counted, which never took more than five minutes anyway. Then I would hurry back to this little room where I first heard those profound words, pick up the Bible and start right back over again asking the questions...and probably from the deepest part of my heart.

Again, I must have somehow asked the right questions. I must have asked, "Father, how does this power work, that you said was in the tongue?" And, I believe HE heard me again. I have no doubt about it. As a matter of fact, HE had heard me all day. HE always hears me. if I would only ask the right questions, from my heart, then listen, I would always get an answer…not only did HE hear me but it seems HE was trying to lead me all day as it turned out, to the only answer HE has ever given any man, concerning how this power works. HE said, by the same principle HE set up since the world began! The same principle HE even gave his son to give to every body on Earth! His word Principle! And His word Principle is:

"If you would first confess with your mouth, and believe in your heart." Romans 10:9

I could not stop reading and listening today it was in Roman: 10:9 but it sounded like he was standing in front of me….. Suddenly I just knew something was about to make sense, and I could feel it in my spirit. Plus, that is the same principal that this Caucasian out there seems to be convinced of, he seemed convinced that, "I could do something"

I remember this Caucasian asking me over and over "What are you going to do?" ….as if, I already had the power or the solution to do something to change the bondage that my People are in, or stop them from shooting my People down. That is the thing we both seemed the most concerned about today, and the thing that seemed to be crushing both of us today. I believe that basically, he was just concerned about his son. I was concerned about me and my people.

Now, here the scripture is pounding on me, something that is piercing my heart. It keeps saying that, I can do something ..it keeps saying repeatedly, If I, If I, If I, If I! Do something…things would change.

That is basically all I have been hearing for some reason, all day long… "I can do something"…plus, now something keeps saying, I got the power in my tongue… Hum!

After I had obviously got the gumption and obviously had the nerve to ask The Creator of the World those profound questions, the scripture definitely started saying to me, If I…If I…If I would do something, If I!…one time it said to me loudly, If I would confess with my mouth and believe in my heart, I could even be saved. or delivered. If I', would do it. Not Him! But, If I, would do it…Me! **Romans 10:9**

I knew what saved meant. I knew that much. I knew it didn't only mean that I get to go to Heaven when I died. But set free, or delivered from any situation of bondage right here on earth, saved! If I, If I do something.

I became seriously confined to this little room now. And this Bible. And this very interesting yet strange conversation, with somebody. That lasted for hours maybe days. All the time still thinking how this black brother of mine, with hand cuffs on behind his back, was shot down by the police, and not many people was really bent out of shape about it. It was like, it's ok! It was suppose to happen....how can we change that attitude about US? That is what I was concerned about.

Brothers and sisters, The Creator of The universe said, WE can! change any negative thing that is in our way ,even the way some one may feel about you, But, it is all up to US! And US only!

Somewhere along the line that day, I remember, I felt the need to get down on my knees and ask the Creator, "Would you step in and save me and my People from this terrible destruction? It looks like people are starting to just kill us, especially our youth, without thinking that we are even important, or even people for that matter. Will you save us?"

And he did answer back. He answered back with about as surprisingly and strong a revelation as I or anyone else probably will ever hear. While I was asking and praying and reading he certainly said, **"I can't! You and your People have to do it!"**

Huh? I know something is wrong now...did I hear HIM say, He, **"Can't?"**...maybe HE means HE just "Won't!" right now.

As soon as I thought that, I immediately heard again.... "No you heard right...I said, **I can't, but you and your people can though! Why don't you use my principals and save yourselves, I already have once."**

Either I had went completely nuts, or these words that I was reading was alive because I was having a conversation with words, and these words that I was reading were answering back!....I really needed to ask this spirit a question then, and get some understanding now. So I immediately asked, " Father, I thought you could do anything, have you run out of power? Don't you care if we perish? I thought you could do anything!"

After that question I know for sure, I heard,

"I can't lie, anything but lie!" (Heb. 6:18)

Whoa! This certainly got interesting. I guess the most profound yet important thing, something that I should even be shouting about, is coming through these scriptures today. That is what I should be happy about. Because it was the solution that has always been available, if we just accept it. And HE didn't stop right there this time HE asked me a question. HE asked, "Why don't you save yourself? Why don't you use my rules, and save yourselves?"

Oh my goodness.... "Save yourself!"....Oh my goodness....and that was without a doubt Him! The Creator of mankind! I'm learning according to the scripture and I'm hearing in my spirit, If I do certain things I can be delivered and it is getting louder and louder as I read. Like a voice....

Some of us are probably going to be terribly surprised when we find out that we may have been complicating the simple answer to all our problems. The solution has always been there, in us.

I also found out this day that The Heavenly Father never tells you about a problem without giving you the absolute solution to it too. It seems to me that The Creator of mankind had found somebody to tell me about a problem that WE have always had. Then he showed me His solution right a long with it. And he added "Time is running out!"

TRAIN IT UP

Only those that will believe The Creator of heaven and earth can be absolutely sure that they will get the results they were after. Those and only those! Because God has said, *"It is up to you; plant what you want to receive."* **Galatians. 6:7 Proverbs. 22:6**

You could hope and wish and pray and cry and moan all day, make new Laws, Vote, demonstrate march and accuse everybody you see, yet still may never get that result you were after. As a matter of fact, those that won't believe that the Savior will do only what he has already said and just accept and agree with that, is really working against him, and playing with themselves. Whether we know it or not, HIS rules can never change. Amos 3:1

He is simply asking us to stop the old spoiled root from growing ,and plant a new seed that is good for us...what kind of seed are you watering? That's what kind of crop you will grow up. If you stamp out the old spoiled root, and plant another seed that is righteous, keep watering it, it has to grow up into a bigger and bigger and bigger crop too.

I also found out that it does not matter, much what kind of plant it is, it will still grow. The only real difference in the crop, HE explained to me is, some roots are roots for destruction, and some roots are roots of righteousness springing up unto everlasting life. But His Law is, they both still have to grow, if they are watered.

My people, I must admit, this Caucasian had me so angry until, I just became sick and tired of being sick and tired. I had to look for the truth about this thing once and for all. Are you?

The Savor's rule is, whatever was planted, accepted by the ground, believed, and watered, (which only means trained or practiced), then that is what has to grow and grow and grow and grow, until it dies. The only way it will ever stop growing is if you stop watering it. Which means training it or practicing it? And God is the only one that can make things grows! And He will allow things to grow, when you water it, it's our choice.

We have often made the mistake in saying, look, what the devil did… no, he didn't, and the devil can't make anything increase. It was the Savior that increased it. Whatever you were watering. HE is the only one that can make anything increase. All the devil can do is suggest then try and destroy something, he can't increase nothing. Paul even warned us that

1 Corinthians 3:6
I have planted, Apollo's watered; but Yahweh {God} gave the increase

So all you really have to ask is what kind of plant have you accepted in your ground. { IN YOUR HEART } What are you practicing or watering everyday? That is what your branches will also be like, your offspring… your children….just like the Root. Generation after generation after generation. It can't stop, growing like the root good or bad.

Even if men got together and passed a bill or made a law on paper that says, "Stop it, you absolutely can't do that no more"…The Creator's law says that plant has to keep right on growing until it dies, if it keeps getting watered. His rule is for all creation.

The rule is, a cabbage root does not have the authority in itself to in the middle of growing, to just turn around and say, " I'm going to stop growing cabbage on this root, and start growing something else. I don't want to be a cabbage anymore; I'm going to be a plum."

The creator's rule says, that root has to continue to grow what was planted. If you don't want cabbage no more, you have to pluck that root up, or stop watering it, or just kill that root and start planting something else different in its place. And whatever you plant in its place has to grow too, if you water it.

His word, which is His law explained something so carefully and so simple to me until a baby should be able to understand it. It explained that. When He spoke his words from the beginning

"Let there be Light" Genesis 1:3

It had to happen… that was, and still is, His rule forever. Even for words. They have to produce whatever He says it is suppose to produce. He is the Almighty! That is the spiritual law from The Highest Authority there is. Here is the never-ending law for any seed planting. It was also established when Yahweh the Heavenly Father first created earth. He said,

Genesis 1:11
Let the earth bring forth grass the herb yielding seed, and the fruit tree yielding fruit, after its kind, whose seed is in itself, upon the earth: and it was so.

You see, the seed is already in the things HE brought forth. Even words are seeds, "Whose seed is in itself"…And it has to produce after its own kind. Or whatever characteristic or Spirit it has in that word. Did you hear him? Did you hear the rules?

He planted a word and it increased, everyday there has been light. Forever! Just because HE said, "Let there be light." It will never quit coming up like HE said, never! Everyday. The word Light produced Light. The word manifested itself into what HE said it was. Light! That's his law. Plus HE enforced the principal with another rule

Gen 8:22
"While the earth remained, seed time and harvest, and cold and heat and summer and winter, and day and night shall not cease".

That is the Savior's principle, His law, or His rule forever. It will never quit until the end of time. Never. For nobody. Nothing can stop that because that is The Creator of the universe's will. That's how he wants things to remain. Do you know anybody who can change His laws for Nature?

The rules are permanent for every Law He set in place until the end of this system. And they shall do exactly what His word says it will do and nothing else but what he says it's supposed to do. He explained

Isaiah 55:11
So shall my word be that goeth forth out of my mouth: It shall not return unto me void, but it shall accomplish that which I

please, and it shall prosper in the thing whereto which I sent it.

That is a statement and a Law forever. That is His rule for everything HE says. "It shall accomplish what ever HE pleases." If his word says "Increase what they plant"….Which is exactly what he said in Galatians 6:7…That's what is going to happen. It has to do just that, because He planted the word. And it accomplished what he said it would accomplish. It can't return to Him without doing it.

We all need to just start believing Yahweh the Creator of heaven and earth and the everlasting fountain of living water, who you probably call, God. That's all. Just believe him The Savior of the World. But he does have a name though. And everybody needs to search that out seriously too.

Yahshua Messiah The son of Yahweh, The Creator of heaven and earth. Whom you probably know as Jesus, who all powers were given to in heaven and on earth by Yahweh. The same power and rules as was his father, gave us this very impressive message. HE said,

"The words (Laws) that I speak unto you, they are spirit, and they are life".
John 6:63

What He was saying was "investigate the words that you say first, because they all have a spirit, they are alive".

If man can't believe his word is alive, he will never be able to see the savior of the world. Or receive anything from HIM. ..The spirit and the word agree. remember his father's rules

"every fruit bearing plant, must produce after its own kind"

They can't do anything else but produce more and more of the same thing. The same kind of spirit. And each word has a life and spirit of its own, its kind. (Genesis 1:11)

If I would call you, "King", everyday, if I would just start saying your highness, king good morning king. Everyday, everyday, everyday. I would probably start treating you like a king! Everyday, everyday, everyday. Then suppose everybody else you know started calling you and treating you like a king. Everyday, everyday, everyday. That would be watering that word, or practicing, or training that word. King!

Do you know that even though you may not have ten dollars that you could put your hands on, and a throne nowhere, but sooner or later, you would start calling yourself king! too?....then after awhile, start to act like you were a king!....you don't have to have an army nowhere, or even an automobile of your own, but for some reason you'll just automatically think that you should be giving orders somewhere, or running something. You'll just subconsciously start to try to imitate a king!

Do you see it? The word itself has a spirit in it, and if you let it sink in, you will sooner than later just develop the characteristics that is in that word. King! It's a spiritual law. That spirit has to produce after itself. It has to, the Creator of man gave the words those instructions to produce that spirit. HE is the father of spirits. Read Hebrews. 12:9 sometimes

He created everything that is, and gave everything it's instructions of how it was supposed to produce. Even spirits.

Now the same thing would happen if I called you a Monkey everyday. That word also carries a spirit in it. If I called, you monkey everyday, and that word ever got planted in your heart, because you accepted it, through some kind of training or watering everyday, in a period of time you would start calling yourself monkey too. Then start sooner or later hunting down banana's and climbing trees for some reason. You may not have the slightest idea why you are just sitting up in that tree. But that is eventually were we would find you most of the time. Just sitting in somebody's tree, and looking for a banana.

The spiritual law still applies and will have to work whether you were aware of it or not. That spirit had to produce after that word. That's what monkeys do, that is just the character in a monkey. That's the creator's law not the devils'.

You know one of the greatest things a man could do for himself, if he likes to talk, is get him a dictionary. And just see what some of the words he is going to use means. Every word in there has a meaning and a spirit that goes with it also. Some are more potent than others, but it still has its own characteristic. You'll probably see a lot of people stop talking so much, but if they did, it would definitely help him.

The word "nigger" has a spirit of it's own. It was created for one purpose, to produce its own character. It was created just for perverseness. It is really one of the devil's pets, just because of the character it was design to create. If accepted in one's spirit and practiced everyday it produces hatred, ignorance, disunity, failure, disrespect for yourself and all creation, selfishness, inferiority, low self-esteem, and paranoia. It's a word created to produce all negative qualities. It also has a spirit contained in itself to make one loud.

You don't even have to know it, but if it is used repeatedly enough it will always bring the results that it was created for. It can't help it, it was designed that way, and it has to produce after its own kind of spirit. That is the spiritual law (Genesis 1:11)

This word was created and promoted to become socially acceptable among black slaves, exclusively for them. Most people today don't even know this, especially young black youth. It will make intelligent people eventually start to back away from you. It produces evilness. That is all it can do.

The word beautiful has its own spirit. If you would say that word enough to anybody, even to yourself, you will just start feeling like you were beautiful. You can't help it that is the spirit it carries. Beautiful! It has to do whatever the spirit is designed to do, make you feel beautiful! No matter who uses it, it will work on whoever accepts that spirit in their heart, even if they favor a possum. You will sooner or later just start acting and feeling beautiful! All of that is the Savior's principle at work.

Even if this thing that you are watering or practicing is not what is best for you, the Savior of mankind still has to let it increase. Even if you don't know what you are watering. The word knows. "It is a seed itself" and it won't return void. It will accomplish whatever it is suppose to. Its purpose is to prosper. It is not up to the creator no more. He told mankind

(Galatians 6:7).
"what so ever you plant"…It'll increase!"

Even a root of bitterness will grow, if it is watered…It has to increase, that is the law of sowing and reaping, planting, and receiving…the branches will have to contain the same thing in them as the root…Even if it is a hundred years later.

———

I have got to confess my people, while sitting in this little room. The creator of the universe seemed to have never stopped trying that day to press on me how important it was for all men to understand that this was the same principle and power that set the world in motion. He wanted us to know that this principle is important, necessary and can never change. For our decision of what we water will determine our destiny. So any man that believes Him will just have to go by His rules. Simple as that...Now what are you going to do about it?

And it was the same principle needed to make a baby. All you have to do is plant a seed, if it is accepted, a baby will start growing. A good implantation or a corrupt implantation will increase. If it is continually watered. A thorn bush will even have to grow, if it is watered it don't matter. Those are the Savior's rules. *You don't have to know it, it will still grow.*

its seed is in itself **(Gensis1:11)**

WHAT ARE YOU GOING
TO DO ABOUT IT?

What are you going to do about it seemed to be the question for the last few days. I don't know when the Creator of heaven and earth took a break from speaking about His very important principles to me, honestly, I think that this conversation proved by scripture went on for days. Because as soon as I would wake up, early every morning, it seems as if He wanted to rap again....truthfully I was delighted those few days.

So almost before I could get my shoes on every morning while sitting on the side of my little bed, I would usually grab my Bible open it and just start listening to this very unusual, but powerful and honest necessary conversation, for all mankind.

Only this particular morning as soon as I got up, I had barely got my shoes on and got my Bible out, and what do I see standing in the doorway of my little room? This same concerned Caucasian from a few days ago, who is the one who actually instigated this very unusual conversation between me and those scriptures in the first place. And instead of a, "good morning," his first reply was, "well!..Did you hear anything? What are you going to do?"

There it is again...the Creator of the universe's principal, telling me again, I can do something. But my answer this time was, "Man! I heard a lot! And you were right about the savior's principal's being a force that cannot be stopped, or altered. I think I just heard that from Him, personally! It is awesome! And, I found out that the same principals that can bring you death, and destruction, can be used to bring you life! Eternal life! Wow!"

This gentleman seemed relieved and elated, to see that at last, maybe

I do see that something can be done to turn this trend around that had plagued my people for generations.

Even though the ones that need something done the most were my people, he seemed as happy as I was as he threw his hands up in the air and said, "Hallelujah brother! Hallelujah!. I thought that is what you were probably doing, shut up in this room for the last few days, listening to the Creator!...hallelujah"

This man was excited. For a while, I thought he might shout. He continued, " You know what man, I would give anything to be a black man in these last days, man, you guys have got a message for your brothers that will help the Creator get His people in!...before it is too late...hallelujah! Man you guys are valuable to The Savior in these last few days, you could deliver your brothers, just like the Jews were delivered."

I replied, "WE!..could be valuable?...what about you?...your people are the ones it seems like that got us all messed up!....bringing us to America, planting that ugly root in us,...why don't YOU try to deliver us?"

"Man I wish I could," he replied,... "If I was black I could though!... but hold it before you take off on that revenge trip....Now that will destroy what the creator is trying to do here...don't worry about those people of over 200 years ago, they don't get away either. I feel worse for some of my people. Just be glad you know the solution now...look what he said he would do to them."

This fellow just invited his own self in now, then sit right down beside me on this little bunk, picked the Bible up and quickly turned to Proverbs 22:..and said to me, *"Man will you just look at who will avenge you."* He *started reading:*

²². Rob not the poor because he is poor, neither oppress the afflicted in the gate ²³. for the lord will plead their cause and spoil the souls of those that spoiled them

He continued explaining, " Do you see?... I really hate that some of my ancestors are not going to be there in the kingdom when I get there, but those are the rules. Even if they had done some good things sometimes, and had high hopes, and expected to go into the kingdom with God. God said they still can't go, if they were still wicked when they died. Listen to the rules:

Proverbs 11:

⁷. When the wicked dies their hopes dies with them"

Do you see now? He has told us 100 times in the scripture, that revenge is his. .No brother, don't waste your time worrying about what somebody did to your ancestor 200 years ago, be happy, that you can now deliver your brothers with this good news, here on earth!...Then go into the king-dom with God, forever!. Hallelujah, man that is something?"

I replied, "That is something isn't it? What are you man, a light unto the gentiles or something?"

He answered back, "Maybe! I don't know, I do work for The Savior though...but I do know who you are...you are a vessel he could use, to get his people that he loves in! If you care enough."

I replied, "Oh I care, this thing has got me almost sick to my stom-ach. Now that I have discovered this BITTER ROOT thing could keep me, not only busted up on this earth, but keep me from having life in the kingdom with Him forever according to **Hebrews 12ᵗʰ chapter**. I most certainly care...I'm just wondering why you think that I could do so much, and not you?"

"My friend,"...He sat back down on the bed again, then opened the Bible again, and began explaining, "Did you know that every time the Creator of the world, sent a message to save a people that HE loved, He never sent a foreigner first?...He always sends one of their brothers first. He has-been doing that every since he delivered the children of Israel out of the same kind of trouble that your people are going through. Will you just look at something? Look

Deuteronomy 18

¹⁷And Yahweh said unto me, they have well spoken that which they have spoken ¹⁸ I will raise them up a prophet from among their brothers, like unto thee, and I will put my words in his mouth, and he shall speak unto them all that I shall command him. ¹⁹And it shall come to pass, who so ever will not harken unto my words, which he shall speak in my name, I will require of him

The Savior knows exactly what he is doing. He has sent every nation a

---

prophet of his own brothers to draw those to him that would be delivered. Even Jesus was sent, just like you, to deliver a people out of their bondage. Before He died on the cross, He was supposed to tell the Jews about the good news. As a matter of fact, He told his disciples not to even go yet, to the Gentile Nations until after He resurrected from the dead, did you ever see that? Look at this from the King James version

Matthews 10:

⁵. These twelve that Jesus sent forth and commanded them saying, go not into the way of the Gentiles and into any city of the Samaritans enter ye not. ⁶. But go rather to the Lost Sheep of the house of Israel. ⁷And as ye go preach, saying the kingdom of heaven is at hand. ⁸Heal the sick, cleanse the Lepers, raise the dead, cast out devils: freely you have received, freely give.

It was not until He was resurrected from dying on the cross, and the curtains were torn, and the veil was lifted did Jesus instruct Paul to go spread this message about what God had promised, that all men can come in now. Those that would accept his Father and was called. It didn't make any difference now whether you were black, white, red, or green. He wanted all people to hear this good news. Paul said, now:

"There is neither Jew nor Greek, there is neither bond, nor free, there is neither male nor female: for ye are all one in Christ Jesus. And if ye be Christ's then you are Abraham's seed and heirs according to the promise"
Galatians. 3:28-29

Let me be honest with you brother, there is no defense for what some of my old ancestor's did to your ancestor's because they were tricks from the devil, that's all there is to it...oh they were clever now, never the less they were powerful tricks using the principals of the creator for their own evil selfish gain consequently it enslaved a people in their heart....a people whom they had kidnapped and kept them from reading the scriptures. So they couldn't know what was happening to them.

If your people had been able to read the Bible, some of this enslaving my ancestor would not have been able to do to them. God had already warned men to be on the look out for the tricks of the devil. But your people never heard it until it was too late. Look right here, **Ephesians 6:** *He had already told us;*

> *¹¹put on the whole amour of God that ye may be able to stand against the wiles of the devil*

Now what are the wiles of the devil? Well we know what they are now. In Webster's dictionary right here, wiles have been identified as,

WHILES
No. 1 A deceitful stratagem or trick
No. 2 A disarming or seductive manner device or procedure
No. 3 Cunning trickery

You see? You and your ancestor's were tricked my friend by the devil's spirit. They weren't just wrestling against my old forefathers, but against a powerful principle set down by God but used by the devil's advocate.... Man, that was the principle for all the power in the universe coming after you. Listen to what you were wrestling with **Ephesians 6:12**

> *For we wrestle not against flesh and blood, but against the principalities, against the powers, against the rulers of the darkness of this world, against spiritual wickedness in high places*

You see, if a ruler takes the Creator of heaven and earth's principle and turns them around and use them for selfish evil purposes that is spiritual wickedness in high places"

"You saying the devil can use God's principals?"

"Oh yes! The devil can use God principles and they will still work. He will use it selfish and unmercifully, used wrong it will bring death. The devil knows that (ll Corinthians 3)

The only thing is, he will use the Savior's principle but not the Savior's mercy with it. The devil has no mercy in him. You see anybody can use God's principle, that's how the devil has deceived so many, because God's principle works for anybody. A person may belong to the devil and don't know it. But yet use God's principle of sowing and reaping. That is why God says HE would prefer mercy rather than sacrifice. **Proverbs.21:3 Hosea 6:6**

Oh yes,...one could sacrifice an offering of going to church, quit smoking and drinking, pay their tithes, one may even do a good deed here and there and still belong to the devil, they may even exercise the principle of sowing and reaping.... all of these are principles that will work into producing something. But if they have no mercy, the creator is still not honored or pleased. That's the way some of my ancestor did.

Yes sir, you guys have survived a mighty war, the devil has been trying to completely destroy you forever, since your beginning here. But he can't...God always sends a people, one of their brothers with HIS message to help first....for whoever will receive it.

God even sent a message to your people long ago that said, 'go ahead, obey that slave master with fear and trembling but not like you are obedient to him but obedient to me, I'll get you out of that mess, I'll send you a messenger...just don't let those words get in your heart'. Listen to him warn you Ephesians.6:

> [5] *Slaves be obedient to them that are your masters according to the flesh... with fear and trembling...in singleness of heart as unto me*
> [6] *Not with eye service as men pleasers...*

Did you hear what he said, In singleness of heart,....in other words, "don't worry about what the slave master is saying, keep your heart, mind, and eyes on me, not men, I'm going to rescue you"...Listen to the conclusion of his statement as to how we are suppose to obey the Savior. It says

> *But as servants of Christ, doing the will of God from the heart*

Yes sir brother...now what are you going to do? The will of God or what?...who are you going to obey, the slave master or God? ..Man look at the power you got on your side, all the power of the universe is working with you guys now. Who knows you may even get the chance to make his holy name known...YAHWEH! Man I wish I could go out with your people and spread this message....you see, I've got a dog in this fight, my kid has got to be delivered too."

I finally quit listening and spoke up, "...I've got to be honest with you, old obedient Caucasian man...light unto the Gentiles...I never seen it like this before, you are right...the Savior's principles are powerful and unchangeable, and they still work!...you just have to use them the way he says use them and they will deliver you. I believe that without a doubt now...so what do you think I'm going to do? I'm going to obey the Savior of mankind, the only help for my people...man if enough of us start to preach this message of, 'Plant another root' with words of righteousness,...man this thing could catch on like wild fire...man that would be something, wouldn't it?...my people are starving for truth...and it all starts, according to the Savior, with just a new set of words."

This enlightening character didn't say much more as it was just about count time again; he just threw his hands back in the air again mumbling something as he walked toward the door saying, "Hallelujah! Hallelujah!" And I sat there with the Bible.

I sat there alone feeling somewhat relieved, yet somewhat terribly guilty. I knew I was going to have to go spread this message to my people, knowing that some of them will be offended from this message in the beginning just like I was at first. I had to ask myself some serious questions this time again... I pondered out loud, "Man I hope our root of courage and understanding haven't been destroyed already, along time ago forever!

Could that really be true what they say about us? Could we really have a viper's spirit in some of us? And just don't even have enough courage left to investigate what we have been saying and accepting through the generations? Have most of us just become basically brain dead from this old poison root of nigger, and don't even know it?... O' man, wonder should we just give up and say, O, well I guess this is just the lot for this race of people forever!"

Frank stops and turns around and says, "The Savior of the world doesn't think so! He keeps saying, if I, if I, if we! If you! Do what He said, mankind could all be delivered. Plant A new Seed"

So I decided, I do have love and concern for my brothers and sisters, And I do trust The true scripture. So, I guess I'm going to have to just do what the Savior said do, and go deliver this message to my people, before it's too late! Let's plant a new seed!

THE SOLUTION

One word, one word my people ,started the deterioration of a whole race...NIGGER! Simply because WE watered it and watered it and watered it down through the generations. Even though unaware of what WE were doing, this word is still trying to manifest itself into a blanket reality. Very few African-Americans escaped accepting this poisonous root. A root designed to destroy all intellectual capabilities, and if one is not careful it can destroy all possibilities of one even receiving eternal life with the Heavenly Father according to the Scriptures. **(Hebrew 12 :)** For the word breeds sooner or later a serpent root, NIGGER!

Our great ancestors were forced to accept this poison root, a word called NIGGER! And handed it down to us through generations, even to now. However evil or unfair that was, it is a reality that WE must get past this unfortunate injustice and move on.

The truth is what ever happened in the past, if we hang on to a poison root from a people who have been dead for hundreds of years, WE will only continue to destroy ourselves more and more and never change in character. Then the devil still wins **(Mathews 6:14-15)**

We absolutely must kill the poisonous root that WE accepted long time ago, and plant a new one, if WE ever intend to become meaningful on this earth or receive life in the kingdom with The Heavenly Father when WE die.

Hebrew 12:15 (The Book of YAHWEH)
So that there is no fornicator nor profane person like Esau, who for one morsel of food sold his birthright.

WE received what has been identified in the scripture as a "Root of

Bitterness" in US that cannot depart under the present seed. According to the scripture. That bitterness root defiles you in Character here on earth. And you will be defiled, then destroyed in the end forever, if that poison root is not ever replaced. And the only way that poisonous root can ever be destroyed is to first quit watering it!

The saddest part about this is that as long as you keep watering that poisonous root in you, The Creator of the Universe has to give it increase even though it is a poisonous root in you...WOW! {1cor.3:6}

Of course there are people that may even be sorry that they, or rather their ancestors planted this evil root in people in the first place. Just the thought of this immoral injustice makes some people of Caucasian descent or other races who have learned what took place in slavery days feel ill. But that doesn't matter much now, they can't stop that root from growing either. Nobody can stop it from growing if you keep watering it... Nobody can stop it from growing but you. Our Savior said, you have to stop it.

What is more pathetic is that the devil is so clever, he has told some of us today that the word NIGGER can mean something else, if you want it to, don't worry about it. The devil has told people who have limited knowledge of the Creator or His, word, that if you put an "A" on NIGGA, you can change the meaning and spirit in which the Creator has said will never change. [Gen.1:11] And some people believed him. Oh, he is deceptive.

The Father of Love himself warned mankind through the scriptures hundreds of years ago to be sure and not accept any bitter root in your heart or it can defile you.

He explained this principle so perfectly in the 12th Chapter of Hebrews, and most of us have been missing it for years; warning us to be aware. Plus, WE and WE alone have to make this important choice. It is not even up to HIM anymore whether WE keep this poisonous Root in US and be destroyed, or whether WE plant a new one and be delivered. He has given all men a free will (**Revelations 22:17-18, 21:2-9...Deut 30**)

It is so vitally important to know if you have accepted a bitter root in you or not .He is saying here in this scripture that not only will it cause trouble for you in this life, but you can't even go into eternal life with Him without destroying that Root and getting yourself connected to an undefiled root. Him, The Father of Living Water. It's all up to us now. Just listen to what he is saying. Plus He tells us exactly what that root of bitterness was designed for.

Hebrews 12:9
⁹Further more we have had Fathers after our flesh which Corrected us and we gave them reference, shall we not much rather be in subjection unto the Father of Spirits and live?

In other words, He is saying, "isn't it better to listen to Him and live, than to keep listening to the slave master's training. We obeyed him and accepted that bitter root , didn't we?" Actually, all that most Black people in America know is the Slave Master's training. That was a bitter root. It was handed down to us through the generations. But now the Savior is saying, why don't we mind Him and Live? Let's listen to the scripture a little more, and not the slave Master's Training.

¹⁰For they verily for a few days chastened us after their own pleasures but HE for our own profit, that we may be partakers of His holiness.

He is saying right here that the slave master trained us for his own selfish benefit, but HE is trying to qualify us to come and live with HIM with HIS training… to be partakers of HIS holiness…because the other training we received from our ancestor's and slave master's training was designed to destroy us. Let's read further

¹¹Now no chastening for the present seemeth to be joyous but grievous:…[some times we just hate to stop what we have been accustom to doing and saying, don't we?]
Nevertheless afterward, it yieldeth the peaceable fruit of righteousness unto them, which are exercised thereby.

What does He mean? No training is joyous is what HE is saying here, but nevertheless His training will deliver the righteous fruits that you need to be healed, .saved, delivered. Did you hear that?

12Wherefore lift up the hands which hang down, and the feeble knees
13And make straight path for your feet, lest that which is lame be turned out of the way: but let it be rather healed
14Follow peace with all men and holiness without which no man shall see the Lord.

He said as clear as it can be said, "follow this, Peace and Holiness, you are going to need it…if you ever expect to be with HIM someday…without it…you cannot see HIM!" Now let's continue listening to Him.

15Looking diligently….

Hold it a minute…now He is saying, do it diligently…train yourself, do it every day! diligently. Now let's let HIM finish that verse it's so important.

LEST ANY ROOT OF BITTERNESS SPRINGING UP TROUBLE YOU AND THEREBY MANY BE DEFILED.

He said brothers, if a root of bitterness grows up in you, who ever holds on to it, will be in big trouble…you will be defiled. You may want to ask HIM, for how long will we be destroyed, Father? You are going to hear from the true scripture:

"Until you stop that root, and plant another one…If not, forever!

The rule is, as long as you water that old root; it will have to grow. However, you can die with that root of bitterness still in your spirit that you never stopped from growing bigger. So you cannot see The Heavenly Father with that thing still in you, that root is not a holy root you have been watering. The 14th verse told us, **WITHOUT HOLINESS YOU CAN NOT SEE THE HOLY FATHER!** Didn't He?

If we hold on to that same root that our ancestors accepted and planted in us, which was a root of bitterness, started by accepting the word, NIG-GER, as being something that you are, then it don't make a bit of difference now that they didn't have a choice. We will just not be able to see the Creator of the World. It's as simple as that. Never!...He gave all men a choice! And the solution! In the 9th verse, He told us plainly

"quit minding those earthly fathers that harmed you and plant HIS root in us of righteousness."

We can accept The Savior's root of righteousness or keep the devil's root. It's up to US.

That was the whole plan of the devils' to get us destroyed here on earth, then through out eternity. All he did in our case was use one word, NIGGER!...and it manifested itself into a bigger and bigger root of bitterness down through the generations

The Savior Himself even warned us to not be like Esau, who would have received the blessing, but didn't because he was a profane person. He said, don't be like that. Stop it! Turn it around! Repent! Stop it from growing! It's a bad root! A root of bitterness. It will make you a profane person. Let's read it for ourselves.

16. Lest there be any fornicator, or profane person, as Esau, who for one morsel of meat sold his birthright 17For ye know that afterwards when he would have inherited the blessing, he was rejected: for he found no place of repentance...

What ?...He wouldn't stop?...Did he say, "WOULD HAVE" inherited the blessing, but he was rejected?...because he wouldn't repent? He let a bad seed keep growing? He was profane ?...He would never repent...so he was rejected for it.

That's what the Creator said. So he couldn't receive the blessing that would have been his. No matter what else he did. He wouldn't stop and plant a new seed. So he could not receive the blessing. Even though he cried and begged and prayed, the Creator said he still could never receive it because. The end of the verse says,

"though he sought it carefully with tears."

Ecclesiastics 11:3
"The way the tree falls is the way it has to lay"

Ezekiel 18:2
Ezekiel even warned us that Yahweh the Heavenly Father said "All the good things that a man may have done will also have to be forgotten"

The heavenly Father has sent us a message to my brothers and sisters that said, "If one dies with a root of bitterness in him, he can not take a root of bitterness like that into the presence of The Father of Light." It's against the Creator's whole principle, His rule. He cannot break His own rule. (Hebrews 6:18)

So I ask you my brothers, don't we absolutely have to stop the old root from growing? Don't we need to plant a new root from new words in our hearts? Don't WE! Absolute need to change something?

That word NIGGER has basically defiled the majority of a nation. It is still all around us daily and still carries the same spirit that it was supposed to carry from its origin. Shouldn't WE do something? Not only to unite and become respected and prosperous in this life, but also to "follow peace with all men" like the 14th verse says we must do? There is an ultimate reward of this whole solution given to us by the heavenly Father. It is then and only then can we go on into eternity with the Heavenly Father

Otherwise, WE will never be able to go into the next life with the Redeemer, according to the scripture. As sad as it is WE as a black nation could live our whole life being basically an outcast divided and in vain then dies and can't even go into the New System with the Savior. { Heb.12:14 }

The problem is WE won't believe the simple solution for our problem sometimes. Some of us can't believe the solution because we won't just believe the Savior. And you do not believe the Creator unless you believe the Holy Scriptures. But those and only those who would dare to just believe HIM only will ever get to see HIM or live again.

Unfortunately, I do understand the problem now, there is usually a veil that covers most of our eyes and hearts whenever the Heavenly Father's rules are read to us, basically because of that serpent's root that has been so deeply planted in some of us. This is not new or of any surprise to the Creator of Mankind. The same thing happened to the Children of Israel when He was trying to deliver them from the hands of the serpent's root. They would not believe Him.

Yet if any people would somehow find the desire to seriously turn to HIS son with HIS new agreement that is administered by HIS SON and our REDEEMER, the veil would be removed and we would understand perfectly. That is also HIS will for us, that WE would hear His son and be freed and have liberty. Not only in this world, but also the world to come. Listen to II Corinthians 3:14

¹⁴ But their minds were blinded. For until this day the same veil remains un-lifted at the reading of the Law, Prophets, and Writings, because only in Messiah is it taken away: the veil taken away and the blindness removed
¹⁵ But even unto this day when the Law given through Moses is read, a veil lies over their hearts; minds

He is saying that when YAWEH'S laws are read, when his rules are read, which has never changed by the way …some of us still can't see it today! Let's continue to the 16th verse

¹⁶ Nevertheless when it shall turn to the Savior the veil shall be taken away

HE's saying here, when you seriously turn your heart to the Savior the blinders will be taken away

¹⁷ Now the Messiah is that Spirit and where the Spirit of the Messiah is there is liberty.

We often think even say that the devil is doing some things to us, but it is not. It is the Savior alone. He lets it happen. His principal allows it to happen. His Rules say if you do certain things this is what has to happen. And He will increase it. Good or bad. So if we turn to His Son. He will also increase goodness and righteousness and understanding. It is all up to us!

The scriptures has explained to us that from the beginning of the earth the Heavenly Father ordained that every fruit bearing seed would have to produce after its own kind Genesis 1:11. That goes for a bird, a cow, the fish in the sea, a pig, a person, a flower or what ever kind of plant that is planted, or anything else that grows. That even goes for WORDS.

A chicken can't produce a cow no matter how many times he would try it. He has to produce nothing else but a chicken. Neither can a bird produce a monkey. It has to produce after its own seed. Neither can a rooster produce a rabbit. It can't happen because The Creator has set the rules for each seed. Nor can corrupt words produce righteous fruits, or actions.

Words are seeds. They also have to produce after their own kind. Words have a spirit. Every word has a spirit of its own. And if it is used it will eventually produce the results it is suppose to. The more you use it the stronger that spirit will become manifest in it. And so came the spirit of bitterness and defilement by the word NIGGER. It is a defiled word, created in extreme hostility and promoted from hate. It carries an evil spirit.

Furthermore, I would seriously urge you to take serious your words. Because you will have to give an account someday of every idle word, you speak. It is what you have said that will determine what will happen to you at the Judgment.

Matthews 12:37
By your words, you shall be justified or by your words, you shall be condemned.

That is why it is so important to know the meaning of words that you are going to use consistently. They can help you or harm you. Words make you react and people react to you. Words will actually start to form your character, negative or positive. It all depends on the words you use.

This rule is firm. We need to know what that word was designed to express. Some words are designed to bring life and joy and peace and some words are designed to bring death And they are spirited. The word and the spirit of that word agree. Haven't you noticed that some words will make you feel one way and some words will make you feel just the opposite. It's the spirit of that word at work.

Furthermore, I would seriously urge you to take serious your words, because you will have to give an account someday of every idle word you speak. It is what you have said that will determine what will happen for you at the Judgment.

By your words, you shall be justified or by your words, you shall be condemned.
Matthews 12:37

What have you been speaking, life or death? What you have been speaking is what you have believed. And what you have believed is what has formed in your being as the Root. Have you been speaking words that formed a root of bitterness? Then you will probably be speaking that same bitterness at your Judgment. Which means you will have to be rejected, according to the scriptures:

Hebrew 12:17
And afterward, when he wanted his fathers blessing, he was rejected. It was too late for repentance, even though he wept bitter tears.

Matthews 12:36
For every word against the work that men shall speak, they will give an account for it in the day of sentencing.

Or, did you ever stop somewhere along the line and plant another root in your spirit, a Root of Righteousness with life bringing words? Whatever is in your heart is what you will speak.

For out of the abundance of the heart the mouth speaks...
Matthews 12:34

My brothers did you know that WE as black people are going to have to learn the importance of words. Words are so vitally important to our future existence. Most of our life WE have been using the wrong words which has resulted into us taking on for the most part the wrong spirit. We are all going to have to even learn the true name of the Heavenly Father before WE can truly honor Him. Not by his office he holds, but by

His Holy Name.

Even using the word Lord, God and Jesus Allah, Jehovah, Christ is really not the honorable correct way to praise The Creator of the Universe that has given mankind the principals in which to be saved. Did you know most of the entire world does not know this? Most men have been deceived by the devil. {Rev.12:9}

The evidence is over whelming that the Creator's true name is YAH-WEH and His son's name is YAHSHUA. We are eventually going to have to learn the personal name of the Father of Israel as written in the Hebrew Scriptures with the four consonants YHWH and is referred to as the Teragrammation. Have you ever considered investigating for your-self The original restored Hebrew Scripture? It is called The book of Yahweh. Are you really serious about righteousness and truth?

At least until the destruction of the First Temple in 586 B.C.E. YAH-WEH's name was pronounced regularly with its proper vowels as is clear from the Lachish Letters, written shortly before that day. However, at least by the third century before YAHSHUA our MESSIAH (Jesus) was born, the pronunciation of the name YAHWEH was avoided, and Adonai, (the Lord) was substituted for it.

Words are a terrible thing to misuse, my brother, they cannot only ruin you in this life, but they can lead you to take on a deceived spirit. They can actually keep you from receiving eternal life. I am even reluctant to use the word God or Lord and Jesus. These are Canaanite and Babylonian titles that really mean "Baal". BAAL is the devil.

For YAWEH men have substituted "Baal" the Babylonian God (EL) and Adonai: the Canaanite God (EL) of the Phoenicians, both corresponding to the English word "Lord". However, I believe that Lord, God and Jesus is probably the only name most of my people are familiar with, so I will resort to it. But only to try and reach my people and lead them to truth before it is too late.

My misinformed dark skin brother, let me just be honest with you… Nigger is not a color, Nigger is a character. A character that was beaten into a people basically…so that they could be easily controlled by the slave master. A beating so vicious, it basically sometimes retarded the brain…. There are plenty of black or dark skin people that are not of Nigger mentality….Some never received this root. Therefore, never claim the title.

This character was bred intentionally to serve a specific purpose. This character of nigger was raised up and trained daily to remain ignorant to all intellectual, productive thinking, so that they would stay useful for physical labor in the fields. They were made to always confess daily that they were only niggers. So consequently, this would be what he would have to teach his young ones, that is all that he knew and believed, and became.

This character was trained through out the generations to believe that he could never be anything else. Don't you see…this character couldn't afford to be taught anything else by the slave master because this knowledge would have changed his character and set him free. This would have spoiled the devil's plan a long time ago.

Romans 10:9 says
That if you confess with your mouth the Messiah Yahshua (Jesus) and believe in your heart that Yahweh {God} raised Him from the dead, you will be saved.

Brothers and Sisters, the scripture says words are important for getting anything. The most important thing for mankind to know especially this generation is it all starts with your mouth. The scripture says

"If you say with your mouth"…{ confess with your mouth }.

It says first, you must say with your mouth!…whatever it is, it starts with saying it with your mouth. Then that will ultimately determine what will inevitably happen to you in action eventually if you persist. HE goes on to say in the tenth verse,

"with the mouth confession is made into salvation"….

Do you need deliverance from anything? Do you need anything? Then do what he said

"say it first".

In other words, what you say can wind up saving you or condemning you in this life or eternally. It's "Made" It's what you have said that started your belief system working. Consequently forming your Character...It's what you say you are that you will wind up believing you are...being or doing or having....one way or the other...the thing was "made" in the spirit, by you saying ,and saying and saying it ,then manifested physically. It is the most important thing you can do, speak with your mouth, words! Because the savior warns us over and over

Matthews 12:
By your words you will be justified and by your words, you will be condemned

Your simple words, my people, will eventually do one thing or the other. Justify you or condemn you. All words have a spirit in which they were created for. And that word has to, by the Creator of Heaven and Earth's Law, work in itself in you. Whatever that spirit in it has!

Nothing else can it do. Whether you know that it is working in you or not. It has to keep working for it is a spirit.

YACHANAN (John) 6:63 (the Book of YAHWEH)
It is the spirit that gives life; the flesh is useless. The laws that I speak to you they are spirit and they are life everlasting....

That word knows what it is suppose to do and produce. For **"Its seed is in itself"**. (Genesis 1:11) All it needs from you is for you to water it daily...say it daily, and it will grow and produce in its subject exactly what it is suppose to produce. All you ever have to do is simply say it, say it, say it, until you believe and it will prosper into the things it was sent for, **"Its seed is in itself"** (Isaiah 55:11)

Not only do every word have a spirit of its own that will work in you if it is unleashed by watering it or we could say, practicing it...but inside each person is installed a belief system that man believes with. It is called, "The Heart"...or mans conscience the scripture says, **"With the heart man believes"**...Romans 10:10

So if the heart believes the thought, that word has produced in him... and he must, if he waters it long enough. Then he will have no choice but to act out of that spirit or like that spirit. Just by constantly hearing this word, he started to believe that spirit. Now he has faith in what he is doing and saying! Confessing it! Hearing it! again and again. And it is growing. For **"Faith cometh by hearing"…. (Romans 10:17)**

It doesn't matter whether or not the word is a negative word working the destruction that it has in its spirit, or NOT. Some words were created with a spirit in them, only to bring destruction. And some words were created to only bring peace Joy and Life, and Eternal Life. No matter which it is, it still has to work the work it is suppose to do, and sooner or later, you will see the results. For **"Its seed is in itself"** **Genesis 1:11**

However, in the case of a negative word or a negative plant, a plant that was created and designed to only bring destruction, it is sin. And when it grows up strong enough, it will bring death

Yaaqob (James) 1:13-15….

¹³Let no one say when he is tempted; I am tempted by Yahweh {God} for Yahweh cannot be tempted with evil, nor does HE tempt anyone. ¹⁴But each one is tempted when he is drawn away by his own lust and enticed ¹⁵Then when lust has conceived, it brings SIN: and SIN, when it is fully matured, brings forth death…

Make no mistake about it my brothers and sisters, if you have planted that negative thing in your heart and is watering it daily, that negative plant cannot do anything other than what it was created for that word to do.

By your words you will be justified and by your words you will be condemned…Matthews 12:37 If I say a word like NIGGER…that word alone, has the potential to do eventually only one thing. That is what ever it was created to do. For who ever will accept it and promote it by watering it, will inevitable take on the spirit that is in that word, eventually. It is a spiritual law from up above.

Let's just examine what the word NIGGER was originally created for, and what does it mean? In what spirit was the word created in? And how was it supposed to be perceived? How was it supposed to explain the character of this people, the attitudes of theses people, the look of this people and destiny of this people.

It was supposed to say in just one expression about a people, and make them and every one that seen them believe that "this people is useless, worthless and ignorant, and repulsive as a human being. So they must always stay in the back. But they can be used in the fields as a mule. So we will call this variety, NIGGERS".

That is some of the original definition of the potent carefully designed words and the reason why most of the time your ancestors, who were the first to receive this word, were instructed by the slave master, who was the arbitrator of this word, to add, as you were identifying yourself,

"I'm a no good NIGGER"

The slave master wanted it to be no doubt about it to the slave and anyone who just saw them or met them, that this was something NO GOOD! And they were made to practice saying this word to themselves and each other over and over until they believed it in their hearts, or be hung. That was the spirit this word was created in. And the name it was purposely given.

This word unaware at that time to these slaves, whom ever it was forced upon, would eventually retard the brain and just by the cruel spirit it was conceived in, it would automatically suggest and start working inferiority to whoever accepted it in their spirit. It has been proven to be one of the most dangerous and cruelest applications known to mankind for corrupting one's spirit. Just from one word NIGGER

So I ask you my brother, are you going to continue to agree with the negative spirit and help it grow? All it needs is watering or practicing everyday and it will grow bigger and bigger and finally completely destroy this whole race. According to the Creator of heaven and earth who says

Whatsoever a man soweth, that shall he reap....
Galatians 6:7

"Out of the abundance of the heart the mouth speaks"..., which is delivered by the tongue... And the tongue that is not wholesome is full of deadly, deadly poison. The scripture has told us

A wholesome tongue is a tree of life: but perverseness therein is a breach in the spirit.
Proverbs 15:4

Did you know that a perverse tongue with foul words in it can destroy all creation and corrupt a spirit and make one be perceived as an abdominal thing, and an outcast, even to society, let alone the Creator? All because of what comes out of your mouth constantly.

The scripture has already told us "the mouth of fools poureth out foolishness"...v. 2 simply because the tongue is a world of iniquity. This combination can and has destroyed a nation, time and time again.

Isaiah 3:8
For Jerusalem is ruined and Judah is fallen: because their TONGUE and their doings are against the Lord, to provoke the eyes of His glory.

Brothers whether WE had a choice in the matter or not, or whether it was handed down to us from our ancestors training, WE basically stay fallen and divided as a whole people by our own doing. WE have set on fire the course of nature according to the scripture and it came from HELL with the foul TONGUE...NIGGER is a foul word, The TONGUE delivers it.

James 3:6
And the TONGUE is a FIRE, a world of iniquity, so is the TONGUE among our members, that it defileth the whole body, and setteth on fire the course of nature; and it is set on fire of HELL

That fire came from HELL, the scripture says these words and this thought to use foul words came from HELL!....A world of iniquity even if we did inherit this habit through our ancestral slave training. We don't have to keep it today. That is why the Saviour tells us over and over.

Either make the tree good, and its fruit good: or else make the tree corrupt and its fruit corrupt: for the tree is known by its fruit.   **Matthews 12:33**

Again, the scriptures have said *"Every idle word that a man shall speak, they shall give an account thereof in the day of judgment"* **Matthews 12:36...**

Have you gotten rid of that root of bitterness that may have been stored up you from a bad seed so that you can speak good things? Even if that nature was inherited. Do you speak good things or evil things?

Oh generation of vipers, how can you being evil speak good things?
Matthews 12:34

Do you see now how your words will judge you? They will tell whether you can come into the Kingdom or not. If not, you are probably still speaking evil words. You can only come in if your heart has been circumcised so that you can speak good things.
Deut. 30:6

A good man out of the good treasure of the heart bringeth forth good things: and an evil man out of the evil treasure bringeth forth evil things   **Matthews 12:35**

My dear brothers and sisters, isn't it time WE get serious and take a good look at ourselves? Nobody else right now but ourselves. Is it not important that WE make sure that WE are right? Would it not be a terrible thing if WE found out too late that some how WE ourselves had inherited a Viper's nature, and kept it without knowing it? O my goodness that sounds like that would be an awful nature to keep. Then die, and can't even go into eternity with the Heavenly Father? Oh my goodness.

Let's just stay honest and accept the truth in this probably painful, yet enlightening and necessary oration, proved by the word of the Creator. The scriptures:

———

And in some ways I hate the fact that some people are probably feeling sadden about their past ancestral history and the burdens that was bestowed upon them. Even I as a black person have sometimes felt angry about being deceived and mistreated and guilty for something I initially had no control over. Especially when I realized that I have been duped into self inflicting pain and degradation upon myself, unaware...Just by practicing negative words in my spirit.

However, WE, of Afro-American descent, should be rejoicing now. Yes rejoicing at the fact that WE now know, not only what caused the problem that has held us back for so many years but WE now have the absolute solution. Yes the solution!...the Creator of The Universe gave it to us. Just for such a time as this. No matter how long awaited it may have been for some of us. WE! now know the solution. The veil has been taken away for those who are honestly seriously looking for the truth.

The Creator of Heaven and Earth does love and care about the future and condition of all people. And when a people turn their hearts to HIM honestly, He will take the blinders off of their hearts.

Never the less when it shall turn to Yahweh {the Lord} the veil shall be taken away.
II Corinthian 3:16

That is a promise from HIM my people. And not only for us, but for any nation of people that gets honest about their future and the Savior. First of all, WE are not the only people who were made to suffer as WE have, or have caused suffering upon our selves. The children of Israel had a miserable existence for even longer than WE had and was delivered. Yes, HE delivered them out of the hands of the oppressor as they finally got wise and started to trust in what HE said would deliver them and WE are going to discuss that in more detail. But, first, to be honest about it, to have this problem of self-destruction solved once and for all. A people or nation must first realize where they stand, then collectively must want to solve this problem once and for all.

Everywhere you turn, there should be a group of black people in some sort of huddle in these last super knowledgeable days talking about the solution. Not the problem, not complaining, not cussing, not criticizing or putting each other down, or even what white people have done to us,

NO! but the solution. The solution My People!

Everywhere you turn, there should be some group or the other of black people talking about WE know the answer, WE have found the solution! WE got the solution now....It was inside of us all the time. However, it is possible that time may not have been right before now for us to all unite, or for The Savior to separate His people from the adversary

Who knows the real big mind of the Creator's timing? Nobody!...But WE now know the solution for everything that troubles us. And WE know it all starts with Respect and WORDS! There is no need what so ever to keep concentrating on the problems any more! The solution is what is important...The solution, the Solution.

WE should be on radio, TV, newspapers, magazines, schools, churches, street corners, little meeting houses in your block, every black person that hears this message should be telling his brothers and sisters. WE found the SOLUTION! We found the SOLUTION! to all of our problems baby, WE know now!......

It starts with our WORDS! And we can't ever solve this deep rotted problem unless WE apply this absolute correct SOLUTION according to the Creator. Hebrew 12:17 WE! can start right now, today

"Training ourselves up in the way WE! Should go and when WE are old WE! Shall stay prosperous" Proverbs. 22:6

That is the Creator's principle and promise for us, and all mankind. However, the only way to do that and the only right answer and honest effective way to make the SOLUTION work is we have to put action behind our positive words and thoughts if WE are going to be real about it. If you are really tired of being, sick and tired.

The only true lasting solution for this same age old problem, if we are going to be real about it, is for us to let the system, our brothers and sisters, and that old ugly mind set that may have thought you were worthless.... Let everybody see you become serious, intelligent, committed, responsible and getting informed of the true facts of all matters in life, qualifying yourself, determined and honest, yet respectful. You must be first respectful of yourself, then, each other and united in this most important cause.

These are all qualities mandatory just for US to qualify in the battle for dignity. And WE must do this first!...First!....The Creator's says,

FIRST!....Not after no bills are passed, not after no new laws are made but FIRST!...Not after WE! straighten out somebody for mistreating you, and get on our feet, NO! FIRST...Not after We get revenge and make them start treating US right, NO! The Creator of the World said this character must be FIRST!

Humble yourself in the sight of the Almighty and He shall lift you up.
James 4:10

We can do one of two things – become a people of the Living Father of Light and be healed or stay like we are and keep saying we are just Niggers.

If my people, which are called by my name, shall humble themselves and pray and seek my face, and turn from their wicked ways; then will I hear from Heaven and will forgive their SINS, and will heal their Land... II Chronicles 7:14

The Creator is the one who furnished this solution for all mankind's troubles and the only solution for this degradation that has snowballed through the generations and has now picked up speed and just about destroyed a nation, US!

Deut. 30:6 Yahweh your Father will circumcise your hearts and the hearts of your descendants so that you may love him with all of your heart and all of your soul and live..

Who?...The Creator of Heaven and Earth. He said He would do that... circumcise our hearts. What are WE saying new?...Everybody knows it is really nothing new that We need to love and pray and unite and all of that...Fine, that's true, every politician, and civil rights leader and preacher you know has said that! That It is good.

However your biggest problem now my brothers is you are vulnerable. Let's be honest, we don't have collectively, no economic power. You don't run nothing. You don't have any money, so you don't have any authority! You don't call no real shots!....and we never will as long as WE think that

We are just NIGGERS…Because then you will always, act like Niggers. Intellectual people of any color just cannot tolerate for long, Niggers.

WE are going to have to finally face the truth of the matter someday brother and sisters if WE are to ever truly over come. No one can really liberate a people, except themselves. Not Abraham Lincoln, nor Kennedy, not Clinton, not Bush, nor Martin Luther King, or any other lawmaker. All that any concerned conscious leader can do is try and get some law or the other passed that could sort of level the playing field. But you yourself and only you have to take the responsibility of performing in a way that demands and deserve respect. Brother, if we don't qualify for respect then people are not going to just automatically give it to you. That is just human nature. That is the only true liberation. And it starts with your TONGUE!

Only then will one be allowed to live a quality existence that would be recognized and accepted and appreciated by all, that is, when you respect yourself. That is true freedom when one sees you as unstoppable, serious, and respectful, no one will really honestly want to stop you. You are just too valuable. People will want to join with you, my brother.

Listen my good brothers and sisters, don't we see, can't WE understand that as long as WE! Just have a dream, just had a dream, keep having a dream and never make it into a reality WE are just fine with the opposition, or the adversary? The adversary is even fine with you just dreaming. You are even welcome to have all the dreams you want, as long as you don't do anything that would make it come true.

WE could even celebrate that dream, forever more, and never get anywhere meaningful to your life's present existence. So what? So you had a dream. As long as it does not manifest itself into a reality, you are just dandy with the adversary, dream, and dream on!

I'm afraid that WE have terribly mis-focused on what Dr. King was really saying in his speeches in relationship to his vision for black people's future. As a matter of fact, Dr. King was not just a dreamer at all, he was a doer! That was just an inspirational motivating projection speech. He never wanted us to just keep celebrate dreaming, but Doing!…This was only to show US the dignity and the prize that could be ours, if WE ever united in righteousness and became dignified WE would all be respected then. He was just saying, " WE can have dignity "

My good people WE can't keep expecting THEM or HIM or nobody else to stop doing anything to you, if they have been doing it. OR start doing anything for you, if they haven't been doing it…If you don't start doing something different for yourself…If WE keep doing what WE have been doing, then WE are going to keep getting what We have been getting….It's as simple as that. Haven't WE learned that after all of these generations?

You could even be serious. You could be as serious as cancer. What does that really mean? If We keep applying the serious wrong Solution to this problem, WE are going to continue to get seriously wrong results. WE must change. We must change. If WE change, the whole world will have to change toward us. Don't ever expect anything else. If WE keep doing what We have been doing, WE have to keep getting what WE have been getting. That is a spiritual and physical law forever from the Heavenly Father.

Galatians 6:7
What so ever a man soweth THAT! Shall he also reap.

Come on my people, at some point, WE are going to have to face the fact. WE are going to have to just be honest with ourselves and face the reality that we have projected and projected and projected the wrong picture of ourselves as a black nation to the world, through out our existence, that mostly is not us for real! It is sad to even say but WE have projected an image and an attitude that says to everybody, and made them believe…"So What? I can kill your brother, lock him up or anything else I feel like doing to him…you are not going to do nothing about it And you too!"

Search yourself brothers and sisters, and see if that feels anyway familiar…No need to look around or discuss it with anybody yet.. Just search yourself honestly….and whether you know it or not, WE are the only race that will allow this….Oh there is a reason for it everybody know that…So what? But first just see if you know this to be true. Does that attitude need to be changed or not?

And are you still honestly expecting that one-day people from other cultures or other races will come along and grab you by the hand and say "Oh you people got a bad break, when your family came over here. So, here, come along with me, I want you to have this money, Oh and by the way I'm going to just split this whole pie here on earth, down the middle

74

evenly with you, regardless whether you qualify or nor, because it is the fair thing to do, you are another human being."

My brothers if you believe that, you are indeed dreaming. Wouldn't it make more sense if a nation that has been exploited for so long to one day says to them-selves,. "Hey, wait a minute I won't stand for any more of this abusing of myself ...and from you either! I want some of this country's respect! I'm going to change the way you feel about me pal...I'm going to show you that I am something that deserve, and you have to respect. I'm better than this."

Doesn't that make more sense than being looked down on, generation after generation? Basically, because we won't change our generation loser's habit and qualify ourselves, regardless of what anybody says.

If that ever did happen, that nation would probably wind up having to say. "I'm going to change my foul language and what I call my brothers and myself. I'm going to change what I say to my children and friends and neighbors. I'm going to plant a different root of respect in myself and I'm going to start respecting you, and you are going to have to start respecting me! I'm going to change, change, change and you are going to quit doing this to me...You are going to have to respect me world."

IF WE don't do these things brothers and sisters and on a massive level, why would WE ever be expecting anything to change?

Why don't we just stop right here and take a look at another culture and a Nation of People who could be a prime example for us, who at one point have experienced the same things we have, but over came. Actually way down the line, they are our brothers, the Jews. The children of Israel.

THE CHILDREN OF ISRAEL

Sometimes it could be good to be a copycat. Yes, if you are copying something worthwhile, a champion, a winner, or over comer. WE copy all the time anyway. But if WE are really going to copy, why not copy the Jewish nation?

You can say what you want to, but most of those people are smart. Yes, they eventually wised up as a culture of people and got super smart, and as a whole developed good character. They are smart and they went through the almost identical same things that We black people are basically going through right now.

Plus these people faced extermination and almost extinction. But they finally turned to the real SOLUTION! And Just look at them now. And the devil hates them for being the first chosen people of THE Creator of the universe. You don't know anybody any smarter or richer than the Jews. It don't make no difference whether you like them or not, you still have got to respect them and somewhere along the line in your business dealings, whatever it is, you may have to deal with them.

However, I do know now what they eventually done collectively to create this undeniable respect and success. They organized and united in Righteousness! And no one can stop them now. According to the Creator they will survive and be saved in the end forever. Let's just take a minute or two or whatever to talk about Jews and how our situation as Black people is more than just related but most identical.

Listen to this. YAHWEH their heavenly Father, which is the true Creator of Heaven and Earth by the way, but there is no need stop and debate that right now either. In any event the Creator Himself had at one point called this people, a stiff-necked evil, ignorant, sinful, and rebellious people. A Nation of people that HE was going to allow all kinds of tragedies and sufferings to come up on. Because they were so divided and disorganized and hateful and disrespectful against each other. And they listened from time to one god to the other, instead of HIM.

He promised then sometimes that HE would let them be murdered, let them be taken slaves, HE would let them wonder around in the wilderness like beggars with no real home to call their own. HE said HE would send cruel and merciless rulers to rule over them, for four hundred years. Then HE would let them go so hungry they would cook their children just to have something to eat. Plus HE said HE would cause the land not to produce anything good for them. And HE did. Ezekiel 5: **Jerimiah19:**

He did that... Just what HE said HE would do... This was a stubborn bunch of people, an ornery and disrespectful people, a stiff-necked generation. But HE was constantly sending somebody to tell these turkeys to "turn, turn, turn, and get right, turn to ME! Organize and get right and I will stop your suffering. Plus I will make you all rich, if you will just stop and do what I tell you"

Does any of that sound at all familiar to you? I believe WE have dealt with some parts of those calamities, haven't WE? And NO, I'm not getting ready to tell you my brothers to grab your gun and let's go and get even with somebody. That is not the solution that is the key to the opportunity for genocide of this whole race brothers and sisters, so don't even think it. But who does that sound like? What people do you know that has gone through just about the same things?

You don't have the slightest idea right?... Good, that is the same way the Jews were, stiff necked and stubborn and pretended that they didn't hear or understand the prophets. They did exactly the same thing. They had a stubborn root planted in them too.

Do you know how many times the Creator would step in and deliver theses people out of the hands of the oppressor and save them from starving to death or just total destruction of themselves by some of the foolishness of theirs?.... Over and over and over and over.

Finally, sometimes they would get beat up so bad, or so hungry and helpless because so many of them may have gotten killed, or somebody would have them in slavery somewhere, or jail, until they would finally have to come running saying "OK, OK, OK, help us Father Yahweh, help us, we'll listen to you now, we'll quit robbing, we'll quit disrespecting each other, we'll quit lying and serving other gods, we'll listen to your prophets, only please come save us, we'll do right. We will organize ourselves in the righteousness and listen to you!" But I guess you know just as soon as HE would deliver these people from their poverty or their bondage and they would start prospering and having good things again and running their own lives again. And it looks like they have it made, they would go right back into their same foolishness again, practicing witchcraft, robbing each other, lying to each other, taking advantage of each other. Everybody had their own god. If they didn't they would get somebody to make them one. They would even turn HIS house into a den of thieves. Then sometimes even tell HIM, we are tired of listening to you, we want our own God like everybody else, just give us a king. **1 Samuel 8:18-19**

So HE would just let them have what they said they wanted. But again HE would have to keep HIS word too. HE would send something worse upon them. He has sometimes threaten them that HE is not going to even save them no more from the merciless adversary, for turning their backs on HIM like that. "You are worthless!" HE would tell them sometimes. He WOULD BE FURIOUS WITH THIS STUBBORN BUNCH OF PEOPLE, AND EVEN KILL A BIG BUNCH OF THEM, **Jere... Ezekiel 11:**

Yet HE would always send somebody else, another prophet to try and reason with these stiff neck people, before they destroy themselves. Prophet after prophet after prophet, message after message after message. pleading with this bunch. "Return O back slider, Return! Return to your only help. Can't you see you are sick? Can't you see your whole nation is in ruin? Turn to ME! I'll save you again what's the matter with you people?.... Don't you know that the time is running out for you?" **Jeremiah 3:**

Poor Jeremiah and Ezekiel, they use to catch the blues trying to warn these rebels about the consequence of being disobedient. And they would explain exquisitely why, and exactly what disaster would happen to this people if they didn't quit being ornery. All of the prophets had trouble trying to turn these stiff necks around, but Jeremiah and Ezekiel may have had it worse. Ezekiel4: **Jeremiah 27:**

These two would be preaching and crying and begging this bunch of knuckleheads, "Stop, Stop, Stop, Yahweh said stop this sinful stuff, HE is going to kill ya'll, me too, if ya'll don't stop and unite and return to HIM. Can't you see He's going to let our nation stay in ruin? Oh please stop this evil stuff! Yahweh said for us to forsake our wrong doing, organize as HIS

78

people, and return to HIM before it is too late!" **Jeremiah 4:9:**

I kind of feel bad for these two guys, more than for any of the other prophets. Because not only would Yahweh make these guys go preach to this rebellious nation, "Return to HIM" But they would also have to take so much abuse from this people. Sometimes physical. Just for trying to warn them. And take their abuse until Yahweh said enough. Which was sometimes for years? Jermiah3:

Whatever the punishment was going to be for Israel, for being disobedient, these two like the rest of the prophets, would have to simulate, or demonstrate it physically on themselves. Just to show them what was going to happen to the whole bunch, if they didn't straighten up. Oh how the prophet of old tried to warn this people to repent. **Jeremiah 12:1-11**

You still don't know who this bunch sounds like, do you? No problem. Well the children of Israel finally got wise. It took them a lot of years and many beatings but they finally realized that the Creator of Heaven and Earth is not joking. He let enough of them get abused and killed and punished but they finally realized HE means exactly what HE says. They finally stopped the nonsense and developed good character.

We especially should know by now, HE will let you get drugged through the mud if you don't stop somewhere along the way and pay attention to HIM. HE is a man of war and HE always wins. He scared the holy stew out of these people. But look at them now. Take a good honest look and examine the children of Israel now.

Some of us are just probably not familiar or informed as to just who really owns just about everything that is of real value in this country and most of the world. And they are united. Although the devil hates them. You would probably find out if you don't already know that you are just not going to be able to do business with the Israelites, if you are not organized and united and serious and respectful in your business dealings. HE is just not going to have much foolishness.

These guys are constantly in a huddle with each other talking about how they can find the solution for something or the other. Every time a problem comes up, they will meet daily if necessary somewhere, get in a huddle, and won't leave, until they have found the sensible workable solution to their problem together.

And they will encourage, sometimes insist, on their people being rich. Or you may have to get out... plus they will help you get rich if you want to… These people have been trained by the Creator of the Universe.

Even if you were born in the middle of Israel, but is not a respectable sincere organized person, you probably won't get too far with these people. He is probably just not going to be interested. They have learned a hard lesson about foolishness. You must be committed to something that is positively prosperous for these people to even get interested.

Even if their own brother decided that he was not going to dedicate himself to a high enough standard or principle and diligently try to prosper, they may just disown him. They just won't claim him, or tolerate his foolishness.

However, neither would they let him stay broke up and busted, if he was honestly trying to become a serious respectful prosperous Jewish brother. What Yahweh did to these people, you don't want. They know HE means business. The scripture explains

Proverb 1:7
the fear of Yahweh is the beginning of wisdom and knowledge: but fools despise wisdom and instructions.

HE does not want you to be a fool. And he honors these people now. Just check these people out honestly, a people who were being beat up and abused just like you may be now. Then you decide whether they are being honored by the Creator or not. And it is because they now honor HIM.

You are rarely going to see an Israelite mistreating an Israelite. You will constantly see him trying to organize and educate and uplift his brother through. That will be common.

So why wouldn't WE take a page and a lesson from that bunch? Could WE use any of that? Their situation was exactly like ours is now. As a matter of fact the scripture says, what happened to them was for our example.
1 Corinthians 10:6-13

ARE YOU REALLY VALUABLE?

No one, No one, no one, not even any group of people can solve the problems we are confronted with today, Black people. No one, No one but US!

Nobody else can solve the problem of poverty, disunity, ignorance, and respect for each other and ourselves, economics stability, or even in what WE call, racial unfairness. NO one can solve these things but us!

Let's be honest if WE don't have any economic power, make no mistake about it, we will never have nothing on this earth of real value. WE may as well face it. And if WE don't get any unity, WE collectively are never going to have any economic power to amount to any thing meaningful. At least not anything that can become a force that has to be considered or recognized as true power.

Plus you may as well forget about all of that "It's not Fair" stuff. Who really cares? Life is not fair. Actually you only get and is entitled to what you qualify for, and that's fair! Qualify yourself to run something my brothers and sisters.. Insist on learning how to do it, you, and another brother. As a matter of fact, why don't you make it a group of your fellow brothers who are insisting and determined to be, not the tail of this thing, but the head. Shouldn't you really want to be a leader or respected? That is the only way that anybody and everybody have to respect you. And that's fair. That is really what fair is, getting what you earned, not a hand out. Be the boss, qualify yourself to be that man. You can do it!

Oh, sure there will always be a hand full of us like it has always been a small hand full of black people who will rise up here and there, now and then and own a few minor operations, or one large company, now and then. But that only represents possibilities. Because truthfully your brother who may be in big business still may have to do business with the ones that has really got a lot of stuff. And that is not only fair, but necessary.

Let's face it, those that make the final decision are those that have the economic power. They run this system because they do have the true power and that is also fair. And even if it was not fair it is a fact.

That's why your brother, who may be big in business, in order to stay in big business , would naturally have to go to those who control the whole system exclusively because you basically don't have anything to bargain with. You don't run nothing, so you can not help him. That is what WE need to change. Because you don't run nothing for real. Really you are expendable. Things could really continue nicely without you. You need to become collectively valuable, even nonexpendable. Otherwise you have no real non-negotiable corrective measures. Let's quit being so dependent on other races. Then every body would prosper. Even other races.

Everybody basically knows about the problems that had happened in the past. So what?... What are you going to do about it that will stop it in the future? In reality, WE need to just quit talking about THEM! as being the problem. WE should be constantly talking and comparing notes and ideas about US! as having the SOLUTION! Just US!

Everywhere you look there should be a group of black people talking about the SOLUTION. Everywhere you go, they should be in a huddle talking calmly and seriously about the SOLUTION, the SOLUTION, the SOLUTION, we found the SOLUTION...Not the problem but the SOLUTION... that is what Jews do,...they always look for the SOLU-TION...We all know that there has been some problems, and there is going to be some more problems, but champions always go looking for the solution .

The SOLUTION, The SOLUTION...Now losers will always keep whining and complaining and accusing and making excuses, and talking about how bad the problem is... but champions will always huddle and try until they find the SOLUTION. The solution is the only thing that will change everything elaborating on the problem can only make it worse.

It is how WE respond to any situation that will ultimately determine the results. Now, let me tell you what the SOLUTION is definitely NOT! The solution has proven time and time again to definitely not be a group of us getting together and march and complain with a bunch of signs for a few days against the white man and the power structure, screaming and hollering like a bunch of morons, "OH look what they done to us!....he's the devil!...stop the oppression of my people! Ya'll are wrong!....What are you all going to do about this? What are you going to do about that? We want justice!"

That nonsense never has and never is going to solve anything!....You want to know The Creator's truth?...That is exactly what WE have been getting, is Justice! Justice for how WE have responded to issues. If WE don't do nothing corrective WE will never get nothing corrected. That is Justice, getting what your hands call for... You are just playing with yourself if you really expect anybody to ever give you anything you haven't earned. Except a little pacifying until you chill out. Isn't that what has always happened throughout history?

So why don't WE just change what our hands call for? Brother WE need to run things. You don't run nothing of value to society that would make anybody have to stop and negotiate with you.

You don't run any banks, no jails, no courtrooms, no major, much needed manufacturing plants, you don't run no schools or colleges. These are the true power structures, these are the rules and decision makers. And more of you brothers need to qualify to run some of this, no matter what it takes, or how hard you have to work or study to qualify yourself to do it. This is the only real authority.

You and your brothers need to respect and just love authority. And desire to have some authority! You should want to be in charge at just about any cost. Why wouldn't you qualify yourself to the point that you are definitely needed? Ask yourself, am I really needed? Are you truly valuable?

Other wise who is ever going to have seriously bargain with you? Why do they have to? And if WE be honest, brothers, that is the real problem. WE don't run nothing, or own nothing of real value enough to make the system have to respect you. But we could, it's up to us exclusively. WE must unite! And that is the only real solid solution to this problem. And it should be always a group of us running or owning something, not just one every now and then. That is the only way WE will ever be in charge of our own destiny. When WE get some economical collective meaningful power, UNITY.

Be honest my people, who do you think is ever going to seriously have to bargain with you fairly without some of this power? Not even your own natural brother will usually. Why does he absolutely have to? Just because

---

you are another human being? Get real.

Are WE still looking for somebody to come along one of these old days and just say, "Ok fellows, we are going to split this pie down the middle with you fairly, because you are another human being. It doesn't matter how you treat each other, or if you qualify for it, or earned it. Here ya'll take this money! Ok?" You still think that will happen anyway huh? Ok, keep dreaming...

So the next time you want to ask, "Why did he shoot that man so cold blooded like that, when he had handcuffs on?" The answer is, "because he can!" He has been doing it hasn't he? He knows he doesn't really have to deal with you in nothing, or answer to you either. You haven't change, so why would he? He hasn't been answering to you, his father, or great, great grandfather didn't either. So what's new? Did we ever stop and organize in righteousness seriously and collectively, turn to the savior and get smart and command respect for ourselves and everybody else? Did WE ever make the world say, oh look at those smart valuable and respectful people, We need them?

Oh sure, WE did go out and sang a few songs, cried and screamed, marched up and down the street a few days, burnt up a few houses...in our own neighborhood, cussed a few people out...But WE still didn't change our life, or unite seriously in righteousness or make up our minds to qualify our self for some of those positions of authority did WE? Only a hand full of blacks did that.

Now do you see the real problem, and see the only real SOLTUTION to it? Let's just stay with the SOLUTION, The SOLUTION. That is the only thing that is ever going to help this people to become a stable economically secure black respected nation. The SOLUTION! The problem has been there forever, but all we need to concentrate on is the SOLUTION!

The Creator of the universe has more than proven that HIS principles work. The SOLUTION, which is nothing more than the Creator of the universe's principles, that is all WE really need, to get the solution to anything. Now, how are WE going to get it? Character... yes with Character! Character will get you respect, respect will get you in the door to qualify to be in authority, authority will get you money, freedom, justice, liberty, and anything else you desire. Character!

CHARACTER IS THE KEY

My brothers, you have got talent, talent, talent. You have got talent coming out of your ears. But your character may not allow you the opportunity to get in the door to present or demonstrate your talent. You may not even get the chance, just because of what you may have projected about your character. Or if you do get the chance, a foul character won't let you stay there and rise to any position of authority.

So there you are again. Because without authority of your own, as a race, a people may have to stay under the rules and mercy of a merciless decision maker. The authority! Didn't the Jews prove that to us in the scripture? They were forced under the rules of merciless rulers, just because they had been so disobedient and ornery and would not unite themselves in righteousness

You can say what ever you want to about the holy Bible. You can say it's a white man's book, or a Jewish man's book, you can say this translator was no good, or that translators did this or that ..It doesn't matter... but what ever you keep saying, history has proven, and it keeps right on proving, that the Bible still has all the answers and directions to get you, or anybody else what ever they are looking for. Or what ever you are trying to do good or bad. And following the true scriptures' rules correctly, you will get there. And that is so very important to know, Now look what it said about character, the very key to our solution.

Proverbs 22:6
Train up a child in the way he should go and when he is old he shall not depart from it.

If WE have never received anything in our lives before, WE need to receive this. And examine it and see if it isn't absolutely true. This is a spiritual and physical law from The Creator of Heaven and Earth and it will never change and we are about to examine the Solution again for those who may have missed what the Creator said in the beginning or who don't already know.

Look what The Creator is saying here. He's telling everybody. Give young people the character you want them to have and train them up... and they will keep it....even when they are old... Good or bad. In other words... if you can plant a root...a type of character is what he is saying..., in a people, or yourself, then keep nourishing it, keep watering it, keep training it, that is what he is saying... Train them how you want them to act, and they will do just that forever.., they will keep that character with them forever.. . That root forever until it dies... Any people, if you haven't matured yet, you would still be considered child like, it has been proven, regardless.

If you have never received anything in your life from the scriptures you need to get this. And examine it. Make sure it is absolutely true or not. It will help you in everything you do from now on. You see, the Savior's principles will work for even an evil man. If he applies what the scripture says apply, like it said do it. Even if you may have to pay dearly for misusing it, if you do misuse it by planting evil things that will also grow. But the principle will still work regardless, it's been proven.

I would advise you to stay with this little oration to conclusion, because this principle is something that cannot change, and has to work in every root. If you plant a root and train it up from a baby that is the way it has to keep growing no matter how old it gets. "It will not depart" HE told us until it dies. No matter who or what is planted. It has to work on a baby chicken, a baby bird, a baby gorilla, or a baby flower.

The only thing here is that the Creator is not talking about flowers. He was as pacific as He could be, HE said A Child" Here he is talking pacifically about people. A Child, a beginning, or an early stage of something... "Train a child up" ... **Proverbs: 22:6.**

HE is saying "Give him the character you want him to have and train it up, when he is a child and he will always keep it until he dies" which means the ROOT... The character comes from the ROOT... You could say give him the Root.

The only possible way for you to get something different is to plant another root and train it up… If you want something to grow in that same place as you have something else right now, you would have to first STOP that root from growing somehow. And plant something else where it use to be

The whole 22 chapter of Proverbs is basically dedicated in talking about a people's character, Which could turn out to be the character of an entire nation. And this principle was set up by the Creator of the entire universe.

The whole key to life's success or failures is determined by what kind of character one has. That goes for any race or people, or anything you do, winner or loser is determined by character, or one's perception of what kind of character it is… Is it of good character or bad character.

In other words, is this something valuable or is this something worthless? Is it something we ought to be proud of or something disgusting and repulsive that we should get rid of. Just what is the natural nature of this thing, is what character explains. Believe it or not, every one judges character, even you.

We talked briefly a minute ago about one having a super amount of talent, ambition, energy, and a lot of things to give. But one's character might not allow the door to open to demonstrate it. Simply because of what somebody perceived or thought was in your character. So let's continue that a little bit more, because it is usually perceived as foul character when one's vocabulary is so poor and limited until they would normally have to spurt out perverseness, just to express themselves.

That is when most people find it hard to welcome you around because you would normally be perceived as a defiled character. These are defiled characteristics. That character is normally perceived as not being valuable, or worth much. So he probably won't even get a chance to demonstrate his talent, no matter how good he was. His character kept him out. A perverse tongue is just hard to take.

The same thing applies if you were a lazy person, or a person that will never unite for any good cause, or if you are an argumentative person a person who will never reason and get serious, un-organized that is a character too. But a bad unbeneficial character is not valuable to any one.

That is called character judgment. Somebody will always be judging the character of you. Is he worthwhile messing with or not. Would it be a good move or a bad move? Could I take these people anywhere with out them embarrassing everybody and me? Sometimes Just an attitude will identify the character of one with out even a word being said.

That is why you will see people of all races and colors rush to see a Michael Jordan type of character or other super heroes, even though they may have never physically seen them before, Just heard about them. They may even want to go there to get their autographs, simply because of what they think is a good quality in a person. Nobody is ever really concerned at that point what color he is, all they know and care about is, they heard he was a winner, he has good qualities, good characteristics because he likes to win. That is character and a good reputation to have.

Those are good characteristics for one to be known for, a winner, something of value. He is always winning, he must be smart, he must not be lazy, we can use him, because we can trust him, he's helpful. Something to be proud of, not something that will embarrass somebody. Those are good characteristic to have, he's something worth going to see, and pay money for, and we want to be identified with knowing a person or a people with those kinds of respected valuable qualities. He has something to bring to the table that's valuable. That's just good character to possess. This kind of characteristic is always thought to be from God, not the devil, he's a leader, not a follower of foolishness, he has positive characteristics, everybody loves that, and will join in to help. Those kinds of characteristics will never harm him. He is respectful, looks rich, he must be important, that's what good character will do for anybody. And we all could have a Michael Jordan character in something, respected. trusted, wanted, liked, if we plant one and train it..

Somewhere along the line a root or character was planted in the man. A root of, "I am somebody, I can win, I am intelligent and respectful, I am a champion, I am not supposed to lose. I can be trusted and I like myself, so I respect other people too. I'm just a great filled with love person with good characteristics from above, not a curser, foul word user, I'm not loud and boisterous and disrespectful, I'm not repulsive to people. They like me around, I always want to help, not tear down"

Somewhere along the line early, somebody planted that positive characteristics root in this man. And somebody watered it and watered it until it became a strong positive implantation. And it was started originally with only WORDS' I bet you he didn't hear everyday nor say everyday." "You ain't nothing but a nigger, you are going nowhere"... bet you that never was accepted in his spirit. They just started him off growing the ways they wanted him to go positive. Then it was practiced and practiced and practiced, which only means they spoke to him that way, trained him to speak and think that way, said what he started believing and according to God, it *will never depart*

Proverbs 22:6

Sooner or later this positive word implantation in this man had to develop into something great and the scriptures says "It will never depart" It will always be great. And his sons will have positive characteristics and their sons and their sons. As long as they train or water that root like that, these characteristics of, "I am something worth while" 'will never depart...

Proverbs 11:6.

What ever you planted, or what ever you accepted, that someone even planted in you, and you accepted it and practiced it, or watered it, is what you will always be like. If you keep watering it. Watering it just means to always be saying it, or listening to it.

So what words do you say and Listen to all the time' Well that's what you will always be like. Let's listen to the Creator again to confirm through yet another scripture that you will always get what ever you planted and practiced. He starts of saying:

Be not deceived: God is not mocked: for whatever a man sowed that shall he reap.
Galatians 6:7

That! That! Nothing else, just THAT! That he planted, is the same thing he will pull up... that's what he will harvest, or that's what he will get., or receive back.., over and over and over. HE even begins with. 'Don't fool yourself'

If you plant collard green seed, you will NOT! receive back watermelons or cantaloupes. You will get collard greens always until the day that plant dies. And if you plant negative and defiled WORDS into one's spirit, they will also develop into the character that the spirit of the words has in it, and produce a negative disrespectful loser, and that is what you will always have also, until it dies. It can't be helped.

That is God's Rule. That is the negative side of sowing and reaping, everything has a positive and a negative. A killer, a rapist, a sicko, a bum, a useless quitter, they will also demonstrate a certain character trait. It will be something negative and basically repulsive but they still have a characteristic, and it will be visible. A loser has characteristics that will show he will prove it over and over, because that's what he is, and that's the way he thinks, he'll just continue accepting losing and saying he is a loser with negative words. A drunk, will be just stumbling, that is the characteristic of alcohol, it will make you stumble if you consume enough. You can count on it That is just what it is suppose to do. That's the characteristics of a drunk, he will stumble over everything. If he planted alcohol, sooner or later if he continues drinking you'll see him stumbling all over everything. That is the God given rule for alcohol.

OK my brothers. I'm sure by now you must understand how important character and character perception is now, I believe we have stayed on this point long enough with the scriptures from the heavenly Father up above as our proof and foundation.

WE, black people, may as well do ourselves a favor and make up our minds to accept truth, then change the situation if WE don't like having certain kinds of characteristics, because the Savior has already made up his mind that HE is not going to change the Rules. Do WE really want to keep characteristics that would label you as negative or a loser. A character that makes people don't mind shooting you down even with hand cuffs on behind your back?

WE were trained to possess that character. Yes, bad character from a baby and from the Rules of The heavenly Father. From the very entrance into this Country of America, is where your root begins. It does not matter what you were in Africa your training how to think and speak started here in America by your American ancestors. That is your root! your beginnings! And whatever root was planted in them is the same root they had to install in you. You and everyone that accepted this implantation of how to think and talk. Which was to be a loser, a slave? If you haven't changed this root.

As a matter of fact, very few blacks or slaves even got away. So most Afro-Americans have this basic characteristic still deep down in us, if it has never been deal with. There is no way around this truth. Your ancestors had a brand new root planted within when they entered this country, a brand new beginning. a brand new nature, a brand new characteristic planted and nourished daily in them from the time they landed in America.

However, the good news is, there is nobody that can make you keep it in you Accept you! You and only you can kill that root, and plant another one! Nobody can stop you from planting another undefiled root, then "Train it up" the way you want it to grow, like you were trained to go the way the old slave trainer wanted you to go. You and you alone have to plant another root, or keep the old one you've got. And there is nothing that anybody else can do about it because that principle is from the Creator of Heaven and Earth. The principle is found in **Galatians 6:7**

If you, if you, if you, if you , whatever you choose and water is what you will get.

This old root, or this nature of disrespecting your self and your brother was bad when it was planted in your ancestors . whether you knew it or not. It was just trained and trained and trained from birth and just grew bigger and worse, by the time it reached you and your off springs.

So you may as well decide if you want to keep it or not. You can be trained to always win, be respectful, positive intelligent and righteous, or you can accept training of negativity inferiority defeat and evilness. But to change anything you would still have o start a brand new root. One way or the other. But it is entirely up to you, as to what your offspring's will be. And according to the Savior of the world, whichever one you decide to water, **"it will never ever depart"** Your children's, children's, children's children will practice that same character training, positive or negative.

Generation after generation after generation. WE have trained the same root the same way that WE learned, instead of stopping somewhere along the line, stopping and planting a brand new thought, a new root. Although it was all because you just didn't know. WE certainly would not have accepted a bad root, if we had known that it was bad would we?

Whether you are aware or not. you by nature do the same things basically that your father and grand daddy did. He did basically the same things his daddy taught him, and his daddy did the basic things his daddy taught him to do and act. And the original ancestor did what they were told to do or forced to do whether they liked it or not, they had to accept that root and train the rest of your ancestors to accept these characteristic or be hung. The original slaves basically had no choice. But my brothers and sisters, you do! You have a choice. Deut 30: explains those blessings or curses.

According to the Creator this basic negative defiled nature **"will never depart"** until that training stop and a new root is planted. **Proverbs 22:6**

Unfortunately WE can wish and pray or dream and march... kick and buck. WE may even be able to get all the man made laws passed that WE want to, put up picket signs and scream out "We deserve this and that!".. all WE want to. But that alone has never solved anything. And never will.

The scripture says *"You will never depart from that character of your root, as long as you will water it."* (**Proverbs 22:6**) You will just have to plant a new root

Let's just make a hypothetical example here. If a person or a race would act as if they were retarded wouldn't that give a people a reason or maybe an excuse not to get involved, or not to help?

You are never too old or young to plant another root, another way of thinking and talking in yourself, if necessary. And the root planting starts with only words. That is all that watering means, practice doing it or saying it. That is training our self to change. Then people will have to change around you and toward you.

Now my brothers and sisters in case you may have missed it from the beginning. I must tell you again what that negative training WE received was for from our beginning. This is our root. You, my brothers and sisters, with the same color skin as me. You who have been deceived just like me... . You who *the* Creator of the world is trying to reach just like me and people that I love.. WE have got to change WE have got to start a new root in our race.

You know most young people are probably not going to be able to remember that intelligent black people had once discovered the deadly poison of the cruel implication bounded up in this popular word NIGGER! And almost had this seed just about dead once. Yes, dead!... Once WE had realized the evil spirit it can produce.

It was back in the early sixties and the civil rights movement was big and on everybody's TV and on everybody's conscience. Black people had finally discovered after generations of calling each other NIGGERS! That they had been ignorantly confessing and accepting the wrong things about themselves. Defeat. And that it was the very single most thing that was most responsible for holding them in sort of bondage as a race. Just by saying and accepting that, you were a NIGGER! Which means, you are worthless"… if you accept that spirit in your Spirit.

So blacks had basically banned that word once for the most part. But somehow by the early eighties, the devil's spirit managed cleverly to resurrect that poisonous word again and it began to show its ugly face among our innocent youth and made a home among this naive bunch. Even on TV, The devil promoted this poisonous word as something hip! and not bad at all but rather something that makes you socially accepted and make you feel and sound like you are hip' Clever HUH?

You may be unaware of this poison root implanted in you through no choice of your own. A root of a character of low self-esteem, inferior, worthless, hatred. That was all that was needed to control you and me forever or destroy you if necessary.., and now you may not know anything else but bitterness, or even why you feel and act the way you do. Yet what ever you do, don't get angry about the past, get glad about the future. You know the solution now! Don't you see, now you know what they know?

First of all, these people that implanted that poisonous root in your ancestors, they are all dead now Dead! Not a one of them are alive to day. But they did know the scripture. They found out exactly what it would take to make anything grow. Good or Bad' and if we don't kill this poisonous root it will kill us one day. They knew this stronger than concrete foundation was from the Creator of the entire world and it had to work forever and ever. That is why they trusted and used nothing else but His principles. So, if it worked for them it will work for you and me. All WE need to do is plant us another root of what WE want in us. Then water it.

The Savior of the world, brothers, has given all mankind the same principles to use HE has also gave all mankind the absolute concrete solution for solving any problem that troubles you, forever and ever. It has to work forever and ever, for who ever will dare to use HIS rules. So all WE really got to do is plant a different root! And "train it up" the way WE want "IT" to go. If we don't like the one that was planted in us to make us inferior.

Proverbs 22:6.

Let's fact it, I was trained to hate you. And you were trained to hate me. You were trained to kill me and that I was no good. And I was trained to think and do the same thing to you. It was drilled in to me daily that you were no good and worthless and nothing. That is what we have heard most of our lives. And it was watered and trained and practiced everyday by you, to feel the same way about me. Simply by saying certain words.

I was told and trained from the root, which mean from our ancestors beginning in America everything black was no good. And anything white was right and good. You were told that also. That is what is maybe imbedded deep down in you and me. And you maybe are still saying it every day with out even knowing it just by practicing calling yourself and your brother foul words. The scripture says if you do that that is what you will become **Proverb 23:7**

The training was so cruel and thorough and repetitious that it had to register because you were forced to say it or do it every day until it just became natural, basically because it was all you knew. And consequently, you may have given that same practiced trained characteristic to your children. This was the devil's plan all the time. Then he could someday destroy a whole nation.

Let me tell you another truth right here that hopefully will make you throws up… to the point of definitely doing something about changing it… But you see I had no idea why every time I seen you I just felt like calling you a foul name, a NIGGER. This is really to say subconsciously "you are one of those worthless nothings just like me. I hate you! And want to kill you' neither one of us are nothing!"

I didn't even know the truth definition of the word NIGGER, until later, and then it was too late. I had already unleashed and spreaded hate around us. And I didn't even know why I always wanted to fight you and destroy you, or compete against you. I didn't know that this word had a spirit in it that made even me defiled if I used it enough.

I don't know why I just thought I was supposed to do that. You see, it started along time ago back when I was a slave. As soon as I would see you I was trained to just put my hands in my pocket on my knife. As a matter of fact every time I would see a blackface, something rose up in me and said, 'Do something to him, or call him something ornery, he ain't nothing, call him a NIGGER!. Like the slave master trained us to do, long ago.'

I didn't even call myself mad at you, or even knew you. But the more I did it, the more natural it became, every time I saw a black face.

Sometime when I thought I was happy and laughing and joking, I would all of a sudden feel like I should just say to you, " my nigger, you ain't worth nothing! I ought to kill you. ...You should have been born dead you worthless piece of crap!" And YOU would be laughing and joking and say the same thing back to me, if you seen me first. I didn't know that it was the devil's way to fill us full of hate. You see the devil had blinded us both, and was trying to get us both dead.

As a matter of fact, I didn't know any other words to say to you but both those whenever 1 felt like talking you didn't either. We thought this was what we were suppose to do to every one that looked like us. That was the only way we knew how to communicate. I was told that you were a N1GGER...and worthless I knew very few positive words.

You see, I didn't hardly hear anything else but those words, and I couldn't read, I didn't like to no how. So that is the only characteristic that grew stronger and stronger in me. As a matter of fact, just to be silently was the only thing difficult for me to do whenever you were around. I even started singing hate words to you in my songs. I basically only listened to hate songs. So I just kept practicing and practicing and training, and training. I tried to find as many words as I could so that I could communicate with you. So my environment would give more hate words, like ho, bitch, dog. Nigger. I trained myself and trained myself and practiced and practiced what few words I knew until I became an almost perfect hater of myself...and you too, you look like me.

So subconsciously, I just thought like the slave master told me to think, that you deserved killing too.. You were a NIGGER.

Proverb 18:8
The words of a tale bear are like wounds that go down into this inner part of the belly.

I Practiced these words until I become an almost perfect hater of myself And you too. You look like me. So subconsciously I just thought you deserved killing too. You was a NIGGER.

I even said those things and taught those words to my children, and planted in them, my same characteristics. Before you know it, they were teaching their children to be and do and think the same way. They didn't know anything else. All they knew was what they heard from me and our environment and all I knew was what I heard from my pop and that environment. Nobody ever told me that words had spirit and sooner or later you'll start acting like the words you use the most. I didn't know that the Creator had told mankind all words are alive.

"The words that I speak are spirit and life." John 6:63

As soon as one of my kids was born, I would pick him up and hug him and say to him in his ear,

"this is my little Nigger here!"

In other words what I told him and planted in his spirit was. "You are my little worthless, no good, useless piece of crap, I hate you, and ought to kill you! You are going to be a loser!" So he just grew up with that same spirit too. Now, that's the way he does his children.

Oh, I know, some of you want me to just quit talking about this awful subject like this and start talking about let's go get some guns and just go kill some of them and show them we are just sick of them for planting that spirit in us and killing us like that. Just start shooting back! righ?

I got news for you, my brothers that is exactly what certain mind sets who do have power is hoping you do. That would make genocide easy. Don't look now but, you don't really have no real guns no way. You are easy to kill, most of you are in jail anyway, or on the way, or just left. That would just confirm that you are never going to just get rid of that spirit and change and compete in the legitimate arena where power is won. If you rather continue hating nor change. Which would give the devil justification to lawfully finish you and this whole race off? He is counting on just that one day.

Some of you may be too young to know or maybe have never read, but your ancestors was brought into this country as slaves and was forced to accept certain kinds of evil training or die. But you don't have to! You don't have to do that no more!

I know it even sounds pitiful, but you ought to be rejoicing now that you know what to do and what not to do. Thank the Creator for giving the Solution! That would be the intelligent thing to do. WE can be intelligent. Or are we just what somebody said we are? Just NIGGERS!

Now it would not be wise, intelligent, or productive to take this information then just go get stupidly mad at some people, and say it's their fault for all black people being in our present position. First of all the people that are responsible for originally planting that root in you are all dead, long ago, dead! And truthfully, it was US that refused for so long to let the negative plant die, we keep watering it. And some of us are still watering it!

If you don't know already, most white folks, and all intelligent white people are saddened and embarrassed and some are even sick to their stomach over this whole situation that they basically had nothing to do with personality. They weren't even born yet. But they are all intelligent enough to know, that you and only you can plant in you and your people another root. And they are all hoping we do. Oh my goodness could this country win if we would unite with it in righteousness. They are waiting on us.

Just wait until you find out how great you really are with that new root in you. Oh man, I can hardly wait to give you a glimpse of yourself. They can't either! Things would be so great for everybody! Plus then you would qualify for eternal life with the Heavenly Father Forever! Some of us may not even qualify to see the Father of all creation at this point now. Why wouldn't we change? **HEB. 12:12-17**

BE CAREFUL WHAT YOU
ASK FOR YOU MAY GET IT

Brothers and sisters there is no other way around it…I wish it was Then maybe we wouldn't have to preach this dreadful message so repetitiously to each other. However, we are going to just have to face something that WE may have never been honest about. There never has been and there will never ever be any economically stability or nothing else of real value in the Black nation as a whole, as long as there is no respect for yourself and your brothers and sisters in noble character. If we don't plant another seed in us of respect, it just cannot ever form a root. So no one else can respect you either. That! My brothers and sisters will stop any nation from economical stability

There is much more at work in this bitter word NIGGER than meets the eye on this earth. Its greatest and ultimate goal that it has been trying to prepare for since the beginning is to actually try and keep you out of the new system with the creator of the world. The enemy knows that if your spirit becomes defiled by this root's implantation, it forms what has been described in the scripture as a bitter root. If you have a bitter root of character, you will not be able to live in peace with all men you will not be able to unite in righteousness with men so that in the end time we simple still will not he able to make the fair and honest decision. Consequently you will have to be rejected from coming into the Kingdom, because you will not be holy. {Hebrews 12: 12-17}

When we see Afro-Americans like Colin Powell who became the Secretary of State, or Condolesa Wright, who became one of the most respected advisers to the President of the United States, or some of the Afro Americans down on Wall Street who some are a actually head of the Stock

Market, or a Michael Jordan who the whole world respects, not just because of his basketball ability but because of their character, or a Tiger Woods or an Opra Winfrey, Bill Cosby, Barack Obama and many more Afro Americans, don't you ever wonder, why these kind of people are so successful and why they, although they are few, are so respected by the entire world?

These are Black people who never accepted that Root that was planted in our ancestors of, "I am worthless!" They never called themselves and their brothers and sisters words that would penetrate their hearts and make them subconsciously believe, they were inferior and only niggers. They all planted a new root in themselves of " I am respectful and useful". Starting with just words. Consequently their off springs will have to become important and respected as long as that root get watered. It is the law from the Creator of Heaven and Earth. Galatians 6:7

That alone should tell us my people that we can do it, we do have it inside of us to succeed if we would only get rid of the old poison root, and plant a new one of, "yes I can, I am not what they called me, worthless"

All we need to do first individually, my people, is to examine our self honestly. Then ask your own self just a few questions, like why do I always feel so negative, or that some one is always doing something to me or taking something away from me? Or denying me something? Or why do I call myself and my people such negative names all the time... why do I have this bad habit? Why am I so insecure and loud?

Then you, may for the first time in your life, face the truth that something was planted in our ancestor's spirit, years, and years ago, and was hereditarily handed down in our character, even till this day. Something that was a negative implantation.

Although this implantation was beyond their control, it unstable their emotions, and destroyed their confidence and respect in themselves and their trust in people in general, and made them feel like somebody was always doing something to them or taking something away from them. And they were. A long time ago the slave master stole our dignity from our ancestors . They simply could not help that they had been kidnapped, then trained to feel paranoid and inferior, never trusting, always expecting the worse, consequently even calling themselves, losers, Niggers!

They were made to do that.

However, today my brothers we do not have to continue accepting that original implantation… We do not have to continue confessing we are worthless, or even carry that thought pattern around anymore. Nobody is making, taking, or doing anything like that to us today my people, Nobody is making us disrespect ourselves and our brothers. Nobody is insisting that we follow the same slave patterns. Nobody! Nobody is making us do that. Nobody but us. O, why don't WE just quit following the slave master's rule of brother against brother? WE don't have to listen to him no more, he's dead' Remember?

WE can stop doing that now my people, not one of them are alive today. We don't have to obey that mind set anymore, they are all dead. We don't have to kill our brothers any more, we don't have to even disrespect him any more every time we see him and remind him that he's still only a nigger. We Don't! Don't! Don't!

That was the slave masters' training, that he made your ancestors do to each other, then by habit, handed it down to US and WE! are suppose to give it to our children, and they will give it to their children. This way we will forever stay uninformed, divided, hateful, and basically just like we say we were in the spirit of that word we teach, Niggers! Worthless!.., That's all it takes. Would you like to remain like that? That's exactly what the slave master would like to see, that's the way he planted it. Do you?

He is dead now Dead! Dead' Dead! Hallelujah, Dead So why don't we do this my people, why don't we start today… Every time another brother disrespect you or call you a Nigger, Let's tell him, We don't have to do that to each other anymore brother, the slave master is dead' Haven't you heard? He's Dead!"

Most of us just do not know how powerful that spirit in that word is and how long it has been around building up potency. It has been working for hundreds of years by getting watered daily by a certain segment in society, all to one day reach its ultimate negative goal. To infest inside themselves an entire nation on this earth bitterness. ultimately making them unworthy of eternal life with The Heavenly Father.

This may be one of the few words created that can actually form a character. A negative character, Just by a period of time of using it or hearing it. As a matter of fact the spirit in this word Nigger is so strong, because of the hostile environment it was created in, and its intended use. If you could stop using it, or hearing it for one month you probably would not he able to stand to even hear that word anymore with out feeling like you were going to throw up.

That is just how strong the sprit in that defiled word has grown. However, from the first day, you stop using It., or hearing it, your inner spirit starts to heal. Because you will be starving it from that defilement. You may not even realize it is healing, but trust me, in about one month , you will probably not be able to comfortably use or hear that word again without feeling ill. The word will start to form a picture in your mind of something repulsively ugly.

However, the sad and most dangerous part about that rebellious thinking in using that defiled root word is, the Creator of the World has made a rule that cannot be changed, that says. As long as a people or nation accepts thinking like that, or wants to act like that, or don't object to being like that spirit produces, then HE has said, "Give them what they want ". I Samuel 8:22.

WOW! Give them what they want! Yes, my people, the Creator of mankind has just allowed man to have whatever they insisted upon. If they are comfortable and want to continue being slaves of an evil sprit. HE has said, "Give them what they want"… But that attitude and that spirit will ultimately completely destroy them some day, if they don't repent. However. "Give them what they want"

The scripture has admonished us that all those with mindsets that feels comfortable with the devil's rules over them, will be completely destroyed someday. And that word is from the devil.This is the rule from the savior of man kind .

Let's examine that statement and see if the Creator of the World would actually allow this degradation and eventually destruction of man forever, if he persist in his ways of disobedience even alter being warned by Him

It was the Children of Israel, The Creator's chosen people that first refused to listen to Him and change. Although the Creator was trying to save them from this destruction, they had just gotten comfortable with this evil thing ruling over them, basically from habit. Their and other nations around them. So they wanted to copy the ways of their enemy, even if it was wicked. The same way some of us do today.

In any event, they continued to desire a king and even asked for it. "Give us a king, Give us a king. Give us a king to rule over us. Give us a king to judge us." Even against the warnings from YAHWEH (God) that this king was going to be an evil thing. **I Samuel 8:**

So Finally the Creator of the Universe after much trying by Samuel the prophet to get these stiff-necked people to change their thinking and choice said, "Give them what they want". Even though it will completely destroy them someday. Yet he said "Give them what they want, they are free to choose". Let's just examine the very important example by scripture.

1 Samuel 8:

⁴ Then all the elders of Israel gathered together and appeared to Samuel when he was at Ramah.

⁵ Saying to him, you are old and your sons do not walk in your way. Appoint us a king to judge us, just like all the other nations.

⁶ But these things displeased Samuyl especially when they said: Give us a king to judge us. Then Samuyl prayed to YAHWEH {God}

⁷ YAHWEH answered Samuyl and said: Listen to all the words the people speak to you, for they have not rejected you: they have rejected ME that I should not reign of them.

⁸ Just as they have done to ME from the day I brought them (out of Egypt. to this very day. they are now doing to you – they are forsaking ME in order to serve god(s) Elohim.

⁹ So listen to them. "However Samuel forewarned them and let them know how the king who will reign over them will behave toward them.

Some of us have rejected the Creator of Heaven and Earth that HE should not reign over us. And selected the devil as our king to reign over us and judge us. One who has no mercy. One whose only motive is to kill, steal and destroy us. John 10:10 and the Savior has allowed it. If we say so.

Romans 6:

¹⁶ Do you know that to whom you yield yourself as servants to obey, his servant You are whom you obey whether of sin which

leads to death, or of obedience which leads to righteousness "
[17] But thank YAHWEH though you were once servants of sin, you have become obedient with all your heart to the form of teaching which was delivered to you.
[18] Being then set free from sin you have become servants of righteousness.

DIVIDE AND CONQUER

Brother and sister and all of those whose conscience may be stirred up and knows for sure that there is something happening that is important and different today . You may be being admonished by the creator of the entire world to do something. We need to be on guard for a cleverly thought out scheme by the devil to destroy America. Then the entire world.

This is a scheme where WE black people may play the major roll. And it is so perfect yet so deceptive until one must look real careful, not only with our natural eyes but with our truthful inward spirit man. Because what the devil is really concocting has been disguised. It will look like he is after one thing but in reality he is after another thing altogether. He just did not go straight to it. The devil is going to make sort of a detour, but trust this, he will return back for it. You may only know the devil as a he! so we will say he!

The devil has a plan to destroy a nation that is very important to the creator of heaven and earth's plan for these last days before they can realize what he is doing. It is US! Afro-Americans. And this scheme is un-folding and approaching rapidly. Even though this plan may look like it is going in another direction, it is still aimed at capturing you. Black brothers and sister! Plus the devil has now only a short time to keep his plan under wrap. So he must hurry.

REVELATIONS 12 {the book of YAHWEH }
9. And the great dragon was cast out that old serpent called the devil and Satan who deceives the whole world. She was cast out into the earth and her angels were cast out with her.
10. And I heard a loud voice saying in heaven now is come

---

salvation and strength and the kingdom of our Father and
the power of His Messiah: for the accuser of our brother is cast
down who accused them before our Father day and night.
11. And they over came her by the blood of the lamb and by the
word of their testimony {The law and the prophets] and they
loved not their lives unto death
12. Therefore rejoice you heavens and you who dwell in them!
Woe to the inhabitants of the earth and of the sea! For the
devil is come down to you having great wrath because she
knows that she has but a short time.

The devil is going to use the events of Sept.11, 2001 as sort of a launching pad to try and turn the heat up so to speak of division among Americans to a degree never seen before. America is who the devil must divide first in order to un-stable the whole world, preferably black America in particular

He is going to for the first time in history provoke white democrats to blame white republicans and republicans blaming democrats for something that can spiral out of control into such a nasty fewd until it could actually divide brother against brother in the same house.

This unraveling of America and division of the politicians coupled with this race problem is going to start first at the Governing level of America. But the fewd will become so nation un-stabling because of the constant fighting between the almost equally divided governing officials that both sides will think that they must have the support of the black community just to stay in their governing positions.

This is where you enter the plot, black brothers and sisters. And hopefully enough of us will have our hearts circumcised in righteousness by then, enough to see this deadly plot unfolding in time. Or heaven help us all

The devil is going to try and get YOU! Black people to start making unfair and undeserving demands on one party then another just for keeping them in their positions. And when your unreasonable demands are not met fast enough that is when the fight for survival from both parties, from their lust and greed will reach a height never seen before of mankind. Both telling you how bad the other side is trying to gain your support, plus giving some of US position that WE! have not been even trained for, or even qualified to handle, just so they can stay in their office.

However, we are going to hold the key my brothers, to whether America survives or whether it goes into complete chaos and self-destructs. It is all going to depend on the righteous or unrighteous decision WE make as a whole people as to being responsible standup, united and honest. The ball will be in our court. This will be a dangerous time in life

The devil is going to tell US something that will divide us even more again soon. Somewhere in the middle of this super heated battle between Democrats and Republicans fight for power, using his favorite line that seem to always work in a portion of misinformed Americans, that the American white man is the devil, and that it is him who is the cause of all black people's problems and always have been. Plus the problem of the whole world is because of this American white man. And some are going to buy that lie because it will look right to some of US.

The devil is going to try and agitate a furious bloody fight in our country of America, of Americans against Americans first. This fighting and accusing between the suppose to be brothers, even white brothers and sister this time, will add fuel and give energy to the devil's confidence that he can win. Although it is a deceptive confidence, he will escalate the battle by his continuous promoting these accusations of each other. Then eventually white America against black America. He knows this way he could keep us so busy distrusting and competing against each other that we will not be able to see, nor defend America against any other enemy, for he knows the scripture has declared:

YAHCHANAN Mark (Mark) *3:* **(The Book of Yahweh)**
24. If a kingdom is divided against itself, that kingdom cannot stand
25 if a house is divided against itself that house cannot stand.
26 So if Satan has risen against herself she is divided and cannot stand—she has come to her end

We are the only people today capable of making or at least allowing a meaningful division to persist in America black people. WE hold the key of solution. WE could cause men to have to drop their foolish divisions and all unite in righteousness or not, basically because of our number and what we have experienced.

Those of us that just refuse to get honest with ourselves and our brothers, or those of us, who just will not become serious and knowledgeable and spiritually discerned and stand in honest truth so that WE can make the right decision at this troubled time, will unfortunately wind up buying this lie from the devil that all white men are our enemies, because it could look true if you have never heard the whole truth from the Heavenly Father of his never changing rules for all mankind. Even though the devil's scenario will be in no way the entire truth. If we black people don't unite in righteousness, we'll wind up putting more fuel on the fire. That absolutely has to happen.

However, unless black America is willing to leave our tradition of dependency, open our eyes up wide, get involved personally and honestly, as a whole united people, about our destiny WE will make the problem worse.. WE should make it our responsibility to stand up for pure righteousness and make aware those brothers and sister who may just not be aware of the honest truth about US! Just US! first. Consequently this could cause US to become accountable and valuable to The Creator if WE united in righteousness. Then WE can without a doubt make the right and fair decision for the whole world .in this prophesied trouble time .

I'm afraid if WE don't do this, WE will have to always buy a lie and be completely destroyed forever. Because the devil is going to use the rehashing of some of the atrocities that happened in the past to black people, which were true, as a justification for US to join him in this deceptive revengeful fight, then destroy the whole America through an in house fight. Preferably US! first. The reason is, you are the prize' It is US! that he wants to destroy so badly. Black America. There are some things you may not know about US! that the devil does. He wants us to stay revengeful and confused so that WE will be un-forgiving in the end time, then WE could actually miss our blessing that The Creator has prepared for us

Here is the devil's hurry for the devil creating this turmoil. WE are the last group of people that are called to come into the kingdom of YAHWEH (GOD) as a united people The Heavenly Father wants desperately for us to be renewed, united, and justified so that WE can enter as a whole nation. WE are the gentiles that the Creator has promised to deliver. And when he gets all of his people in, that will come in, HE is going to start a brand new system, right here on this earth. And some of us! Will rule as kings and queens. You may want to ask , " when will The Creator set HIS kingdom up here on earth ?" The scripture says

Romans 11:25
"After the fullness of the gentiles is complete"

This will happen. But the devil wants to stop us! He knows that time is running out and he wants to keep as many of us as he can, hearts and minds confused, bitter, and revengeful so that he can keep us out of the kingdom forever.

The devil is actually trying to prolong the sitting up of, the Kingdom of YAHWEH {God} on this earth, we can never enter into his Kingdom with a root of bitterness still within us! Hebrews 12:12-17

It would only be the natural and honest and necessary thing for any serious people to ask, Just how could one get his heart and soul in righteousness, so that they could make the absolute right decision that would please The heavenly Father in trouble times especially, so that WE could inherit eternal life as time is about to close. And HE has given all mankind the only way it can be done. He promised.

Deuteronomy 30: 6-7
YAHWEH your FATHER will circumcise your hearts, and the hearts of your descendants, so that YOU may love him with all your heart and with all your soul and live. Then YAHWEH your Father will put all these curses upon your enemies and upon those who hated and persecuted you.

My brothers and sisters it is the only way for us to ever be able to come into the kingdom of ever lasting life that the Creator of the world has prepared for us? We need a heart circumcision. Destroying an old bitter root planted by the enemy, But saved by the Father of Life and It is our just for the asking then receiving He said

Romans 10: 9-11
9.that if you confess with your mouth, the Messiah, YAHSHUA (Jesus), and believe in your heart that Yahweh(God) has raised Him from the dead, you will be saved. 10. For with the heart one believes unto righteousness, and with the mouth confession

*is made into salvation. 11.For the scripture says: whosoever
believes on Him will not be put to shame.*

Romans 11:25
*I do not want you to be ignorant of this great secret brothers so
that you may not he wise in your own conceits; that blindness
in part has come upon Israel, until the full number of the
Gentiles has come.*

Isn't it time for us to get honest and serious brothers and sisters? Isn't it time for us to try and unite and search out the true Father from Heaven and save our youth? And ourselves? Haven't WE spent too much time already listening to old traditional fables and solutions that will never work? Isn't it time to try and find and obey the Creator of Heaven and Earth?

11 Timothy 2:15-16
*Study to show yourself approved to Yahweh: a workman
who does not need to he ashamed, rightly dividing the word
of truth. (The law and the prophets) But shun profane, vain
bubbling, for this will only grow into more unholiness.*

As long as the devil can deceitfully keep you busy listening to him in his lies the more he will try and pervert your mind and tongue, consequently forming a root of defilement and bitterness in your heart.

Hebrews 12:
*"Searching diligently so that no one falls short of the honor of
Yahweh, so that no root of bitterness grows up to cause trouble
— for because of this many are defiled. '16So that there is no
fornication, nor profane person, like Esau, who for one morsel
of food sold his birthright 17For you know that afterwards,
when he wanted to inherit the blessing, he was rejected for he
found no way for repentance though with tears sought it out.*

The devil knows clearly that if you don't repent of a bitter root and profane and perverseness, he can destroy you forever. These rules are from the Creator. A perverse tongue will destroy you and all creation around you eventually according to James 3:6 the scripture also warns us that perverseness breaks up the communication and fellowship with us and the Heavenly Father. It states that it helps the devil work on you.

A wholesome tongue is a tree of life, but perverseness in it breaks the spirit.
Proverbs 15:4

When there is a breach or a break up of a relation, there is no communication. So you probably will not study and accept truth and righteousness from The Heavenly Father of Light, which is the law and the prophets, just because of this breach. The devil knows this Well. That is why he will encourage a perverse tongue. This way he is almost guaranteed to eventually destroy you. All of this was a part of a endtime plan to destroy America.

If the devil can in any way keep one in a mentally confused state of mind. Even though you may be unaware of it, he knows that you will probably never check to see if maybe you have been ignorant of something that is vitally important to your salvation. And a perverse tongue will eventually confuse the brain.

That is why it is so vitally important for all mankind to study, study diligently. For the mind eats words and information. It is food for the brain. Perverse words will bring destruction. Life giving words will cause the brains to lead you to life, then eternal life.

An alarming number of black youngsters have went back into a basic slave mentally, unaware of it, voluntarily Just by simply repeating over and over and over certain words and phrases that has made them perverted and defiled. These words, even though they are unaware, has entered their hearts, and altered their thought process, consequently defiling their spirit. It has revived a bitter root inside of these hearts that is most difficult for them to detect, or be delivered from.

Most of them have never studied, nor even heard about what happened to their forefathers years and years ago, back when they were first kidnapped and brought into this country of America, and made to accept certain satanic rules and behavior or be hung.

This teaching was designed to instill hatred among a people, by promoting repetitiously one slave against another. The principle was called

Divide and Conquer done mostly with only words. A powerful principle that is also supported by the Scripture Galatians 6:7 & Proverbs 22:6

Now the devil is trying to use that same principle today that he used on a Nation of Black Slaves of brothers against brothers to divide up the whole of America. Divide them up and keep them from truth and knowledge and unity. For he knows that only through truth and knowledge can one be made free.

Proverbs 23: So as a man think it, so is he.

It is a proven fact that a person's belief system is just naturally started and established by what they hear… "Faith cometh by hearing" **Romans 10:17**

That is just the way the Creator made all mankind. Negative words carries a negative spirit, positive words carries a positive life giving spirit, If one listens to a suggestion long enough, even in a song or a melody, they will just naturally sooner or later began to accept that suggestion deep in their spirit as a normal part of their thinking. That is why the savior of mankind has warned us to be careful what we lend our ears to. **"Faith comes by hearing".**

The devil has revised and is promoting vigorously an old ancient but effective tactic of his today, that this present generation did not experience or live through, nor have most of them even heard about. At least in truth. Therefore most of them have no idea of how

Proverbs 15:22
Folly seems delightful to him who is "Destitute" of Wisdom, but a man of understanding walks uprightly.

The scripture has identified this situation as one that has become one of "Desperation". He says, "Destitute". The defilement of these particular youngsters spirit of this generation usually starts with this poison root word "NIGGER" then escalates into more and more poison and perverted suggestions of hatred, killing, murder as the devil has made these thoughts seem harmless and justified through just the clever continuous use of such terms. And his new method today is first to just get you to agree and promise to do these evils through a simple song until it penetrates your heart and becomes well with your soul. However, it has been identified by the savior of man as something that will destroy you! Folly! {foolishness}

One time the scripture identified this folly and deception as the equivalent of shooting death and fire at your brothers. It reads

Proverbs 26:
18.Like a madman throwing firebrands, arrows and death. 19 is the man who deceives his brother then says: I was only joking

The true message is that the Creator of the world is seriously concerned about this generation and warns us that our youth are not in just a little bit of trouble in these last days from accepting what has proven to be a multiplying poisonous root that has taken years to mature to be a poisonous degree, but according to Him, it can make some literally brain dead from its repetitious use. For they do not know that all words have power and its own spirit. – The scripture said, they are now "Destitute"…

the words I speak are spirit and they are life (John 6:63)

This poison root has become "Delightful" to them somehow through this just popular acceptable use of certain words even though it is absolutely wicked and working to defile their spirit man they the don't know it. But they are now "Destitute of Wisdom". There is probably no one who would accept destruction of themselves and their brothers, knowingly and willingly. However: Prov.5:22 says

The Wicked man is entrapped by his own iniquities, he is caught in the ropes of his own sin. 23He will die for lack of discipline and instruction in the greatness of his folly he will be led astray.

The most important thing for any person born to do today is know for sure for yourself the word of YAHWEH, The Creator of Heaven, and Earth. In the last days it is fore told that men will not know how to identify for sure what is wicked and what is not! If do not know the word of the Creator. Plus mankind will have to already believe that the scripture is true, before he could trust that was, and still is the only answer to bring

---

help or save him.

So in these last days, if men don't know what the word of the Creator said for sure, for himself he will be hopelessly lost then destroyed forever without a remedy. Proverbs 29: 1 He simply won't know what he should or shouldn't do for sure.

Simply because in the last days sin will have abounded so much and more and Men will have ,just gotten use to doing certain things that are so evil and wicked just from habit. Yet to them they will seem merciful and sociable and right. The scripture even warns...

There is a way that seems right to men. But the end thereof is the way of death"
Proverbs 16:25

Again the scripture tells us, by then, sin will have increased to a level of unconsciousness to sin, and your good deeds and mercies may be even cruel. You may be condemning yourself more through just habit and don't even know it. He says that He is desperately trying to get mankind to hear Him because some men conscience has been seared as with a hot iron.

1 Timothy 4:
Now the spirit speaks very plainly, that in the latter times, some will depart from the faith, giving heed to seducing spirits and doctrines of demons (Elohim) Speaking lies in hypocrisy, having THEIR CONSCIENCE SEARED as with a HOT IRON

Proverbs 12:10
The tender mercies of the wicked are cruel

James 1:15
Then when lust has conceived it brings forth sin when it is fully matured it bring forth death.

LET'S TALK ABOUT
NOBODY BUT US! FOR A WHILE

My dear brothers and sisters who are black we are just going to have to face a serious truth before it is too late, if we are ever going to realistically overcome as a whole people. We must stop delaying this inevitable chore. And no, we have not overcome as a black nation, just a few of us happen to be doing fairly well, but not nearly as well as we should be doing. But as a united nation we are still in trouble.

We are just going to have to get honest and face something that is and should be embarrassing, degrading, and insulting. Yet, could be helped. We must face that we or at least our ancestors bought something a long time ago that was a lie that made us build inside of us hereditarily a root of bitterness.

Yes my brothers and sisters. I hate to admit it but we have a poison root in most of us that was planted there upon our very entrance into this country that we must get rid of. It makes us enemies to ourselves, our brothers and everybody else This root of bitterness inside of us, make people think they are justified to not help us, even kill us.

Deuteronomy 30:6
Yahweh (God) your Father will circumcise your hearts and the hearts of your descendants, so that you may love him with all your heart and all your soul and live.

Do we really want to be looked at as the enemy? If that root is not finally faced and dealt with by getting a new heart transformation, then we will always be viewed as being at least a potential enemy by society at large. And our children's, children's children will always be too.

If we don't start to teach and preach to ourselves on a massive basis about the error of accepting in your spirit an inferior title, then our black youth have no choice but to copy and call themselves the same negative character that your great ancestors called themselves. NIGGERS! Which is really to say,..? "I want to return back to the days of my ancestors when I was looked down on, dependent upon the slave master because I am ignorant and irresponsible."

So I ask you my people is that what you want to do, return back to the days when it was legal to beat you with a whip because you were thought to be the same as a mule? Is that the way you feel about yourself, that you are really incapable of being responsible? Do you feel like you are really still just a Nigger? Is that what you want to do?" That's what the word means… So do you? Are you really still more comfortable putting yourself and your brothers down? Do you really want to teach your off springs to feel and talk like you?"

My people if you don't respect or even like yourself or your brothers, how can you be liked, respected or even be valuable to anyone else?

So why don't we do this, why don't we change the way people feel about us, by changing the way we feel about ourselves? It starts simply by saying that you are important. Or would you rather just stay a Nigger?

The word itself Nigger, means and always will mean, "A character of little worth and low self esteem. And a potential enemy to himself and all those around him"

This particular word was created out of hostility and was designed to be controlling from a negative ambition.

The Creator of Heaven and Earth has admonished us that once any plant or word has taken on a spirit that spirit and meaning can never change in that seed. For its seed is in itself Genesis 1:11

We continue my people to enslave ourselves generation after generation, after generation. we and we alone are, and should be responsible for our own future and destiny. And nobody can really do anything about it at first but you One way or the other

Every law and rule necessary for us to progress or gain self esteem is already in place now days my people. Nobody can legally hold you back from nothing worthwhile if you qualify for it today brothers and sisters, not even the president of the United States. It is only what you think and say about yourself that can stop you.

However, it is how we apply ourselves and what we apply for that will make the difference and has always made the difference. And above all the character and attitude we apply with. It is not your color any more, it is your character that will determine the outcome one-way or the other. It is what you sow that you will reap. Galatians 6:7. Plus no one can do it for us but us, It is mandatory, according to the Creator.

There is another sickening thing WE must correct my people, even after we may be in a position to make a difference, is to see some of our brothers continue to get on radio and TV and complain and cry about "0 'look what they've done to me... they want let us do this... or, they won't let us do that"

Truthfully my people that makes us look so pitiful and weak and sloth-ful, always still depending on what someone will allow us to do. When the truth is, we don't need nobody's permission to exist or to earn any dignity. Let's just go possess it ourselves, nobody is trying for the most part to stop US! We are naturally strong, if we want to be.

What is missing though, we need to just go and qualify our own selves in ability and character and we may he surprised at the people who would jump to invite you in and assist you. That would be a much better solu-tion than waiting and hoping or wanting somebody else to do it, or give it to us for free based on an old excuse of something that happened over two hundred years ago when neither you nor them were even born, "They owe me"

Brothers, what about black accountability, in ability and character? And righteous aggressiveness. We can have it, and teach it to our youth. And according to the Creator it would never depart.

Proverbs 22:6

When one use words that suggest or refer to themselves as an idiot, or words that means you are worthless, but yet, ask or demand that some-body else give you the respect of a king, or even an intelligent being, how can that be? Is that honest to expect that?

Here is another good one my brother that we should examine. We, ourselves are still asking the same old slave mentality questions, when an opportunity or something presents itself for this country's progress. "OH

I wonder how that is going to turn out for us?"

The answer is my surprised people, one that is engraved in stone. It is going to turn out just the way we make it turn out for us. The more of us that get involved, honestly and diligently the better anything will turn out in our favor. And history has proven over and over again that is the only way it will turn out in your favor. Haven't WE learned that yet?

Or listen to this beauty, that we are also famous for, "Oh look, the government is building something new, I wonder how many contracts were given to us?" The honest answer is, and should be brothers, "How many of US! Applied? How many different areas? How hard did you try to make sure you were qualified for that position?"

Let's be honest and fair with ourselves first, my people, and not look so much for someone to pick us up and say. "Here ya'll, come and get it!"... But rather why don't we determine ourselves to just go after it then say, "Hold it pal, some of' that is mine, I'm here to claim it."

Let's quit just sitting on the sideline, observing ,just waiting so we can criticize after the fact. Let's get actually in the fight as a participating partner, and help. Then you have a justified reason to demand something. Let's stop playing the blame game.

WE my people, must open our eyes and recognize not only what is happening to us as a whole people, but also why it is happening. That is most important. We could stop most of the negative stuff before it even gets started by getting more aggressively involved in what would be the fair solution. But we can't keep waiting until it happens then complain.

Just voting, does not give us any automatic power, It is in deed a good thing that we finally got the authority to exercise our opinions. Sometimes we just go vote, then go back home and sit down and say, " now let's see what are they going to do!"

What WE are really saying with that attitude is " let somebody else do it"... .We have got to learn to vote, plus go and help or at least make sure that person is getting the job done you voted for. Then they will know you are serious. It may not happen automatically.

The first thing we are going to have to do my people is insist from us, ourselves, and any other black leaders we elect, or anybody else that represent our interest that they give us some truth telling. For only by the whole truth can we make right decisions.

It is mandatory, if we are ever going to get anywhere meaningful to ourselves or the world, is to be known as a people who can be trusted, for truth. The truth of the matter is there is a big responsibility that comes in being a just people. First to respect other people as you would like to be respected. But it all comes with telling and accepting truth

We have absolutely got to start facing the truth my people. Not what we wish it was, or what we think it ought to be, but rather the truth. Whatever it is!… History should have taught us by now that WE and WE alone must first take charge of our own destiny. If we don't, WE nor our children's, children's, children will never become economically secure, or united in righteousness or have any dignity as a whole black nation, Never! And no one else can do it for us but us with our own determination… .We have got to finally say enough is enough of coming up in last place.

We need to just cease from accusing other people and other races of not helping us become successful or dignified when the leadership responsibility lies exclusively with us. And only us! That is such a sad and somewhat hypocritical pitiful complaint. That is really shifting the responsibility and blame on some one else that is truly ours

Brothers and sisters, let's just step to the plate. We can do it. Let's just quit using that old pitiful helpless slave mentality excuse of "Oh we just can't make it with out master!"

That is exactly what we are saying subconsciously when we continue to march, and complain and argue and demand that, "We would be alright but, he has got to give us this and he has got to give us that!" .. That seems to be the story of our lives, "He has got to give us something!".., When clearly, all we need to do is get up and get moving towards it ourselves,

My people ,we may just find out that people would assist you in what ever it is you don't have. They would have no choice, if we would only unite in true righteousness. We would be profitable to them' IF we took the absolute leadership role fist! All we need to do is unite in righteousness my people. That is wisdom.

YARQOB (James) 3: (the book of YAHWEH)
*13 Who is wise and understanding among you? Let him
show it by his righteous conduct, by works done in meekness,
humility that comes from wisdom.
14 But if you have bitter rivalry and strife in your heart do not
boast and lie against the truth.*

---

15. this wisdom does not descend from above, but is earthly sensual and demonic.
16 for where rivalry and strife are there is confusion and every evil work.
17 But the wisdom that comes from above is first pure, then peaceable gentle and easy to be entreated of mercies and righteous fruits without partiality and without hypocrisy
18 And the fruit of righteousness is sown in peace. For those who make peace.

It is so essential my brothers that we make peace. It is extremely important that in our quest to become stable and united with ourselves that you don't become enemies of others in the house that we live in. The enemy would just love to see us become angry revengeful and proud; over zealous and self-righteous, accusing and blaming and pointing fingers at the white man. So that we would cause unrest then a war with in a war, in our own house. Then he could surely destroy us all. That is the devil's ultimate goal.

YAHCHANAN MARK (Mark) 3: (The Book of Yahweh)
24.If a kingdom is divided against itself that kingdom cannot stand
25.If a house is divided against itself that house cannot stand
26.So if Satan has risen against herself: she is divided and cannot stand. She has come to her end.

One of the very first things we must do as a black nation, that we have neglected to do for so long, is learn to organize, orderly and diligently and participate by the rules. The sooner the better. We could do ourselves a much needed favor right now by starting today with our youth. Somehow convincing them that life's success comes basically from asserting yourself in unity and going by rules. All of life has rules. These rules were given to all mankind by the Heavenly Father of Loves. It is the key to everything successful. **Galatians 6:7**

WORDS HAVE POWER! REJOICE

What we didn't know my people is, words have power. That's basically all it was to it. Words are powerful. Words are the most powerful element there is. With words you can speak life to yourself and somebody else, or you can speak death, with just words. (**Proverbs I 8:21**)

The slave masters knew this, but you didn't. They knew the scriptures, your ancestor didn't. They knew the deep principle of scriptures like.

Proverbs 6:2 (the book of Yahweh)
"You are trapped by the words of your own mouth".

The old slave masters knew if you say certain words until one believes them, or just hear those words until one receive them in their hearts, the words itself will form sort of a picture that you could start believing is true. You could eventually start acting the word out. I don't know how long it might take for each person, but I do know, just as soon as any one believes something is true, they will act according to their belief. And it all starts with just words.

If you said a word that even meant you were a monkey enough, you would eventually start to act like a monkey. But you did not know this two hundred years ago, and this is how you and your ancestors may have gotten molded. They had no idea they were being molded. And according to the scripture you can get, even destroyed, not for what you do know, but for what you don't know.

Isaiah 5:13
Therefore my people are gone into captivity, because they have

no knowledge: and their honorable men are famished, and
their multitude, dried up with thirst.

II Peter 1:5
And besides this, giving all diligence add to your faith virtue;
and to virtue KNOWLEDGE

Let's just take another look right here, and listen to what the Creator told Soloman that words can do. HE said

Proverbs 6:2
You are snared ('trapped or captured) with the words of your
mouth. Thou art taken with the words of your mouth

The Creator of mankind never tells you about a problem without giving you also the absolute solution. Always, Always. He always tells you even how to do **it.** Here, right after HE revealed to us that your words had gotten you captured or in trouble, He gives us the only way out by saying in the third verse

3."Do this now my son and deliver thyself make sure!

Not only did the scripture identify who had you captured, but HE revealed to us the only thing that would ever want you captured, a hunter, a fowler, your enemy, but HE is telling us also to **"Do this! Make sure!:**

Deliver thyself as a roe from the hands of the hunter, and as a
bird from the fowler

The first thing WE probably need to understand is, these instructions and principles are from the highest authority there is. And they cannot be changed they are all written down in the book of instructions The Bible. The law book.. And the right words will start to deliver you Just like the wrong words captured you.

These principles will work for anyone that will use them. Your ancestor's capturers knew the scriptures were true, they knew that if these principles were applied in the way the savior of the world said, they would work, they would increase. They can be used for good purposes or evil purposes. They knew you could use words to set a trap for a man or words to free a man. But your ancestors didn't, they couldn't read.

Our ancestors, brothers, had some words forced upon them that were cruel and – created just for that purpose. And they were so potent and delivered with such intensity, persistence, repetition and cruel force until it didn't take long at all, in their case, for those words that bring captivity to start penetrating their hearts.

Let's just reiterate in fine disgusting details. Sometimes one or the other of your ancestors may have been given a big knife or big club or pick handle or something and ordered to beat the other ancestor of yours until he or she admitted with conviction that they were a worthless, lazy, no-good piece of garbage. Just a NIGGER and deserved to be punished. And if you couldn't beat him or her, or kick them bad enough to make them admit this to the slave owners satisfaction, then you got beat or sometimes hung, for being disobedient and no good either. Sometimes the slave master was not satisfied with either one of your performances, so you both got hung while the rest of the slaves were made to watch. All of this just for not admitting and accepting that you are a no good NIGGER

Now according to the Creator of the Universe, words alone spoken long enough and convincing enough can eventually enter into a person's belief system, by themselves. And if you practice saying those words long enough, you could automatically start just believing them, then start to act out the spirit of that word, which the word NIGGER means worthless or monkey like.., a NIGGER"

Again according to the Creator, words can form a root of belief in your heart good or bad. And unless that believing root is replaced, "it will never depart" **Proverbs 22:6**

"For with the heart man believeth"
Romans 10:10.

The character that emerged from such a training of that root word, NIGGER!, generation after generation was a character that was in no way a surprise to the administrator or I should say, slave owner, but rather a character that he was well pleased with, which had been bred by him from a fundamental principle powered from up above. The Heavenly Father. The slave owner also knew

Roman: 10:17
"Faith cometh by hearing, hearing, hearing"

A character was planted in a human being from just continually hearing certain words basically that he believed, and admitted that "I realize that I am inferior to white people, without you I am nothing. So I'll work for you. I will honor you, I will obey you, and I will never disagree with you. And I will never try and defend myself against you because I realize I am only a useless, defenseless ignored piece of garbage compared to you. I am only a NIGGER. Please do not be angry master."

Now should WE keep saying that? Should WE keep that character? WE keep watering that word, NIGGER' Should WE keep doing that?

This agreement worked well for the slave owners and the developer of that character, for years and years and years. As a mater of fact, as one generation of slaves with this mind set died off, it became easier and easier for the next generation to just follow that set down accepted rule for their existence. After all it was being taught to them by the ones that gave birth to them now.

The slave's mothers and fathers were reminding them by this time, from birth that they were only NIGGERS and don't ever believe that they can become anything else. Or change the way you are. You were born nothing and that is the way you will always be. Plus it is OK, because Mr. Charlie is smart enough to tell us what to do.

Even when one slave or the other died, it was not a big thing to the other slaves. By now you had witness a beating or a public hanging of a worthless NIGGER who disobeyed his owner. Mr. Charlie was usually applauded or praised by the rest of the slaves for giving a worthless NIGGER just what he deserved for not being obedient to Mr. Charles. Plus he might have been one who was reported to have been trying to slip and learn how to think for himself anyway. Even after Mr. Charlie and the rest of the slaves had warned him and warned him that he was too ignorant to ever learn how to think or even read, "That is not for you, that's for decent folks, and you are just a NIGGER."

You are supposed to be happy about these revelations my people. You should be so happy that you should be jumping and shouting on the in-side. You now know what the problem was, and you have the solution. You now know the only solution to any problem you did have or have. The Creator's Rules.

Th Savior of the world said, "Stop the old root and start planting an-other undefiled Root". You know the solution now. I don't think even the Creator, himself, can do anymore than what HE has given us. Accept let us continue to get into a little deeper degradation, then maybe WE will stop and just believe HIM. Maybe then WE will turn to his Rules and advice.

WE could start today planting a new way of thinking about ourselves right now. Then everybody else would be forced to think different about us. If WE could get enough brothers and sisters to just start trusting the Creator's undeniable, guaranteed to work, respectful rules for all creation, I believe that maybe inside of one year every black person on earth may get a hold of this revelation and start preaching to the world and each other, "we got the solution, we got the solution It's Savior's Rules! The solu-tion how is the creator of heaven and earth's answer for everything"

Why would you NOT! want to start planting another root in you, one just the opposite of what was planted in you without your permission?. Plant a root of, "Oh Yes I can, I'm not what they said I was, Halleluyah I can do it, and I can win! I am not a NIGGER, I am not a worthless being, that's a lie! They just told me that. I am not a dog. Ho or bitch! They just planted that negative quality in me...l am really a winner, I am somebody special, I just need to he trained up in the way I want to grow, Oh I've got the solution, I've got the solution, I've got the solution! My Heavenly Father gave it to me. I believe him over the slave master" (Hebrews 12:9) "Words have power, rejoice!"

The worse thing WE could do that would definitely stop even God's plan for us in these last days, my people is just get mad because of this revelations and start going around blaming people.

NO! NO! NO! NO! The white people that planted that poison root in our ancestors are all dead. Every single one of them, dead! It is all about what you do and call yourself now. Who are you? What are you? What do you want to do? Nobody can stop you now, but you!

Did you know that the majority of white people that are living today are just as disgusted as you are at their ancestors of long ago for such a barbaric act? And wish that it had never happened like that. Most of them are even too embarrassed at their ancestors to try and talk to you about a subject like that. And they will not... until they are positive that you are intelligent enough, and have the kind of mindset that could deal with the honest truth with out anger or revenge. They just will not even acknowledge such a subject. But trust this my brother, most of these people would be happier than you are, if you would stop and plant another root in yourself, a root that showed the beautiful black talented people WE really are that has never really been shown to the world on any massive scale. It has been covered by our own insecurities and lack of knowledge.

They know that they can't plant a root of, "Yes I am somebody" in you. That has to start by you realizing it. Then confessing it with *you mouth*. Then believing it in your heart. According to the Savior. Romans 10:9

As a matter of fact, you haven't heard a white man call you a NIGGER in over forty years. And you probably will not. There are just not many of them that would call you a "worthless piece of scum", and most of them are truly uncomfortable, paranoid and embarrassed just to hear you call yourself that ugly word.

Believe it or not, there are a lot of' white people just waiting and believing for that day when WE as a whole united people decide to stop playing the blame game and plant a new root of' respecting ourselves. A root where they could stand around you in the same room without you disrespecting yourself and threatening them. A people that they could trust that wouldn't call yourself and your friend a bunch of "useless no good NIGGERS!" Loud and ridiculous.

Most of them are hoping for the day that they could sit down beside you and discuss some multi-million dollar plan with you and you understand it. Some are actually hoping for the day that WE become sick and tired of being sick and tired of our condition, and not scream and yell in anger about the situation like a savage, but actually do something corrective about it, and show the newly planted root that WE are training up of self worth and real value. They know that WE can do it like anybody else, maybe better. But only WE can do it.

That my brothers and sisters is the answer. And the only time any people will think, that they can't get away with doing anything they want, to you, is when you show them that they can't. It is not automatic. Sorry but life just does not go that way.

When a person thinks you are somebody or something to have to reckon with, or something of value to be useful, trust me, they will hesitate before they just shoot you. WE must insist by our own actions that certain attitudes and perceptions about US! STOP. WE must let the world see WE are somebody, who will unite and fight And with the right tools, the holy scripture's rules.

WE are somebody. WE do deserve to be respected by the Creator's rules. However, it is still up to us to demand. "How dare you treat me like that, don't you know who I am?...I am a king's son {or daughter}, I am intelligent, as a matter of fact, I am really Royalty ..I am not a Nigger and I'm not your dog, and don't say that to me any more, OK my brother? I don't act like that any more, and I don't talk like that any more, because I'm not like that anymore. I buried that character."

WHILE WE ARE AT IT

Let us take this great opportunity right here to try and make another very obstinate assumption clearer. Every person you see that is in a decision making position about your future or that has a white face, is not against you. Or against minorities progress by no means.

However, let us take a look at a situation that WE have allowed to linger for decades that could make it appear that every one is against us. When it simply could be the ball was just in our court. And WE may have dropped it

If you were a minority or black and you were the only minority, or one of a handful that was seated among an army of majorities, and let's just say, a bill or a decision came up to either build another jail to warehouse and store this problem bunch of minorities out of the way, or a build a school and training center to educate this bunch of so called trouble makers. What decision do you think would more than likely take precedent? Which one though the years has usually taken precedent ?

Yet I don't think that would necessarily be your thinking or your solution to the problem. Build another jail? …would it black brothers? No way do I believe you are happy with that as a solution for your black youth.

This could be that it was just not enough of you minorities sitting there to suggest or present another option. These majorities were probably just waiting for some more suggestions from the minority side. And it is our responsibility to present another option.

Truthfully there may not even be one sitting there to just purposely block or oppose you black brothers. This is just the general normal consensus that has been tolerated by all. Especially by you, black brothers. Did you really object furiously to them building another jail for your brothers? WE don't seem to make sure that there is enough of us in there to object furiously enough. So do you see what WE have to do black brothers? Not THEM!. But WE! Otherwise WE stay powerless and accusing. It is not their responsibility really to liberate you. It is ours.

And while we are at it, I would greatly appreciate it, if my brothers don't start attacking me for telling pure truth. Check it out first brothers, scriptures and all. All this entire oration really needs is, Amen!

That is one of our greatest obstacles that WE are going to have to learn to overcome, the unconstructive criticism, not from THEM! But from US!

One of the main ingredients to our success as prospering new black nation is, WE have definitely got to learn how to be less reluctant and contrary to positive change. And become more united. Change must happen, don't be afraid and argue. Trust what the Creator said. And I agree, that is not all there is to the solution, but character change with new language must be First! Deuteronomy 30: 6

And YAHWEH thy Father will circumcise your heart and the heart of thy seed, so that thy will love Him with all of thy heart, and with all thy soul so that thou mayeth live

WE can point to other people and say that THEY are the problem, and point out their wrong doings the rest of our lives. But what does that really mean? What WE need to do, and what is going to help US! Is the solution that the scriptures have so plainly demonstrated for us, the Creator gave us the solution.

Truthfully all WE really need to do is stir up our conscience, yours, and mine, to a level of' 0 tolerance to bondage. What is the matter with shooting for 0 tolerance to anymore bondage whatsoever?

Let's stay realistic though. There is still a thinking out there whose minds WE must change that thinks WE have always accepted bondage, and WE will always accept bondage and the bondage is OK, for US. So let's show the world the beautiful people WE really can be

I remember so well now, at the time of this breaking News flash, that I heard on television, while I was incarcerated, about this helpless man being shot and killed by the police while having his hands cuffed behind his back and me being in jail my self for a technical violation.

In any event, this mind set that ordered me back to jail said, "well, we think you should go back and do twelve more months in jail, that is our rule... you see we feel you probably went out and maybe had a good time or some kind of party or something. Because it has been reported to us that you had a dirty urine, so take these twelve months you owe and go on back to jail because that is wrong, and we must obey our policy the law is the law."

Of course it is, for some people.....That same mindset also reasoned that, "well, the police did shoot this guy, multible times with a magnum, and we realize that he had hand cuffs on behind his back, but that was only to protect this madman from harming anybody. So that is nothing to get all worked up about."

Wow!... "that is nothing to get all worked up about" However this authority just continued saying "After all that is the police's job, that is what their job is all about, protecting the people... So there is really no need for you people to stir up all this trouble, trying to send these fine officers to jail, or even to charge them with any wrong doings. That want help anything, besides, this too will all go away. So ya'll just calm down after all this will all past soon this is nothing that important, or new."

WOW!... I do have to admit she was right about something WE must change, change societies assessment of our worth. And that's important. And WE are going to have to do a much better job of our monitoring system of ourselves.

If we allow any person to be in a position that represents black people's interest WE must make sure that person is genuinely qualified for every righteousness decision that effects us. That is another one of our responsibilities and ours alone. WE must make sure that they are not just qualified enough to help the oppressor, oppress us, not help us, even if they were black and in a decision making position.

Plus WE need to become our own worse critic to guarantee us to become a solid ethical and moral strong black nation. And guard against that deceptive feeling of WE individually may have overcame and is now part of the system alone because of maybe our individual high looking job. I believe WE should have learned that by now, because history has certainly taught us a lesson and proved to us that some of us who are black and in high looking positions could do us worse harms being in that position. If they are not truly committed from their heart to the strongly well-being of all black people. Not just ourselves or our immediate family, but all black people.

Wait a minute. We are not getting ready to criticize or try and put anybody down for no reason. We are only going to try and lift us up. However, the only thing that is ever going to lift us up is to deal with the complete truth and apply the correct solution diligently. As a mater of fact that is The Solution.

Let's just go straight to the point. Some of us Afro-Americans descendants were extremely perplexed the day the news media interrupted regular programming to inform the people that the grand jury had, just refused to indict a white policeman for shooting a black man who was in their custody with hand cuffs on, locked behind his back. That was truly disturbing to me.

Because directly after that newsbreak with the news reporters pointing out how, and with no discretion this hand cuffed black man was killed, the mayor of the city showed up on TV with his newly chosen chief of police, probably to show the black community how un-bias he was and how fairly we are being represented, and how he was the mayor to all people, black and white. And they did both stand there shoulder to shoulder to try and explain away how they saw no flaws in the grand jury's decision, not to even charge this police officer with any wrong doing....

Oh how the two of them did stand there, looking right into the camera explaining and telling black people not to jump to any conclusions or even be upset or get carried away with any non-purpose serving demonstrations or any ill feelings. "Everything is alright … You see we even got one of your own people in the leadership role. We are fair here, and don't let those outsiders spoil what we have got going on by agitating. Just go on home" …and on and on. That was pretty much the whole theme and suggestions of the interview.

However the news reporters seem to have seen a different picture and were determined to shine the Light on the true evidence and expose any hypocrisy of this situation in clear detail, so that every honest and intelligent person could be perfectly clear as to just what exactly happened, and let somebody know exactly where they stood.

It seems perfectly clear to me, that some one's conscience in that news room was trying to let a race of people know and see exactly what they had to do for themselves, if they wanted anything done. Plus they were trying to keep anything from being swept under the rug the best they could. I kept hearing the evidence they were presenting to us on TV say, "Here is the truth black people, we have applied the pressure and raised the lid up on the system. What are you all going to do? The ball is in you people's court now. We've done all we could."

Sometimes my brothers, WE have got to admit that WE don't take advantage of our opportunities to bring us all together in unity and righteousness. There are a lot of good conscience fair-minded people out there trying to warn us to unite in righteousness and overcome these injustices, by pointing out the true facts of the matter. But sometimes WE even attack the people that is honestly trying to "inform US!" so to speak ,when a blatant injustice may be happening to us.

I have heard commentators say in my spirit sometimes, "Here are the facts brothers, but you people need to get busy and responsible and save yourselves. We can't solve your people problems, or unite you, no one can, but you. You people need to get smart right here and you can solve this problem. Don't you see what is happening to you all'? See what they think of you? why don't you people change?".

So many times I have seen us reject that revelation and then begin to attack the mindset that was honestly trying to warn us.

In any event, very obviously, that light shinning, and uncovering of the true evidence in this police shooting of a hand cuffed black male didn't seem to set well at all with our new black chief for some reason. This pressure by the news media could make one to have to make a decision about where they honestly stood and what their priorities were.

Whatever, it was pretty clear to every one watching that this newly appointed chief, was not thrilled at all with all of this newly discovered evidence against the predominately-white police department. Because after the news men had laid out the facts so clear and the pressure began to mount, calling for fair action of this seemingly barbaric act, the chief began responding rather angrily' to the news media as he stood there shoulder to shoulder with the mayor.

"I will not be intimidated by the press or anybody else to make a decision. I am going to do what I think is right regardless" He insisted

I'm sure his boss and colleagues all loved that comment and felt a little more secure. His boss was probably sure at that point that he had made the right decision in selecting this man. They probably all put their arms around him back at headquarters and congratulated him for standing up like that, even took him to dinner with them that day, all telling him, "what a guy! what a good job! Yes sir! That's our man"... .And they all probably gave him a big pat on the back. "I will not be intimidated by the press ".Oh my goodness, what a guy.

Is not the press the people? And aren't some of the people, US!...Black People? My, my, my. And aren't fair minded people suppose to tell it like it is? No matter where the chips fall . I wonder who he would listen to. Who exactly is he there for? Hum!.. A very interesting man.

I guess at that point I was forced to face the fact of what my Caucasian friend who was in jail *with* me had been trying to tell me for *sometime,* the scriptures are true. This was another revelation of the principles working from the Creator of heaven and Earth. If you just listen closely enough to what a person says out of their mouth you won't be mystified for long as to exactly what is in one's heart or where their heart is. The scriptures have pointed that out to us clearly. WE just sometimes won't believe them. Because it does state clearly.

Matthews 12:34
Out of the abundance of the heart the mouth speaks.

Oh when are *WE* ever going to start to believe the Heavenly Father? Because HE also tell us in HIS words,

Matthews 6:21
Where your treasure is, there also will be your heart

Let's hold it right here for a minute and discuss something that is very essential to our progress and to all mankind. Now you can say whatever you want to about this Holy Bible. You can say that it is a white man's Book, you can say that its translators were bias, or this and that. But what ever you say, it still has proven to have all the answers and directions to get you or anybody else wherever they are trying to go. And it will identify every single situation that you will ever have to encounter in life. And supply the solution. Listen to this

---

A poor man that oppresseth the poor, is like a sweeping rain that leaveth no food.

Proverbs 28:3

What did HE just say to us? HE is saying some of US! Oppress some of US! and destroy our everything, even our food. Because WE may think that WE personally have overcame and is rich, but in reality WE may be still poor and just don't know it. That is called, "A poor man oppressing a poor man".

The Creator does not just give us one scripture to try and identify a situation, HE gives you multible. If WE would only listen and trust HIM. Listen to HIM confirm the last Scripture Revelation 3:

16. I know thy works that thou art neither cold nor hot. I would thou were cold or hot, so then because thou art lukewarm and neither cold nor hot I will spue thee out of my mouth.
17. Because thou sayeth I am rich and increased with good and have need of nothing, and knowest not that thou art wretched and miserable and poor and blind and naked.

He. said, some of US! are still wretched, before his eyes. Plus, miserable poor, blind, and naked. Although you think you are rich. HE sees a poor man oppressing a poor man. So HE is going to vomit you out of HIS mouth. Some of us are in a position to help us… but, WE help oppress us. That is a poor man oppressing a poor man

Now do you see why WE should just trust the scriptures? They will help us with every decision we have to make in life. And why WE must be careful in selecting any representative to represent or protect our interest. Our representatives are really the main key they must, must, be solid in word and heart.

WE have got to get serious, thorough, and diligent in our plight to get anywhere meaningful in this world my people. Brothers, you have got to understand that the mindset that is opposed to your meaningful progress in life for the most part is no dummy. He is really smart and knows the scriptures.

HE knows what to do if he was trying to stop you. He know who he can use and how he can use the scripture's basic principles. It will work for an evil man or a righteous man, depending on how you use them, they will work for whoever use them. yahshua (Jesus) himself, dropped us a hint a long time ago. And WE would be wise to consider its value for us even today. HE said

> *Some of you men honor me with your mouth but your heart is not with me.* **Matthews 15:7-8**

We have searched the scriptures. We have talked about past problems. So let' all now concentrate on the most important thing of all, the solution. The Creator of the Universe is the ultimate solution and HE has given himself to us through His word. What HE says is true and will work.

There are a lot of problems and there will be problems so long as the world exist. But the solution is all WE need to solve each one of them anytime they show up. Now WE have the solution. Our problems black people have been around for generation after generation after generation but this time, hopefully WE will see the solution and take advantage of it a lot different

HOW DID WE GET HERE ?

Over two hundred years ago obedient soldiers for the devil like Willy Lynch and Jim Crow did something that was so terrifying, ornery, hateful, and heartless until it's effect is still felt today. They instilled fear, which was designed to result into permanent insecurity in black slave's hearts. And this implantation became basically hereditary.

They made blacks beat blacks, kill blacks, insult blacks, and brainwash blacks, under the threat of being beat, hanged, or killed themselves if they didn't do it. He stated that this action would destroy black's confidence and dignity forever.

His most effective tool was the words and labels he insisted they wear. Words!... words like nigger, shiftless, lazy, ignorant, no-good, dog, coon, ho, bitch... all titles... Titles that we black people carry on still today... Daily'... Even in jest to each other!

Willy's whole theory was based around getting black people to accept certain words and attitudes. He felt, if these people would only accept these negative words as being truth about themselves, spoken long enough and violent enough to each other, they would naturally hate each other on sight and eventually destroy each other forever. Never gaining respect from other cultures on a massive level or respect themselves.

What Willy Lynch did back then was indeed a terrible thing, installing hatred, fear, and disgust in black people's heart against each other. But that is not nearly the problem after all of these years. Oh there is no question who planted the seed, but it is US! US! US!... .that keeps watering it!! We keep watering it! You keep watering It' we keep watering it, so that it has to continue to grow! Isn't that pitiful?

But here is who I really am, I am a child of The King! . .I am a child of The Creator with love in my heart that just got a bad break once!. ...But wait a minute it's alright because I am not fragile I'm not weak, I'm not pitiful I'm tough!...and I'm made with the Right stuff!...So I'm not going to deteriorate I'm going to appreciate. And I am bound to overcome this thing and quit calling me those insulting names!....Because that is not ME!....You are not talking to me, so I want be answering you no more!

That is absolutely the first thing that has to stop' this seed of telling your brother, "You are nothing! You are a Nigger! You are a hoe, a bitch, a M F' you are my dog!" It has to absolutely STOP! Growing! Or we cannot go forward' Its impossible! According to the creator of the universe. Proverbs 23

Can you agree that the seed of hatred has to stop growing? If we can't face the first part, we are not going anywhere meaningful in life no way, so until we can face that we will stay in trouble, according to the scripture Matt. 12:33

We have the key, black people! WE and Only WE...to our problem. We must clearly, let that old thinking Die! Die! Die! That whole attitude and thinking about ourselves, let it Die'.. We ourselves keep hanging on to that old attitude, generation after generation. And that in it's self becomes an excuse that WE are part of the problem, and not part of the solution.

We need to learn how to be part of the solution. Only then will WE be valuable and acceptable, desirable, and wanted by our race and every other race of people but only when we are valuable.

We black people ourselves, have presented an ugly picture of dis-unity that everybody can basically do without! We can even do without some of us. They have even replaced that cheap labor force we use to be so valuable for with either a machine or another culture of people. We need to be a people – needed not a people dreaded.

WE need desperately to get rid of that old label and thinking that we are a people who are disrespectful, shiftless, slothful never willing to unite when it comes to something constructive ,and take responsibility for their own destiny We have also been labeled a people who are never willing to learn plum ignorant, with no love in them, always willing to put his brother down, no consideration for his fellow man, foul mouth people usually to each other.

These are just some of the labels we have accepted, and attitudes we ourselves projected. We did it! And we are still doing it! And we refuse to let it go! We want let it Die !by continuing to practice what we have been labeled. Yet we say ,"It's their Fault! White Folks!"

No! No! No! No! No!. ..It is not their fault! It is our Fault ..And it is our responsibility to insist that it stop! Every Black person that is alive today! brothers, there is no white man born today that is so tough that he can make me nor is he trying to make me do something that I should not be doing to myself. Or you either! No Man' but if you continue calling yourself names ,and practicing behavior that somebody else first said you were... .Then it is your fault and you want to be like that!...You want let it Die! And it will never get any better for us economically or spiritually as a whole Black people until we make up our minds to get some love in our hearts so that we can let that old ugly attitude Die! Yes, get some love back in our hearts is the only way for us to come out of this degraded state. The Creator of you said it was the answer and the only way back to Him

LUKE 8:17
TRULY I SAY TO YOU: WHOEVER WILL NOT ACCEPT THE KINGDOM OF YAHWEH LIKE A LITTLE CHILD,WILL CERTAINLY NEVER ENTER INTO IT

Let's not hold on to that old Ornery Edomite attitude. The same attitude that refused to let the children of Israyl. Pass through their land-Or that Amorite attitude ,who was just as unloving. Or that Moabite attitude that wanted people cursed {NUMBERS 22}

Not only that but we have got to start some where, loving ourselves basically by practicing using good life giving words.. .And keep saying them say them till you believe them !till they get way deep down in your spirit!.. -Just start saying, "I am somebody! I am somebody! I am somebody! I am somebody! I am somebody valuable' I am not a nigger I am not a MF,.I am not a bitch or a hoe I am not and I am not your DOG!..I am not! . I am Not! I am Not! .1 am Not! I am Not!"

Brothers if we do not do this, WE are never coming out as a whole valuable dignified Black nation... – Plus you will never really be welcome anywhere. .As a matter of fact most races will hate to see you coming with that mouth of yours... .Oh sure a few Black people will be accepted here and there but that is not nearly enough to represent us as a race

WE GOT SEPARATED

We got separated from the Creator brothers. It probably want make you feel proud to here that we got separated from the Heavenly Father brothers and sisters, but we did., and he wants us back!

My brothers, let's go back and take a look at a natural, but ornery attitude of a people that angered and displeased The Heavenly Father, sometimes definitely not nice that made Him do something that we can still feel the effects of today. He has set civil war in Egypt and, Ethiopia. That's is US! (deut.23:3-6)

Oh, I know there is going to be debates concerning this truth, but trace it back, and Scripture will prove it. I'm not going to debate it with you, but if you ever got serious about your own salvation you would check it out good! For yourself. But I will help you get on the right path though. You are suppose to do your own research, remember you are suppose to hear him for yourself. (II Tim. 2:15) For starters let's read from the book of Isayah. 19th chapter says:

2. And I will set Egyptians against the Egyptians, they will fight-every one against his brother, and every one against his neighbor, city against city, Kingdom against Kingdom.

This is the Egyptian civil war that occurred in the late 1940's.. If one would study the 18th chapter to Isayah and the 19th chapter, you will see history repeating it's self over and over. The 20th chapters reveals this to us:

3. Then Yahweh said: Just as my servant Isayah has walked naked and barefoot three years as a sign and wonder against Egypt and Ethiopia.

---

4. So will the King of Assyria lead away the Egyptians as prisoners, and the Ethiopians as captives, young and old naked and barefoot with their buttocks uncovered, to the shame of Egypt.

The Creator's word is true, and what ever He promises will come true and has always came true, we just have to get serious and investigate His word. But let's leave that for a minute and go on to establish another truth that is needed at this time to confirm this particular oration.

When the Jews were being delivered out of the land of Egypt, and was trying to get to the land that was promised Abraham and his descendants, there was a people that wouldn't let them pass through their land to get there. Now wasn't that ornery?.. He said this people didn't have enough compassion, way back then, to just let them pass through their land!... Even though they had offered to pay, and not disturb anything on the land, they still wouldn't help them!....Let's look at something merciless, from The Scripture a minute. Then you can decide whether or not we need a circumcision from the creator of heaven and earth

Numbers 20:
14. Moses sent messengers from Kadesh to the King of Edom saying: This is what your brother Israyl says: You know about all the hardship that has come up on us.
15. Our fore fathers went down into Egypt, and we lived there many Years. The Egyptians afflicted us and our forefathers
16. When we cried out to Yahweh, He heard our cry a and sent the Malak (angel) and brought us out of Egypt. Now here we are in Kadesh a city on the edge of your territory.
17. Please let us pass through your country. We will not go through any field or vineyard, or drink water from any well. We will travel along the king's highway and we will not turn to the right or to the left until we have passed through your country.
18. But Edom answered him, you may not pass through my land. If you try, we will march out and attack you with the sword.
19. So the children of Israel said to him, we will go along the

main road, and if we are our livestock, drink any of your
water, we will pay for it. We only want to pass through on foot
nothing more.
20. But they replied again, you may not pass through. Then
Edom came out against them with a large and powerful Army.
21. Because Edom refused to let them go through their
territory, Israel then turned away from them.

Now I ask you, was that ornery?. Oh yes that was ornery! Wasn't it? Brothers, it is so easy for us to talk about that old white man isn't it? Oh he did this: and he did that, to us, Oh, he is the devil, he is just no good, he just don't have no love in him, and it's his fault that we are in trouble! That's easy for us to do, isn't it?.. .You see, that will release us from being: responsible, or accountable for what is in our hearts most of the times.

Then we can always lay it on "Oh, if it hadn't been for these old drugs, and them old guns and things, this wouldn't have happened, or that' wouldn't have happened in the first place Right? But let's talk about no-body but US! for a minute brothers, honestly. Let's talk about something even worse than that lead us to drugs and guns, let's get to the root of the matter, then go to the solution for this problem, Let's just, face the facts for maybe the first time in our lives, for some of us as a whole people trying honestly to get together! Sone of us definitely need a characted change. But first we must read some more truthful Scripture to get some factual documents out on the table so we can deal with this problem intelligently. Take a look at these people.

NUMBERS 21:
21. Then Israel sent messengers to Sihon, King of the Amorites,
saying
22. Let us pass through your country, we will not turn aside
into any field or vineyard, or drink water from any well.
We will travel a long the King's highway till we have passed
through your territory.
23.But Sihon would not let Israel pass through his territory
He gathered all his people together and, came out against
Israel in the wilderness. When he reached Yatzah he fought
with Israel

Wait a minute! I think we need one more Scripture, for solid proof. We have absolutely got to know ourselves and where we have been, so that we can be sure of where we are heading, and for solid foundation. Let's read from the Scripture again:

NUMBERS 22

2. Now Balak the son of Zippor saw all that Israel had done to the Amorites.
3. And Moab was terrified because there were so many people. Moab was filled with dread because of the children of Israel
4. So Moab said to the elders of Midian, this horde is going to lick up everything around us just like an ox licks up grass from the field. So Balak son of Zippor, who was King of Moab at the time
5. Sent messengers to summon Balaam son of Beor, who was at Pethor, near the Euphrates River in his native land. Balak said a people has come out of Egypt. They cover the face of the land and has settled next to me
6. Now come and put a curse upon these people, because they are too powerful for me. Then maybe I will be able to defeat them and drive them from the country. For I know that those whom you bless are blessed, and those whom you curse are cursed

Those are our Ancestors right there brothers!... Yes, the ones that want those people cursed so bad. Whether you know it or not, that is them! Trace them back as far as you can go and you will see you and me. Yes, you and me. Now was that ornery of us or not?

Although The CREATOR of the world had selected and delivered out of bondage, a special people so that through this people, He could redeem the whole human race from the curse of the devil, still another people want let them just pass through their land to safety!...Was that or was it not an ornery attitude for any bunch of people to have? Here the SAVIOR.., is trying to Love and help us all, but you and me won't help the people HE chose, so that HE can do it!.. Let us just look at what kind of people we were trying to curse. And you are going to find that we are still, cursing our-selves and our brothers today. Look at these people?

DEUT. 7:

6. For you are a people Holy to Yahweh (God) your Father. Yahweh your Father has chosen you to be a people for Himself, a special treasure above all other people, on the face of the earth

7. Yahweh did not set His love upon you nor choose you because you were more numerous than any other people, for you are the fewest of all people.

8. But because Yahweh love you, and because He would keep the oath He vowed with up lifted hands to your father to bring you out with a mighty hand, and to redeem you from the house of bondage, from the hand of Pharaoh King of Egypt

I believe that should be enough right now brothers to plunge us back up to date to where we are this very moment in history, and to give us a solid foundation for where we are trying to go with this lesson.

Although I do bear in mind, with out the original true Hebrew translation of these Scriptures, you are going to hear some things new to the ear, (like YAHWEH the creator's name) but I believe that if you are serious and honest with yourself, The Spirit will still lead you to all Truths. Yahchanan (John) 16:13

What we have seen in the last few pages is a retrospect look at our life, Black People, our ancestral history. And this should give US proof that some changes should be made in US from within. THE Creator said, return to him He would circumcise our hearts.

Deut. 30:6

Brothers, to have good success in anything you do, or that you are trying to build, it is mandatory that a people have good communication and good character. There is virtually no way around this sound principal. On the other hand, with out good character you are probably just not going to be very successful in anything of a positive nature.

Here is the point that we have been trying so long to get to Brothers and Sisters, our youth has inherited a very dangerous character that our ancestors, then our parents, then finally we ourselves handed down to them. As you read you will see it basically all came about through simply the wrong, word use.

When a peoples vocabulary and understanding is so small that they must simply disrespect you, and themselves, just to try and communicate, this is truly a people who is in a serious spiritually condemned condition, and in desperate need of help, and probably don't even know it. Even his vocabulary has been identified in the Scripture as a wicked condemned man's deed. It is our vocabulary that basically keeps us in bondage.

When a people have been deceived for so long, as a result, practiced being slothful, and basically self centered, yet is unaware that they need help, that is a serious problem that is not that easily addressed. Then there is little wonder why intelligent folks are afraid, or at the very least, reluctant to get involved with this people one-way or the other. Because to just simply try and commune with this people is usually dreadful. Because he has now displayed himself as a destroyer. One may have to actually back slide just to try and fellowship to commune with such a character.

My people it is a sad thing, but The Creator of man kind has labeled this person as a saboteur Because he doesn't build up, this kind of nature can only tear down destroying everything in it's path. The Scripture calls them brothers

PROVERBS 18:9
He that is slothful in his work is the brother to him that is a great waster (Destroyer)

Brothers, If any of us did posses a Saboteur's nature, which is no more than a disrespectful mouth, an un-thoughtful attitude. That is a selfish and inconsiderably way of existing, then in this sad and desperate condition, any intelligent person or any even concerned race of people, would have to be willing to be disrespected by you, even insulted by you, just to try to communicate with you to try and love you. Now isn't that pitiful?

Plus, with a saboteur nature, if the other party did not come down to your level of communication, which is probably vulgar, then he would more than likely be thought of by you as the one no good, un-sociable, or, inconsiderate. When in fact, you may be your own worse enemy, by just not knowing you are a destroyer…Oh yes, it is a sad and complex issue But it can be, and must be fixed!…with the only thing that can fix it ,and that is Love and understanding

If any people of any nation, or any race of people are ever going to get any where meaningful in life, economically, spiritually, or any useful place in society, they have first got to learn how to be respectful and honest with themselves. Yes your self-first!…only then could you learn how to be honest and respectful. To your brothers or any body else.

I address this oration in particular to my own brothers first!.. Black Men!- Because I am concerned about my own house first. You see, we are suppose to clean up your own house first, then it will be easier to teach others this principal. Charity starts at home, then spreads abroad.

Although this principal of respect applies to all people of the earth and we are concerned about all people of the earth, and we are going to try and unite all people of the earth with this honesty and respect principal still I feel there is a trend of disrespect and misplaced values arising rapidly in Black Youth more than any other people that needs to be brought to their immediately attention.

Truthfully no other race of people can preach this message to Black People except black people, Neither is there any other people who has been Conditioned to disrespect themselves, and each other more than Black People have. So let's just get honest about it and get pass it

Brothers and Sisters, we have absolutely got to stop expecting and depending on some other person or some other race or some other force to come along, one of these old days, and do some kind of Miracle or work some kind of Magic, that will do something for us that will make us complete and prosperous and united as a people, Black nation!.. .When the answer lies clearly with US stopping the harmful and hinder us things WE, and WE alone do to ourselves! ..,And except WE ourselves stop doing certain things to ourselves, we will always be like Crabs in a basket. One person tries to get up and the other one tries to pull him right back down again! A training that came from our long ago slave training.

The alarming thing is, most of the time this attitude is basically an un-conscience one of the harm that WE are really doing to our brother, ourselves and to our race as a whole. ..And there is really no other words that can explain this error except Ignorance… Yes Ignorance If we are going to be real and honest about this situation. It is just simply something WE did not know

The Scripture says, it was for "THE LACK OF KNOWLEDGE"…So let's take this golden opportunity to examine some things that WE have probably never done before as a whole Black nation. Something that is vital to our whole future and our salvation

Let us, probably for the first time for some of us if you will, come to grips with a serious reality we got a problem! The main problem with our race brothers is not with the white man, not with the red man, not with the china man it is not even with drugs. None of these will or can solve this problem for US. The problem is one that can be fixed, but it lies clearly with US, and up to US! Exclusively!...As a Black nation... .Brothers you are going to find out that WE have got to have a Heart Renewal! ...Transformation!...Circumcision... A Change of Heart!   Rom.2:29

We have got to find the strength to start loving ourselves again.. Yes loving yourself. I didn't say you need to get some more money, I said loving yourself. When and only When you start honestly loving yourself will you find the strength to start loving your brother sister and neighbor Or even The Creator above that made you, when you start loving yourself... WE have got to find out all over again what true love is and what true love means that is absolutely mandatory we have even got to learn how to love The Heavenly Father again:.

I know some of US are going to say, " OH he is putting us down" But No! I am trying to bring US! up!...And WE are going to have to first start being honest with ourselves and stop blaming other people for something WE need to do. And something only we can do.

Let's start first with ourselves. We are going to ask ourselves some honest serious hard questions in the next few pages, but be honest with yourself this time. And just accept the answer you get from your honesty to yourself, if it is true. If you do, there will never ,ever again be a shadow of doubt in your mind no more as to just what WE as a whole people have to do for our selves that will begin to solve our problem of disunity forever! .,And that WE also have a problem that even displeases The Creator. Now that is terrible.

You see, most white people are just too polite, or mostly embarrassed to even try and preach a message like this to us, something they know WE should be preaching to ourselves, and our own house, or to our own people .They are just not going to do this on no clear and massive scale. They know WE were taught to hate from our very entrance into this country, slavery days

This doesn't mean by a long shot that nobody out there really cares. On the contrary, it is just too uncomfortable to do for the most part. And it would probably be miserably miss-understood by the masses in the first place.

"BUT WHAT DOES RIGHTEOUSNESS SAY? THE WORD IS NEAR YOU. IN YOUR MOUTH AND IN YOUR HEART. THAT IS THE WORD OF FAITH WHICH WE PREACH" ROMANS 10:8

So today we are going to identify the problem, and the solution with our Black culture. And it is simply LOVE! And WORDS! ..Nothing else,...just LOVE and WORDS! ...that's all. Strangely enough it is the problem and the solution. You see, destruction and deterioration also starts first with WORDS. Yes WORDS!

Scripture after Scripture have told us, and history have proven to us over and over, that it is WORDS! That has the most effect on us in life. Positive or negative WORDS!. ..What you say out of your mouth, and what is in your heart.

"DEATH OR LIFE IS IN THE POWER OF THE TONGUE, A MAN WILL EAT THE FRUIT HIS TONGUE CHOOSES" Prov. 18:21

THE ANSWER IS IN YOUR MOUTH! What?. In the tongue? .Did the scripture just say I could solve my problems with my tongue?

Yes,...according to The Creator of man, it lies in the tongue!...whether or not we live or die!...Sometimes spiritually, sometimes economically, sometimes even physically...,or whether we kill or give life! spiritually or physically it all depends on the tongue. But the creator don't stop there, He goes on and on in The Scriptures about the tongue being such an evil tool to use for destruction.

"YOU ARE TRAPPED BY THE WORDS FROM YOUR OWN MOUTH, YOU ARE CAUGHT BY WHAT YOU HAVE PROMISED {Spoken} Prov.6:2 (THE BOOK OF YAHWEH)

He don't stop there either, He continues on and on in The Scripture to try and get our attention to just WORDS!.. and the devastating effect they can have positive or negative. He explained that:

"THE WORDS OF A TALE BEARER ARE LIKE WOUNDS WHICH GO DOWN TO THE INNERMOST PART OF THE BODY"
(PROV.18:8)

The tongue is by far the most destructive weapon one could have to destroy with, even more dangerous than a gun. The gun may hit just one person, but the tongue may effect a whole nation. That is why Brothers and Sisters, we must start to do something right now, that we have neglected for a long time. That is, start to insist! Yes Insist on our people becoming knowledgeable about our tongue. And intelligent and respectful. But most of all more loving of first ourselves then of each other or we are forever doomed! Not by any other race or people, but destroyed by the ones close to you!.. And basically with using only the tongues! ...Yes it is US hurting US with only our tongues, WORDS!1

Hopefully somewhere along this truthfully researched oration you will discover and be comforted, that there is no one set of people out there engineering a plot to hurt us Black people .Most of the time, no one is even paying that much attention that you are Black, until you mention it Or open your mouth. No one of significant is out there purposely engineering this dreadful plan to keep all Black people down except maybe The KKK, which is basically irrelevant.

However, it is the devil's spirit still at work keeping us down following up on a seed he planted years ago that WE black people refuse to let die! ...The seed was Black against Black using basically WORDS to destroy

Even so, time has come though that people are doing something to us. People all over the world are just standing back and allowing us to be what ever it looks like we have determined to be, even if it is Nothing!

Yes, people have finally decided to just' let us control and determine our own destiny. Now in some ways that is hurting us. As sad as it is to say, but If WE be honest with ourselves, WE will see that the ones closest to US! ..the ones that looks the most like US! .and the ones that talks like US! are the ones that talks the worst to US! And acts the worse toward US! Hating the most! ..According to their WORDS!

Now that is sad.. These WORDS consequently kills my hopes, it destroys my confidence, and it usually destroys or depreciates my self worth, usually only with their tongues.

That is why it is of the utmost importance, that if we are a sincere people and looking for answers to this desperate situation, we must stop and ask ourselves some of these hard question that we have outlined. Then make a decision, hopefully it will be to stop hating me and your brothers, and I stop hating you. .Let's not ask any body but ourselves first. Then answer your self from within.

We are going to get to the questions in just a minute but first let's get just a little bit more proof that our problem comes from our WORDS the problem is definitely the tongue. And the Scripture will testify to that. But it came out of your heart. Yes, and it may even be from an evil heart. Most of us don't like to hear that, but THE CREATOR who is our final plus honest and fair Judge says, that evilness that WE are destroying our brothers with, was delivered by the tongue, and came from our hearts. That is why The Savior is asking us to return to HIM and be made whole again.

Black People, the devil has given US a suggestion to use some WORDS!...that WE call each other daily, that in the pass was thought to be harmless communication or just slang WORDS but has now been identified by THE CREATOR OF HEAVEN AND EARTH as weapon of destruction to eventually cunningly destroy you and the ones closest to you, plus all creation around you According to James 3:6 with just Words!"

The WORDS! are so potent until administered long enough they can actually penetrate your heart by constantly returning back through your mouth. making you and who eve receives them defiled and unrighteous. Eventually causing death to somebody, all done by the .tongue...So let us first now by THE CREATOR'S WORD identify the weapon used to kill us with.

YAAQOB (JAMES) 3:
5. In the same way the tongue is a little member and boast great things behold how great a forest a little fire kindles!
6. And the tongue is like a fire a world of iniquity ,so the tongue is set among our members defiling the whole body and destroying all creation. And for this is subject to the fire of Gehenna.

---

7. For every kind of beast and bird of reptile and sea creature can be tamed and has been tamed by mankind
8. But the tongue can no man tame, it is an unruly evil, full of deadly poison.

Did you hear HIM?. .The scripture said armed with the right ammunition which is nothing but poisoned WORDS!....the tongue is full of DEADLY POISON! You see the devil don't need to give you no gun now days, all he got to do is get you to accept those potent words of his in your vocabulary, and it is more effective than a gun.

That is why THE CREATOR is saying so plain to US Black people WE have got to make a choice soon! ...HE said, return to HIM HE is the only one that could fix our hearts, so that our tongue, which we can't control, won't shoot DEAD POISON! killing each other spiritually and physically when WE speak! THE CREATOR say's it's as plain and simple as this:

MATTITHYAH (Matthew) 12:

33 Either make the tree Righteous and it's fruit Righteous or make the tree evil and it's fruit iniquity for a tree is known by it's fruit
34 Brood of vipers! How can you being evil speak Righteous things? For OUT OF THE ABUNDANCE OF THE HEART THE MOUTH TRULY SPEAKS
35 A Righteous man from the Righteous treasure of the heart, bring forth Righteous things but an evil man from the evil treasure bring forth evil things
36 And I say to you that every word against the Work that men will speak they will give account for it in the day of sentencing;
37 For by your words you will be justified or by your words you will be condemned

Your Words! Your Words! my People your Words will identify you whether you are a Righteous tree or a evil tree What is in your heart will come through your mouth eventually your tongue will speak it!...You can't control the tongue. We can only let THE CREATOR fix our hearts so that when our tongue do speak it won't kill it will give life! According to THE HEAVENLY FATHER, there is no in between you will do one or the other. But only He can control the tongue

Let's look at this simple word " NIGGER" that was promoted for US to use by the devil. This word was abandoned for the most part in the early sixties by the masses of intelligent Black people, people who had marched in civil right rallies, some died in racial riots just to keep from being labeled as an inferior being or an idiot, all suggested by the name, "NIGGER! "...That is what the word NIGGER means. A fool, an irresponsible and lazy person, basically an idiot!

Although this word was once taken out of our repertoire to a strong degree among thoughtful and prudent Blacks who knew the long range implication or damage it could do it was still taken back up for some reason again voluntarily by a new breed or later generation of Black youth on a wide scale basis that obviously have very little idea of it's purposely intended destructiveness. Yet the devil will suggest that even an ignorant and degrading vocabulary such as that is a social able and smart and harmless thing to promote.

The word "NIGGER" was designed to first identify you and to make you seem ridiculous to any intelligent being. Then make you feel inferior so that it can dilute your self worth. Plus it's wide spread implication will suggest to anyone that see any Blackface, "There is another one of those!"

Even before one see what is in your heart or hear what is in your vocabulary you will more times than not, automatically be categorized as an one of those Idiots simply because of the vocabulary and actions of the last bunch they seen that was the same color as you, because the majority usually follows the same pattern of language. The devil knew this would happen if the masses would only accept this negative word in your heart to be "It's alright!" And claim them as a description of you, or just a jokingly communication. Listen to The Scripture identify this error

PROVERBS 26:18-19
LIKE A MADMAN THROWING FIREBRANDS ARROWS
AND DEATH IS THE MAN WHO DECEIVES HIS
BROTHER, THEN SAYS:I WAS ONLY JOKING!

Then if the devil who is the source of all perverseness can plant just a few more poisonous words into your vocabulary some how to keep your vocabulary so small that you would basically need those words just to communicate, then he will reinforce his hold on you and make the venomous vocabulary more potent and wide spread. He has now successfully implanted him a machine going twenty-four-seven that is spitting out death for him with only WORDS!…Isn't that awful brothers. Well that is exactly what is happening to our black youth today

All the devil really needs now installed in the machine is ammunition like the WORDS that will cause a fight an argument an embarrassment or a controversy or an insult or anything else of a negative nature and eventually it will bring death, simply by saying words like M.F. Nigger, hoe, Bitch, Dog. All of these words are words of put down weapons of hate and destruction all suggested by the devil and are cleverly designed to cause your whole body to be defiled by your tongue speaking them along with destroying all creation around you with just simple WORD! And THE CREATOR of mankind is so furious about this ignorance and disrespect to his creation by the tongue .HE says "FOR this it is subject to the fires of Ghenna!" Yaaqob (James) 3:6

THE CREATOR goes even further than I wanted to, HE has told us that not only does our tongue need taming by HIM but our hearts must have a circumcision that only HE can do… Other wise, when the tongue is used in this reckless manner, HE has labeled us as still wicked! Even when we are trying to be social able ,or merciful, we wind up doing wickedness to each other. If you use words of destruction, even in a greeting, it is wickedness in the tongue. The Scripture says

PROV:12: 10
A RIGHTEOUS MAN CARES FOR THE LIFE OF HIS ANIMAL BUT THE TENDER MERCIES OF THE WICKED ARE CRUEL

We have definitely got to wake up Brothers and Sisters. And first and foremost, this intelligence and respect that we absolutely must acquire, must also be measured by THE CREATOR OF THE UNIVERSES standards. Not by what no white man said not what no Black man thinks ,no red man or no other man's opinion, but by THE HEAVENLY- FATHER'S rules or precepts

That is why we are going to have to have TRUE Scripture after Scripture to provide us a Truthful foundation that we can all rely on before asking ourselves these most important questions. ..I think every man will agree that He is our final and Faithful Authority...Who other can we absolutely trust.

While we are at it and without getting too deep ,I think we should face one other necessary Truth then we will ask ourselves some important questions. You know a lot of times we have said "Well I just believe what the Bible said because All Scripture is inspired by God" And that constellations, came basically by the King James version of the scriptures. It reads:

II Tim.2:15
ALL SCRIPTURE IS GIVEN BY INSPIRATION OF GOD AND IS PROFITABLE FOR DOCTRINE FOR REPROOF FOR CORRECTION FOR INSTRUCTION IN RIGHTEOUSNESS

However, that is far from the Truth! The king James version is also one of the most mistranslated. That little beauty there could cause one to believe some translations that is against the will of The creator of the universe... With a little more careful study I'm afraid we are going to find out that some of these Scripture from the King James version are not profitable to us, but rather men's opinions and are actually harmful to us. If they are not Truth.. Actually here is what The Creator of the World really said about His Word... He said

All Scripture .."**That is** ..... Given through inspiration of YAHWEH {God }....is PROFITABLE... ECT (The Book of YAHWEH)

Do you see how we must get Truth?... He never said All Scripture is Profitable... Because men sometimes make their own Scripture!... He said rather All Scripture **THAT is** ...given through inspiration of Him... is PROFITABLE....

Sometimes men can leave out just one word and change the whole meaning of what The Heavenly Father is telling us, Like in this case, **"That"**

I thought that right there might be worth mentioning so that if a controversy should arise any where through out this carefully researched oration, and it is sure to . However we do have a final authority to go to for clarification.

Even most of your scholars will agree that the restored Hebrew text translation, the book of YAHWEH, is the most accurate. So let's try and stay with Truth I know there is going to be some controversy here because of tradition but isn't it time for us to search out and preach absolute Truth? Most Bibles are filled with little errors like up above but that should not stop us from searching out what THE CREATOR is really saying.

We have blamed the white man we have blamed slavery we have blamed poverty and we; all agree that the devil is the culprit which is behind all confusion and destruction, but none of that complaining or accusing has relieved the problem of Black disunity only made it worse

So let's take a look now at something else we may have over looked. I believe that we will soon discover after answering some of these honest questions, purposely asked below, that we really don't have but one common enemy and that is "The spirit of Ignorance!" that is directed by the devil that has just about finished it's purposed assignment and is just about in the right position to kill us all if we do not do something wise and quick!... The Savior said the answer to this is Return to HIM! ... The one that: made us! YEREMYAH 3:

Before we go any further let's find out something that will probably amaze you but awaken you too. And necessarily so. This is how the enemy really works. Let's Identify how what and who the devil could use the most to be the worse enemy to you whether you were aware or not. Would it be the people who are not close around you at all and never even seen you before and you never seen them. Yet you say they are the ones killing you!...Or could it be the ones that are closest to you that you see everyday? ..Let's identify this problem by The Creator's standard. And was he Black or White?.. Check one answer or the other in this little box... ..But be honest with yourself was he Black or White? The devil will try and use color against color to try and keep us from being united as brothers

SERIOUS PERSONAL QUESTIONS   BLACK? OR WHITE?
☐   ☐

1.   Who disrespects you the most daily by calling you degrading names like nigger , hoe, and bitch Punk, dog, M.F. to your face?

---

2. Who told you " these words are not harmful, you are my nigger"
3. Who do you associate with most on a daily basis?
4. Who do you get most of your daily information from?
5. Who showed you how to sell drugs?
6. Who showed you how to use drug?
7. Who told you it is better not to go to school, but selling drugs is hip?
8. Who was it that told the Police you were selling drugs that got you arrested?
9. Who knows where they can find you most times?
10. Who was it that suggested to you we use drugs because the white man brought them over here, it's his fault?
11. Who did you learn that bad language you use from?
12. Who was it that said, you don't have to listen to that teacher , she's white?
13. Who was it that threatened the teacher because she was trying to keep you from being dumb?
14. Who said you don't need no education, you need money?
15. Who said, "Let him alone you can't make him do nothing, he's alright just like he is?"
16. Who suggested you quit school?
17. Who told you when you wear your pants down and show your booty you are hip! You are cool! Smart.. Who said that?
18. Who have told you to your face the most, you are nothing! By calling you a nigger?

Ok let's pause right here to prove something by what THE HEAVENLY FATHER said by Scripture again concerning that last verse. HE said the longer you tell yourself you are nothing! ...The longer you will be nothing! The longer you tell your Brother the is Nothing!...That is what he will probably be if he accepts that in his spirit. Let's look at it by Scripture.

PROV.23:7
"FOR AS HE THINKS IN HIS MIND SO THE SAME WAY HE IS"

Do you see?…Do you see why we have got to stop programming death and negativity and inferiority into our minds and into our race's mind in general by calling each other degrading and inferior words? Because that is the way you will eventually have to start thinking about yourself and your brothers and your race!:… ..Then you would have to fail at everything you do that is constructive, because you have accepted subconsciously.. That you are suppose to fail ! You think, YOU ARE NOTHING! Isn't that what you just said about you and your brother, " You are my nigger" which means "YOU ARE NOTHING!"….Ok, let's go on ,and ask our- selves, a few more serious questions.

19. Who has personally lied to you, that you know?
20. who was it that said cussing is not disrespecting each other, it is alright it's a Black thing?"
21. Who said we are suppose to act like that It's cool? That's just us?
22. Who told you not to worry about having no intelligent vocabulary, they can feel me?
23. Who do you sell most of your drugs of destruction to?
24. Who sells you most of your drugs?
25. Who said you cannot win in this society without selling drugs unless you are white?
26. Who do you think get together the most to vote and plan and communicate to make things better for their race?
27. Who was close enough to steal from you that you know of personally?
28. Who told you ,don't go looking for no Savior that's square and a white man's thing?
29. Who was it that told you the savior is a White man?
30. Who was it that told you, you don't need to watch no educational or news program, or informative program, that's for white folks?
31. Who have you honestly sit down and ,talked to the most?
32. What kind of people do you know the most of?
33. What kind of person said to you they would come to your aid if you were ever in trouble but didn't?
34. Who do you think controls the most money?

35. Who do you think has access to the most positive information?
36. Who was it that told you all white folks are against you they are the devil?
37. Who gave you the most bad information personally, even if it was not intentional?
38. Who did you learn from personally to lie or steal?
39. If a program was on TV, maybe like C-Span,...A program that was designed to show you how to vote or maybe change a law or to educate you to something that could help you to prosper in society! Who would most likely tell you, that's square! ... That's for white folks! Let' watch Jerry Springer or B.E.T they got some perverted freaks on!...They are off the chain today?

Now let's hold it right there again for a minute Brothers, and sister,... Did you know that The Creator that loves you and The SAVIOR OF THE WORLD absolutely hates that kind of stuff?...I'm talking about when people encourage other people to be against other people?...Or when people's feet are swift to run to mischief? Did you know that? .Did you know that HE would not answer your prayers with kindness as long as you are in that degraded state? Did you? HE did not just say HE dislikes that kind of stuff HE said HE Hates It! You want to hear it? Listen to HIM.

PROVERBS 6:
16. THERE ARE SIX THINGS YAHWEH (God) HATES, YES SEVEN ARE AN ABOMINATION TO HIM:
17. A PROUD LOOK, A LYING TONGUE, HANDS THAT SHED INNOCENT BLOOD
18. A MIND THAT DEVISES WICKED IMAGINATIONS; {plans}FEET THAT ARE SWIFT IN RUNNING TO EVIL...
19. A FALSE WITTNESS WHO SPEAKS LIES, AND ONE WHO SOWS DISCORD AMONG BROTHERS!

Have you ever ask yourself, I! Why is it some of us don't seem to get too far with THE SAVIOR OF MANKIND most times? And why is it taking HIM so long? I have heard People say, "I sacrifice and pray to HIM all the times, but still nothing much seem to Happen" What most of us did not know was, HE had already warned in The Scripture

THE SACRIFICE OF THE WICKED IS AN ABOMINATION TO YAHWEH, BUT THE PRAYER OF THE UPRIGHT IS HIS DELIGHT.
PROV. 15: 8

So the answer could very well be, although we are basically a fun loving people, it may be high time we just stop and get serious and honest and examine some of our negative qualities that may not be pleasing to THE CREATOR according to The Scripture. Let's continue

40.   Who do you think actually run this country of America?
41.   What kind of information station do you Listen to most times?
42.   Where do you get most of your, information about white people?
43.   Who raised you?
44.   Who makes the most noise, so they don't have to think?
45.   What do you think would honestly profit you the most, being knowledgeable, intelligent, and respectful and being involved with the up lifting of this country and your people? Or is it better to remain wishing, guessing, and having fun? Off the chain so to speak

These are just a few of the honest questions we need to seriously stop and ask ourselves Black people .Black parents, Black teachers ,Black so called friends.

Then you may want to ask yourself another question., like, "Why is my people like this?" Naturally that will only be if you had honestly asked. And accepted some of these questions as truth

THE CREATOR of Heaven and Earth has carefully and mercifully explained clearly in the Holy Scriptures to everyone that is seeking a truthful answer just why this is. Plus, HE has given us the answer and the solution to the problem because HE loves us. But He cannot deliver us ,unless we want HIM. To

HE is saying in The Scripture it is because of our love. Yes we have forgot how to love. So WE have absolutely got to return to THE FATHER OF LIVING WATER let HIM show us how to love again. We did the same thing our fore fathers did

---

YEREMYAH 2: 13 Jeremiah}

For my people have committed too evils – they have forsaken me, the Fountain of Living Waters and have dug their own cisterns, cisterns that crack and cannot hold water

When one loves they become concerned, they becomes responsible, they becomes respectful and considerate of not just their but of also other people's feelings and well-being. But first they must love something from their heart to really care. And they must learn to love themselves first before they can love anything; else. It just does not work any other way

We have defiantly got to learn to love again Brothers and Sisters that is mandatory Then WE need to make a serious conscience decision from our hearts to no longer be part of the problem that is definitely destroying your Brothers and yourself, with your mouth! It started with Your WORDS! Wait a minute, let's ask one more question before we quit.

"Who was it that Shot at you ,or your friend, when they drove by, were they black or white?

Oh yes , good questions, aren't they? But we should start to feel a little ashamed! Right now. We could find every little excuse there in the world to justify our behavior if WE wanted to. But if we ever decide personally ,then let it spread through our people that WE have determined to become respectful first to ourselves then to our Brothers. And our fellow man. That right there would be the beginning of Loving!

And Oh what a wonderful, soulful, desired people we would turn out to be. And we can!...All it takes Is for somebody to start right now! Just say right now," I am never going to call myself or my brother another degrading name again! .like, My Nigger or My dog ..Or hoe and Bitch! ,never! ...I am never going to accept in my spirit that suggestion if some one calls me that! Never!"

SHOULD WE ASK QUESTIONS ABOUT THE BIBLE, OUR SALVATION AND ALL RELIGIONS?

For hundreds of years now, most scholars of the Holy Scriptures have known that the Holy Scriptures have been misused and abused, not only by the early scribes, but also by the translators themselves. In specific instances, certain words or phrases were left un-translated; at times, changes were made to hide the meaning of the words or phrases. In other cases, words were deleted from the original text, either by copyist error, or by flagrant intention. At times, copyists, scribes, or translators would write footnotes in their manuscripts of the Holy Scriptures, in the same way we would make notes in our books; however, these footnotes would later be included in the text by other copyists, who would write these as supposedly "inspired" Scripture to be read by later generations as part of the original text. Many phrases have been deliberately mistranslated, in order to hide their true meaning. so that Scripture would not bring to light the deceitful teachings of the established and popular religious organizations. The alteration of Yahweh's Scriptures, either by untranslating or mistranslating. has caused the True Work, which Yahweh's Prophets spoke of, to be hidden in most translations of the Scriptures, and this has been damaging to those who are searching the Holy Scriptures for the way to Eternal life. However, the most damaging error in all the Holy Scriptures, was the error of removing YAHWEH'S NAME from the very Scriptures He inspired to be written, and writing in its place the pagan titles of GODS (ELOHIM) and SATAN HERSELF! Because of this grave error, those who are calling upon the names of gods (elohim) and Satan, even though ignorantly, are actually worshiping the gods (elohim) and Satan-for they are not calling upon, and with, The NAME of YAHWEH! These detrimental facts are not hidden. In fact, an abundance of data confirming these statements has been published for many years, but generally confined only to footnotes, Scriptural commentaries, dictionaries, encyclopedias, lexicons, concordances, and technical publications. These facts are indeed plenteous; they are openly admitted not only among scholars of the Holy Scriptures, but also among the religious denominations as well. Joseph Bryant Rotherham, in The Emphasized Bible; A New Translation, The Standard Publishing Company, Cincinnati, Ohio, Copyright 1902, says in the Introduction, The Incommunicable Name:

The Name Suppressed: THE FACT

It Is willingly admitted that the suppression has not been absolute; at least so far as Hebrew and English are concerned. The Name, In Its four essential letters (YHWH), was reverently transcribed by the Hebrew copyist, and therefore was necessarily placed before the eye of the Hebrew reader. The latter, however, was Instructed not to pronounce It but to utter Instead a less sacred name-ADONAY or ELOHIM. In this way The Name was not suffered to reach the ear of the listener. To that degree It was suppressed. The Septuagint, or ancient Greek version (LXX), made the concealment complete by regularly substituting Kurlos, as the Vulgate. In like manner, employed Dominus, both Kurlos and Dominus having at the same time their own proper service to render as correctly answering to the Hebrew ADONAY, confessedly meaning "Lord". The English versions do nearly the same things, In rendering The Name as LORD, and occasionally GOD; these terms also having their own rightful office to fill as fitly representing the Hebrew titles Adonay and Elohim and EL, so that the Tetrogrammaton Is nearly hidden In our public English versions.

The IMMEDIATE CONSEQUENCES
of the Suppression

(I.) Partly lIteral though more than that. Reference Is here made to the confusion Into which many things are thrown through this abnormal state of things. "Baal" Is "lord", and so Is "Adon" { Adonay} -that Is distressing: but why add to the embarrassment by rendering YHWH also as "Lord"? Worst of all Is the confusion when "Y" and Adonay occur together. as they do many times In the Book of Ezekiel (Yechetzqyah). Inasmuch as to say, "Lord ,LORD" for "Adonay Y", was too grotesque and misleading (positively false to the ear), the new device had to be resorted to of rendering this combination by "Lord GOD" -"GOD" In this case. and not "Lord" at all, standing for The Name. Even YH (the shorter form) and YHWH (the full form) of the tetrogrammaton, coming together caused a dilemma; though In these Instances, the acuteness of the trouble compelled the adoption of a partial remedy. and "the LORD JEHOVAH"; is the result. "Confusion", then, Is a term not a whit too strong to apply to these varying devices. No wonder that even Intelligent and educated people are continually forgetting what they have heard or read concerning so Involved a matter.

Rotherham then gives reasons why the Name Yahweh must be restored, and from now on

retained in the Holy Scriptures. I. Because Its suppression was a mistake. So grave a mistake cannot be corrected too soon. An unwarrantable liberty has been taken: the path of humility is to retrace our steps...It Is too heavily burdened with merited critical condemnation-as modern, as a compromise. "mongrel" word, "hybrid", "fantastic", "monstrous". The facts have only to be known to Justify this verdict, and to vindicate the propriety of not employing It In a new and independent translation. What are the facts? And first as to age. "The pronunciation Jehovah was unknown until 1520, when It was Introduced by Galatinus; but was contested by Le Mercier. J. Drusius, and L.Capellus, as against grammatical and historical propriety." (Oxford Gesenlus, P. 218.) Next, as to formation. "Erroneously written and pronounced Jehovah which Is merely a combination of the sacred Tetro grammaton and the vowels In the Hebrew for Lord, substituted by the Jews (Yahdaim) for JHVH (YHWH), because they shrank from pronouncing The Name, owing to an old misconception of the two passages (Exodus xx. 7 and Leviticus xxiv. 16)...To give the name JHVH the vowels of the word for Lord (Heb. Adonai) and pronounce It Jehovah Is about as hybrid a combination as It would be to spell the name Germany with the vowels In the name Portugal-viz., Gormuna...Jehovah Is not older than about 1520 c.e

The Ancient, and Honored Name of Yahweh

The very oldest Scriptural text ever found, dating back almost 2,600 years, was found in a tiny silver amulet which contains a Seventh Century b.c.e. extract from the Book of Numbers (6:24-26), the Priestly Blessing. The rolled up amulet was part of a treasure hoard found by a Tel Aviv University archeologist in a First Temple Period family tomb in Yerusalem, Isray!. When this amulet was written, the Temple of Solomon still stood, the heirs of King David still ruled on the throne, and the Dead Sea Scrolls would not be written for another 400 years .It was three years after its discovery before this fragile amulet could be unrolled by technical experts at the Israyl Museum. On this amulet the NAME OF YAHWEH could be clearly read. Complete details of this magnificent find can be read in the 6-28-86 and 8-9 86 issues of The Jerusalem Post, and the 6-87 issue of The Readers Digest.

THE UNDENIABLE NAME OF YAHWEH

There is no doubt that the True NAME of our Creator is Yahweh. In fact, the evidence is overwhelming *Unger's Bible Dictionary*, Merrill F. Unger, 1957, Moody Press, Chicago, Page 1177, says: Yahweh {ya'we} The Hebrew tetragrammaton (YHWH) traditionally pronounced Jehovah *(q. v.)* is now known to be correctly vocalized *yahwe*. New inscriptional evidence from the second and first millennia B. C. point toward this fact. The old view of Le Clerc, modernly propounded by Paul Haupt and developed by W. F. Albright, has commended itself in the light of the phonetic development and grammatical evidence of increased knowledge of Northwest Semitic and kindred tongues. This thesis holds *Yahwe* to be originally a finite causstive verb from the Northwest Semitic root *hwy* "to be, to come into being," so that the divine name would mean "he causes to be, or exist," i. e., "he creates." Amorite personal names after 2,000 B. C. lend support to the Haupt-Albright view, demonstrating that the employment of the causstive stem *yahwe* "he creates" was in vogue in the linguistic background of early Hebrew.

The Wycliffe Bible Encyclopedia, 1975, Volume 1, Page 690, Moody Press, Chicago, tells us:

The Name par excellence for the Creator of Israyl Is *Yahweh*, found 6.823 times In the OT. Through Israyl's deliverance from bondage In Egypt, adoption as a nation, and guidance to the Promised Land. the Re-

---

deemer-Creator is especially known by THIS NAME." (Emphasis ours.)

The Interpreter's Dictionary of the Bible, 1962, Volume 4, Page 923, Abingdon Press, Nashville, says: "YAHWEH-The vocalization of the four consonants of the Israyllte name for the Creator, which scholars believe to approximate the original pronunciation.

James Moffatt, in his translation, The Bible: A New Translation, 1935, Harper and Brothers, informs us in his introduction:

Strictly speaking this ought to be rendered 'Yahweh' which Is familiar to modern readers In the erroneous form of "Jehovah". Were this version intended for students of the original, there would be no hesitation whatever In printing 'Yahweh'." Although Moffatt substitutes the title , the Eternal in the place of the Name of Yahweh, he fully admits a distinct loss of meaning in this .

The Encyclopedia Judaica, 1972, Keter Publishing House, P.O.B. 7145, Jerusalem, Israel, Volume 7, Page 680, states emphatically:

The TRUE PRONUNCTION of the NAME YHWH WAS NEVER LOST. Several early Greek writers of the Christian Church testify that the Name was pronounced 'YAHWEH

The personal Name of the Father of Israyl is written in the Hebrew Scriptures with the four consonants YHWH, and is referred to as the "Tetragrammaton". At least until the destruction of the First Temple in 586 b.c.e., Yahweh's NAME was pronounced regularly with its proper vowels, as is clear from the Lachish Letters, written shortly before that day. However, at least by the third century before Yahshua our Messiah was born, the pronunciation of the Name YAHWEH was avoided, and Adonai, "the Lord", was substituted for it.

THE LAST FEW PAGES WAS TAKEN FROM A PORTION OF ONE OF THE MOST IMPORTANT BOOKS OF OUR TIME . We at F.S.O. would strongly urge all mankind, especially any real truth seeker to

SEARCH OUT THE BOOK OF YAHWEH AND READ
Isayah 34:16

THE HOUSE OF YAHWEH
1025 TRUTH & PROPHECY LANE
P.O. BOX 2498 ABILENE,TEXAS 79604

MAN'S LAST DAYS ON EARTH

America...We absolutely do hold the key to the solution of war today! It has been prophesied in the Holy Scriptures, long, long ago. Actually, this answer given to humanity, from the Creator, could save the world.

In the very near future, I personally believe, and my belief is because of, and according to the Scripture and because of some of the prophecies spoken through the inspiration of the Holy Spirit, that black America is soon going to rise up in a majority, and in an abundance of chaos against the present American system. This action will cause havoc that could weaken America to the point that its present enemies could actually defeat it. That is if we are not careful in approaching this extremely sensitive situation and apply the only true healing solution to it. Plus, the solution must be applied the way we have been admonished years and years ago, by the Holy Spirit. Is that interesting?

There are some twisted allegations that will be promoted soon, that will become blatant lies perpetuated by the devil's spirit in these last days, that will basically be the straw that broke the camels back, so to speak. This will bring on a lewd action in America.

America's present enemies will be the principal force behind this chaos in an effort to divide America and instigate a civil blood bath. Yes, they are going to propagandize these lies to America. Yet the Holy Scriptures has explained clearly and precisely who is really powering the dreadful plot. It is the devil. The scripture has also explained to us what exactly, can be done to avoid a worldwide nuclear war!

In reality, it is the devil's spirit. In every nation YAHWEH'S (God's) laws are being broken and millions of people are suffering the consequences. War is the result of this law breaking, along with crime, sickness, and disease.

The aggressor's real purpose in this present war is disguised purposely. The real reason is that the enemy is against the Creator of the world. Let us explain by the Scriptures, some lewd things that are approaching that we could and should avoid.

YAHCHANAN MARK (Mark) 3:

23. **Then He summoned them and said to them is parable: How can Satan cast out Satan?**
24. **If a kingdom is divided against itself, that kingdom cannot STAND.**
25. **If a house is divided against itself, that house cannot STAND.**
26. **Therefore, if Satan has risen against her self, she is divide and CANNOT STAND.**

The Savior of the world is explaining a very important law to us, right here. So let us all listen clearly. He goes on to explain:

27. **No man can enter a strong man's house and plunder his possessions UNLESS, he first binds the strong man, and then he can rob his house.**

That last verse, people, describes perfectly, what the enemy of man is going to try to do, and how she believes she can do it. **BIND THE STRONG MAN**, first! Then you can plunder his possessions.

This attempt to **BIND THE STRONG MAN**, which in this case is America, will be tried first by creating a civil war again in America. In addition, it is being tried today, presently, as we speak. This should not surprise you. Democrats against Republicans, blacks and whites against each other, Hispanics against illegal immigrants; and basically an overall attempt to put Democracy on trial, period. By the way, did you know that it was the Creator of the Universe Himself, who set up democracy for us, in America? We will prove that also (Deut. 30: 19)

America, the Savior of the world has already given to us and to all humanity, without question or one single doubt, **The Solution** to this fast approaching, yet final, last day complex problem that will certainly destroy all of those who do not get wise and righteously unite.

We could just ignore the Savior's warning to all humanity, pretend ignorance, and perish, or we can heed his warnings, obey his rules, and live! Forever! It is just as plain and simple as that, now! And it is every person's individual personal choice.

This inciting and encouragement of civil disobedience in America will certainly **BIND THE STRONG MAN** as the Scriptures have promised it will do, while the enemy plunders his possessions. The devil knows that the Holy Scriptures' principals are certainly, without a doubt, unchangeable, true, and cannot fail or be altered. She (the devil) is actually depending on the Scriptures, which we say we believe in, to work and destroy us. She (the devil) knows they are true. Don't forget, she was there in the beginning when it was all put together. She (the devil) knows that if these laws work like they are supposed to, and has been doing for over six thousand (6,000) years, they have to destroy us!

Are you concerned that I keep calling her (the devil) a woman? Well, she is! That will also be proven. And proven to every honest and serious person, or scholar's satisfaction. But to do this, of course, you must have the true translation of the Holy Scripture, "The book of YAHWEH (Yechetzgyeh 28:) But hold on! That is the least of the problem. Her gender is the easiest thing to prove by scripture. Therefore, that needs to be put on hold for a minute.

In this last, go round of humanity, or in this last dispensation, according to the Creator of the world, as in Mark 3:25, as long as you are willing to be divided in the same one big house, it is just a matter of time before it collapses from within. That is His law. That is exactly what the Savior came for, to separate his flock from the rest of the world, meaning those who will just believe Him and obey His Father's Laws.

Matthew 10:

34. **Do not think that I am come to send peace on the earth! I did not come to Send peace, but a sword.**
35. **For I have come to set a man against his father, and the daughter against her mother, and the daughter-in-law against her mother-in-law:**
36. **And a man's enemy will be those of his own house.**

Wake up my people! The Creator of the world, Father YAHWEH'S (God's) laws has not changed or been done away with as some will say. They can never change. That is religious garbage that has been preached to most of us for most of our lives, from misprints, mistranslations, and sometimes, from deliberate mistranslations. That is not from the Savior, but against Him! He has not gotten rid of the Law; it still applies to all mankind. And they still work. The Savior Himself said in

Matthew 5:

12. **Do not think that I have come to destroy the Law or the Prophets: I have not Come to destroy them, but to establish them.**
18. **For truly I say to you; unless heaven and earth pass away, one yodh – the Smallest of the letters – will in no way pass from the law until they are Perfected.**

However, black America will have the most important and most effective role in these coming last days, through this tribulation period, which will determine whether America will survive as a whole nation, or if just a few will be left. The Scripture explains again

Isayah (Isaiah) 2:4
Because of this, the curse has devoured the earth, and they who dwell therein are desolate: therefore, the inhabitants of the earth are burned, and few men left.

America will survive to some extent, according to the Scripture. This is the nation where the Savior of the world prophesied He would place His Name, His laws, and His teaching for the last time. Humanity must repent of his iniquities, and start following YAHEWH'S laws, which were given by Moses, or be burned. This will be the end of man's government by man.

Matthew 24:14
In addition, **this message of the Kingdom will be preached to the entire world by the one who bears witness to all nations, and then the end will come.**

As a matter of the truth, the only solid solution for America to be saved, and the whole world for that matter, will be a two-fold solution. Repent! And Unite! Repent and unite first with the Savior, and start following YAHWEH'S law for peace. In black America it will be a unique two-fold message. We must do the same two things, and we can. We will explain how those two things must be done shortly.

One of the two witnesses from Isayah's (Isaiah) forty-third, forty-forth, and forty-ninth chapters, that was sent to America with the last day solution is on the earth now, in America, speaking right now as we speak. Speaking about the same thing. This was prophesied to happen a long time ago specifically for this time period. (Matt. 24)

A plan was designed years ago by evil men to one day destroy America using an in-house fight initially to do it. It would be the vehicle mainly, so to speak, to jump-start it. We can just call it civil war. Of course, it was the devil's spirit powering it, as it is in all evil. Yet it has been tried and tested and it works!

So if black America, especially the youth, are not made aware of the depths of this deception we may all perish. If we are not all taught how massive and wide spread this evil plot is, and are not educated to the fact of this plot, a plot that has and will continue to bring only division, thoughts of revenge, false accusations, miss-trust, ignorance, cultural dis-functioning, and crime among our people, if we don't make them know these things, then I am afraid that black America, as a whole, will more than likely NOT be able to contain themselves in this particular prophesied period of time, when the heat is turned up just a little bit more.

The truth is African America may NOT be able to stop and rationalize and come up with any good reason why they SHOULD NOT rise up in heavy numbers as a whole United Black Nation and wage there own war of defense. Just to defend them selves. Because all the devil will be preaching at this time is Revenge! Revenge from a long time ago. She (the devil) will repeatedly say, DEFEND YOUR SELF! Do you get it? Do you see the trap forming and approaching? We must not go for it though. It is a trick!

You may be asking, "When is this deadly plot and new up-rising in America supposed to unfold and manifest itself?"

According to the Holy Scriptures it could be any day now. It has been brewing for some time. The only thing that is holding back some of the trouble is the Creator's mercy right now, giving men an opportunity to repent from their iniquity. He is right now having the Quartet of Revelation sixth and seventh chapters hold back the nuclear explosions for us until all of the Gentiles that are going to come in have a chance to get in. You were a Gentile African American but you can become a Saint.

The United Nations, Russia, E U union, and the United States of America, that is the Quartet spoken of in Revelation Chapters six and seven. They are the Quartet, the four winds that are holding back the winds of war right now. That is their job as spoken of in the Scripture, "**on the four corners of the earth, holding back the wind.**" Rev. 7:1

Romans 11:25
I do not want you to be ignorant of this great secret, brothers, so that you may not be wise in your own conceit; that blindness has in part come upon Israel UNTIL THE FULL NUMBER OF THE GENTILES HAS COME IN.

We need to hurry and get in America, especially Black America. We need to just COME IN! Like the Scripture has said. He is holding back the wars until all who are coming get in. He is saying, "COME IN NOW, GENTILES!" Everybody should be able to see the way the wars, and events around the wars, are shaping up, along with the propaganda, the divisions in America, and the prophesied Scripture that promised these things, that some of us could actually rise up and think we ought to join America's enemies.

So to answer the question of "when will these deadly plots un-fold?"..............

I would say that this thing, if it did explode, would probably be somewhere in the middle of this new surge, when the heat is turned up again, to it's maximum strength, hunting down a self confessed enemy of America, by the name of Bin Ladin. Make sense?

Keep this in your calculations. Without the whole truth and honest evaluation of the facts, especially in these evil days of super deception by the propaganda of man, George Bush, the President of the United States, will be painted in some circles as a worse enemy to black America than Bin Ladin.

Of course, no true, fair, and impartial people or scholars armed with the facts could ever come anywhere near that conclusion, but it will still be promoted in some circles as truth. That will also be part of the enemies design to promote division and encourage animosity between black and white America. For America must first be destroyed before the enemy can go further.

For numerous reasons, given the prophesied evil period in time, if we are not carefully, truthfully, and factually informed, a certain substantial segment of black America could be duped into believing that it would make more sense, in all fairness, to stand up in our own defense and adapt Bin Ladin's thinking. That would be justice as far as they could conclude. But this is really the enemy's ace in the hole. He is depending on just this to happen. In addition, based on the Scriptures, he can expect that it will work. Needless to say, this kind of agitated CIVIL WAR would do exactly what the Savior of mankind said it would do to our nation; completely divide it.

A KINGDOM DIVIDED CANNOT STAND (Mark 3:)

However, we in America have been given the one and only absolute solution that would prevent this over-due prophecy that will be so catastrophic it would completely destroy America. We could and we should head off any more chaos or any deeper division of America. This decision lies with man. This is one subject that will be unavoidable.

There is definitely going to be a debate soon on "the unfair and catastrophic results and effects of slavery on black people." That subject cannot be avoided. It is necessary. But revenge is not the solution; it is the vehicle for destruction.

African Americans are certainly the key to the final results of these wars in this time period; whether positive or negative. Black Americans have the distinction of being the largest minority in America. They have the largest potential for voting in America. We are Americans. So black America, at this time, MUST be made aware honestly, of where they stand in America; good or bad, concerning what is coming up through these wars, or America sinks, period!

Oh, please listen, America, and you, the rest of the world, but especially African Americans! These instructions and revelations are vital in these last days for America's survival and for your salvation. It is our last chance for peace in these last dangerous days. And the reason the Creator set up America in the first place, for the most part, was so that all men from all over the world would have this one last chance to receive eternal life in the kingdom of YAHWEH, and a choice. He set democracy in America so that mankind could legally choose the true Savior of the world. If you were living in most countries outside the United States you would have to choose the god of that country in order to worship legally. But in America you are free to worship whatever or whom ever you choose. You could choose a frog as your savior if you wanted to. So you are certainly free to choose the only true Savior of the world. He is YAHWEH. He has never changed the rules. He said in **Deut. 30:19,**

"I call heaven and earth as a witness against you this day, that I have set before you life and death, blessings and curses (because you, as a free agent, can make your own choice between righteousness and evil) therefore, choose life, so that both you and your children may live.

That is democracy people! That is what democracy means; a free choice. Notice, he did not say, "**Choose revenge**." He said, "**Choose life, so that both you and your children may live!**"

The Scriptures have already clearly declared that it will be America, the chief of the Nations and it will not be Jerusalem in the last days where he will choose to set up His Name, His word (laws), and His house to go forth to the rest of the world, teaching the only true way to salvation, but from America! Listen to the Scripture:

Isayah 2: (Isaiah) (The Book of YAHWEH)

2. **It will come to pass in the last days, that the mountain** (promotion) **of the House of YAHWEH will be established in the CHIEF of the nations, and will be Raised above all congregations and all nations will eventually flow to it. And many people will go and say; come and let us go to the mountain** (Go where YAHWEH is lifted up) **of YAHWEH, to the house of the father of Yaaqob** (Jacob) **and He will teach us His ways, and we will walk in His Path, FOR THE LAW WILL DEPART FROM ZION AND THE WORD OF YAHWEH WILL DEPART FROM YERUSALEM.**

That particular Scripture may have never been explained correctly, re-searched, and proved absolutely clearly to most of us. But it is absolutely clear and true! Research it! Check it out to your complete satisfaction! Don't just say, "Oh, that is not what I have been taught," and then just drop it. America is undisputedly the CHIEF of all nations. This is the place that will launch the very last opportunity for mankind to be saved, and African Americans will play a major roll for peace.

In addition, those two witnesses' in Isayah's (Isaiah) forty-third and forty-forth chapters, Jacob and Israel, were also sent to America to call out to all men everywhere. But from America. He called them clearly by name; names He had chosen. In **Isayah** (Isaiah) **44:1,** He said: **"Yet now hear, Oh Yaaqob** (Jacob)**, and Yisrayl** (Israel) **whom I have chosen from the womb."**

What could be clearer than Jacob and Israel? Not only would these two brothers, chosen from one womb, Sir name themselves Jacob and Israel, but they are also doing exactly what the Savior said they would be doing, today! Right Now! But let us continue:

Isayah {Isaiah} **44:** (The Book of YAHWEH)

5. **One will say; I belong to YAHWEH), and the same will call himself Yaaqob** (Jacob)**. The other will subscribe with his hand, and write: I belong to YAHWEH, and surname himself with the name of Yisrayl** (Israel).

The Scripture prophesied and identified clearly the two that would witness for Him, a long time ago. It was the Savior who gave them those names for the last days to help man kind chose the true Savior, Father Yahweh!.

Isayah (Isaiah) **49:1**

1. **Listen O Isles** (countries)**; to me! Listen you people from afar. YAHWEH has called me from the womb; from the bowels of my mother He has made mention of my name.**

2. **And He made my mouth like a sharp sword; in the shadow of His hand He has hidden me; and made me a polished shaft; in His quiver He has hidden me.**
   Zecharyah (Zechariah) **5:** (The Book of YAHWEH)

10. **Then I said to the Malak** (Angel)**, who was speaking to me, where are they** (the two witnesses) **going with the ephah** (the standard of perfection)?

11. **And he said to me: To build The House of YAHWEH according to the Standard of perfection set by YAHWEH'S laws, in a babylonish land**
    Which does not exist yet. And it will be established at that time (when

The two witnesses are called out to do their work) **as the estab-**

lished
**Place; the Habitation of YAHWEH: THE HOUSE OF YAH-
WEH.**

It is America, my people, and The House of YAHWEH has now been established, in America. It is in Abilene, Texas, right now! Today! It does exist. And Israel, one of the two brothers from one womb, is there, right now! The savior of mankind sent this teaching **"The standard of perfection."** He is giving all mankind one last chance for salvation.

Keep in mind, so that you don't become doubtful or confused as to whether you can trust The Original Book of The Law or not, which is called the Bible now days.It was the devil that changed the Book, and The Creator's Holy days, His Name, His laws and even the way He would have His people to worship Him.

She (the devil) wants to hide any and everything or any information that would cause man to be lead to the only way of salvation. She (the devil) actually wants the world to be deceived so that it would automatically, unconsciously worship her! She said: **"I will ascend above the heights of the clouds; I will be like the most High."** Isayah {Isaiah} **14:14**

Daniyl (Daniel) 7: (The Book of YAHWEH)

25. **And she** (the devil) **will speak great words against YAH-
WEH, and will wear out** (Mentally attack to cause to fall away) **the saints of YAHWEH, and
Think to change times: (YAHWEH) feast days, and laws;
and they will
Be given into his hand until a time and times and the dividing of times.**

This time and times and dividing of times, is actually speaking of the prophesied seven year peace plan. **Daniyl [Daniel} 9:27**

And he will confirm a covenant with many for one week {seven years} and in the midst of the week, he will cause the sacrifice and the oblations to cease ; instead he will cause the prevalence of The Lord of Heaven even until the destruction that is determined will be poured upon the desolator.

This Peace Plan has now come and just about gone. We are now, presently, as we speak, in the last half of that time. All the while ministers, who are supposed to tell us these things, are still running around screaming and hollering! Every thing is going to be all right, all you have to do is believe. And some are still telling us that we don't have to worry and that we don't even have to keep YAHWEH'S laws anymore. That is very interesting, when the Savior himself told us plainly in **Matthew 5:17-18**

> **17 Do not even think that I have come to destroy the Law or the Prophets;**
> **I have not come to destroy them, but to establish them.**
> **18. For truly I say to you, unless heaven and earth pass away, one yodh**
> (The smallest of the letters) **will in no way pass from the law until all**
> **Be perfected.**

We have absolutely no more time for deception, people! We must get it right or perish. Now! We do not have much time left! WAKE UP!!

Let's face it people, the whole world has basically been deceived and is in serious trouble. It was the devil that deceived us, and most of the world is still being deceived.

Revelation 12:

> **9. And the great dragon was cast out, that old serpent, called the Devil, and Satan, who deceives the whole world. She was cast out into the earth, and her Angels were cast out with her.**

However, in the last few days of man's government by man, The Creator of the world has given all humanity one last chance to listen, learn, and repent! He has given us one last chance to be delivered from her lies. We have an excellent chance today with clear teaching by His two witnesses on this earth. All of us could heed the words of YAHWEH as written in:

Isayah (Isaiah) 34:16 (The Book of YAHWEH)

Search out the Book of YAHWEH, and read. Not on of these will be neglected. For it is written; YAHWEH is their Shepherd: they shall not want; for His mouth has commanded it, and His Spirit has gathered them.

However, soon there is going to be another curve ball thrown here in America. It will come with such speed and deception and will look so tempting and acceptable, at least to African Americans primarily, that if we are not careful and spiritually discerning, some of us could easily take a big swing at it and strike out. Again! It is being perfectly prepared as we speak, largely through TV. It will be preaching, for the most part, nothing but hatred, division, and revenge. Many of us will accept it because it will come through the same religious venue that some of us have bought for years.

For a clearer and closer understanding of just what the enemy of peace and democracy is up to today, as we speak, listen! Listen carefully to this most necessary oration of all time. First, we need to go back, and listen to the rest of the last verses of Mark's third chapter, where the Savior Himself will be explaining how a house (or a nation) divided would not stand. Actually, this is prophesy, but if we listen to the Savior closely we will know for sure what can be done, and how it has to be done to avoid such calamities.

Not only will the enemy be trying to divide us more and more in this chaotic period of time that has been prophesied to happen, but she (the devil) will be blaspheming the Holy Spirit all the while she is doing her thing. She (the devil) will be claiming that these ornery acts that are causing all of this hatred, murder, diseases, sickness, war, and division is done by the power of the Holy Spirit! People, that is the highest level of blasphemy that there is or ever has been! On top of that, she (the devil) is going to persuade some people that there is a reward when you die for killing the Savior's people. **"They will kill you and think to do their god a favor"**

That is blasphemy, as you will hear the Savior explain. There is absolutely no forgiveness for that. That is what is going to force the Savior of mankind to step in, shorten the days, and then close the whole dispensation. (Matthew 24:22). As you read you will see that the enemy has gone much too far.

Yahchanan Mark (Mark) **3:** (The Book of YAHWEH)
28. **Today I say to you: "All sins will be forgiven the son of men and whatever**
    Blasphemous things they utter.
29. **However, he who blasphemes against the Holy Spirit will never have**

Forgiveness but is bound to an everlasting sin.

30. Because they said: He has an unclean Spirit.

The Book of YAHWEH, which all scholars will agree is the closest translation we have today to the original Hebrew scroll. Plus **The Prophetic Word magazine, Feb., 2007 issue**, had some very interesting and enlightening comments concerning the above Scriptures, relating them to the last day war and troubles. It speaks of how Satan would do some evil work here on earth in this end time, knowing that some people, under her (Satan), deception would claim that it was a good work, done by the power of their god. She (the devil) would even claim that it was done by the power of The Holy Spirit. That is an abominable blasphemy! Some people are going to be persuaded that some god or the other of theirs is actually helping them through these evil deeds. They won't even realize that these deeds will condemn them!

This is the same blasphemy as when a good work that has been done by the Holy Spirit is credited to the devil, or any god. As we know, there are many gods and many lords but there is only One Authority.

1 Cor. 8: (The Book of YAHWEH)

5. **For although there are many called gods** (elohim) **whether in heaven or on**
   Earth (as there are many gods; elohim, and many lords; Baalim).

6. **Yet to us there is only One Authority, the Father from whom all things came and for whom we live. And there is only one King YAHSHUA MESSIAH, on whose account are all things, and on whose account we live.**

That is an unforgivable sin to even associate any god to Yahweh. According to the Scripture. There is a commentary, taken from the Book of YAHWEH that we should all hear. Plus, **The Prophetic Word** magazine Feb. 2007 issue orates on this subject. It reads:

Is it not astonishing that men who have ever read these words, should doubt what Blasphemy against the Holy Spirit is? Can any words declare more plainly that Blasphemy against the Holy Spirit is attributing to the devil the miracles of YAHSHUA (Jesus), the Prophets, the Apostles, or any other man of YAHWEH, wrought by the power of the Holy Spirit?

That is amazing! However, the effect of these lies and the power of this instigating by the devil in these last evil days on earth, will add fuel to the ongoing feud during this dangerous period in history. The effectiveness of these lies is going to boost America's enemies' confidence that they could win and (depending on the position that African Americans take) make a peaceable ending almost impossible. Even the elect of YAHWEH will have to sharpen up their Spiritual wit in this time of treachery and deceit or they may be fooled by the enemy's wiles.

Matthew 24:

21. **For then will be great tribulation such as has not come to pass since the**
    Beginning or the world to this time – no nor ever will be.
22. **And unless that time were shortened, there would no flesh be saved: but**
    For the elect's sake, those days will be shortened.

There is an important truth, which is probably not going to sit very well with African Americans, and a great majority of the rest of the World's cultures, in these last few days of man's government by man on earth. However, we absolutely must learn to distinguish the Savior of the world's laws from the lies of the enemy if we ever intend to receive eternal life with the Creator of the world or avoid this last day nuclear war. We do hold the key. The enemy would have you worshipping a beast that is a liar, a thief and a murderer if she (the devil) had her way. And some of us have been doing just that for most of our lives, unaware!

Also, some people will tell us, don't worry about it we are fine just like we are. The Savior got rid of the law a long time ago. However, as much as we might love them, they are false Prophets if they say that. Some have even told us that we do not need a special Sabbath Day; any day is all right as long as you just believe. They are false Prophets! Strict adherence to the Law and observance of the Sabbath day are mandatory to eternal life with the Savior. Let's look at something Solomon said for a minute. Then we will go back.

Proverbs 14: (The Book of YAHWEH)

15. **The simple (ignorant and untutored) believes every word he hears;**

But the prudent (discerning and wise) **looks carefully where he is going.**

16. **The wise show reverence to YAHWEH** (God) **and depart from evil;**
But the fool rages on and is confident.

17. **He who is quick-tempered acts foolishly, and a man of wicked devices is hated.**

18. **The simple** (ignorant and untutored) **inherit folly, but the prudent are crowned with knowledge. The evil will bow before the righteous**

19. **The evil will bow before the righteous; the wicked will bow at the gates of the righteous.**

20. **The poor man is shunned even by this neighbor, but a rich man has many Friends.**

21. **He who despises his brother sins, but he who has mercy on the poor, joyful is he**

22. **Do they not go astray who devise evil? But mercy and truth will be to those Who devise righteousness.**

America, we need to listen! The only possible way to avoid the total destruction from the raging wars today, is to listen, and do what the Creator of all mankind says is the solution. And the only way this particular chaos and upcoming atrocity will be prevented according to the Scripture is if, black Americans primarily, are made aware on a national and international scale of how this division in African America was first perpetrated, what it was for, and how the enemy is about to try to manipulate us again into becoming enemies and an untrusted partner in this equation.

If we all could just hear that story told clear and true, African Americans, would finally know, once and for all, just what it was leading up to. For all the deceptions perpetrated through the years, was leading up to an eventual, big split and division in America. First between America and African Americans. Finally, there will be a split between America, Muslims, and African Americans.

I found out just lately, my ministry and message was for me to tell my own brethren about what I found, through the Savior's mercy, African Americans first! Then, Every nation. I found, every nation is supposed to warn their own people. We are supposed to be telling them that, **"WE CAN AVOID THIS COMING DISTRUCTION"**. (Deut. 18:18-19).

If this message gets delivered properly, timely, and honestly, then, for the first time we are going to realize as a united people, what happened in the past don't matter any more than a hill of beans when we realize what we are facing now. All that will matter then will be **The SOLUTION!** **The SOLUTION!** For our **SURVIVAL!** **The SOLUTION!**

This message that has been given to man for deliverance in this end time is crucial to hear and to speak, for it is life saving. Those who survive these upcoming atrocities will live forever. They are the ones who will take heed and obey YAHWEH'S law for peace. Those who don't will die in the flames.

This division, perpetrated a long time ago, first in America on black slaves, was supposed to result in a scraping over superiority; then over land and property. That would ultimately result in a civil war at home; then a war between countries; then more countries; then world war, which would destroy the whole world, a **nuclear war!** That is what was designed by the devil. That is all she (the devil) wanted to eventually happen, by the last dispensation; destruction of all mankind. That is all!

Yahchanan (John) 10:10
The thief comes only to steal, and kill and destroy. I have come that they might have life, and that they might have it more abundantly.

That is the total, final objective of the enemy. This plot was cunning, long ranged, but carefully calculated. It is all identified in the Scriptures.

Nevertheless, the Creator of the entire world had a solution for preventing this nuclear war all the time. None of this was a surprise to the Creator of the world. He knew what She (the devil) would be up to during the end time. But He left the choice to us, mankind, in America. We could choose life or death. **Deut.30:19**

America! World! Will you please, for your own salvation, listen to the only Solution given to mankind in this dispensation that will avoid nuclear war? Listen, before time runs out! There is only one solution! There is only one law that will bring peace. There is only one lawgiver.

James 4:
10. **Do not speak evil against one another brothers. He who speaks evil against His brother and condemns his brother speaks evil against the law and condemns the law. And if**

you condemn the law you are not a doer of the law, but a judge of the law.

11. There is one lawgiver, who is able to save and destroy. Who are you who condemns another?

The solution for the saving of mankind has boiled down to a simple decision of whether or not men are willing to accept the Savior's rule, forgive, unite and be delivered. Because Ismayl and Isaac, are both Abraham's children. We read in

Romans 3:23,
"For all have sinned and came short of the glory of YAHWEH."

The method the Savior has given mankind for uniting these two brothers lies in revelation that Yechetzqyah (Ezekiel) saw in a vision for rebuilding the Temple again, which turned out to be the blue print for Peace in the world. Let's listen to what was written by one of the two witnesses sent by YAHWEH to explain the solution to this last day confusion, in an oration from **The Prophetic Word magazine.** (Jan. 2007 issue) He wrote:

The same creator, who inspired the Prophet Yechetzqyah to write of Tyre's destruction, also inspired a set of laws to be written: Laws, which would assure Peace for all nations. The leaders of the nations would do well to take heed to these laws and apply them to the governments in existence today. We have historical records showing that when these laws were applied, taught earnestly, and enforced strictly, the nation obeying them had Peace. The Prophet Mosheh (Moses) was inspired to write in

Deut. 4:
5. See, I have taught you statutes and judgments just as YAH-WEH my Father
   Commanded me, so that you may follow them in the land you are entering to
   Take possession of.
6. Therefore, be careful to observe and do them; for this is your wisdom and your understanding in the sight of the nations who will hear of these statutes and say; surely this great nation is a wise and understanding people
7. What other nation is so great as to have their God (Elohim)

with them the way
YAHWEH our Father is near us whenever we pray to him.

The absolute solution for peace is simple, according to the Creator of the world, but man complicates it through their lust, greed, and pride. However, it can still be reached. Of course, honest men would have to want peace. And if any man knew what just one small nuclear explosion would do to the whole world, they would all want peace. They would see that in the event of a nuclear war, there would be no winners. There is no way whatsoever now days to bring peace with our weapons or our armies any more. Everybody and every nation have weapons or bombs that could destroy our world. Even small nations that we refer to as "third world countries."

So let us go now and look at one-half of the only true, lasting solution for peace in these perilous times. As strange as it may seem, the Book of Yechetzqyah (Ezekiel) had already solved the great problem of great division and turmoil that brings war and death, a long time ago. YAHWEH, the Creator of the world, gave the solution to him in a vision. According to Yechetzqyah (Ezekiel) chapters 40 to 48, all men have to do, on both sides of this equation, is go ahead and vigorously build that promised Temple again, The House of YAHWEH. It was prophesied that it would be built again. It cannot be stopped. But nothing has to be torn down. Just build it, just a little North of The Dome of the Rock; which has been given to the Gentiles according to the Holy Scriptures:

Rev. 11:

1. **And there was given to me a reed like a measuring rod.**
   And the Malak(Angel) **stood saying: Rise and measure the**
   Temple of YAHWEH,
   And the altar, and its confines; (where they worship within)
2. **But the court which is outside the Temple leave out, and**
   measure it not;
   For it is given to the Gentiles. And the Holy City they will
   tread under foot Three and one half years.

These measurements have never made sense to any scholars before. Scholars in the past have said, "These measurements are just not consistent with the building of The House of YAHWEH as it was built before. Some space is missing."

I would think so! However if men had truly studied the prophecies

---

honestly we would know why...We just heard the Malak (angel) say in;

Rev. 11:
"But the court which is outside the Temple, LEAVE OUT and MEASURE IT NOT! For it is given to the GENTILES."

Let men just go ahead and build the temple again, with the dividing wall in place, as seen in Yechetzqyah's {Ezekiel}prophecy, in the 40th chapter: Just like the Creator of heaven and earth said to do. Then just let the Arabs worship in the Dome on the rock and the Jews worship in the House of YAHWEH and let both of them apply the only set of laws that was given by Moseh (Moses) for all mankind to bring peace. It is simple! According to the Creator of the world, these laws given by Moseh (Moses), is the only law that would eventually cause men to: **"Beat their swords into plow shares and their spears into pruning hooks, and will learn war against each other NO MORE."** {Isayah 2:4}

These laws given by Moseh {Moses} are the only laws that would bring peace to the Jewish Nation and the Arab Nations and to all mankind. If men would only start to teach Yahweh's laws again. We have un-disputable documented proof that the only time any nation has ever been at complete peace was when those laws were being taught. It was when Soloman was King.

The solution has been laid out for man in the Holy Scriptures. Of course, this information must be taken from the Original Holy Scriptures. We could all prove this to ourselves if we wanted to. Although proving that the solution is there, to our selves, would require a little digging and patience and listening to the Scripture as they explain just how it is supposed to be done. But it is all there. And the Savior of man gives us precise instructions and exact measurements of how to build the New Temple. You will find this information in Yechetzqyah (Ezekiel) chapter 40 and 43. I do believe, though, that He intended for man to dig for the solution because in Isayah (Isaiah) he said:

Isayah (Isaiah) 28:
9 **To whom will he teach knowledge? To whom will he make to understand Doctrine? Those who are weaned from the milk and drawn from the breast.**

10   For precept must be upon precept: precept upon precept;
     line upon line; line upon line; here a little and there a lit-
     tle.

Today! America, we have now in our midst, what we had been promised from the Savior of mankind for decades. One of the Two Witnesses
that we all have waited for, seems like forever, is here to give us truth from
the Scriptures. Yes, The Standard of Perfection, the Ephah. We can now
know for sure, exactly what the Savior of mankind has said and know exactly what He means. The Witness has opened the Scripture for us. Please
allow me to quote something from the Witness Magazine. It is called **The
Prophetic Word** magazine. On page 14 of the January, 2007 issue, he
wrote:

**"In my many years of study, of which you will see only a part in
this article, I have discovered that the Prophet Yechetzqyah (Ezekiel)
wrote about a temple and a time period for the day in which we now
live. Yechetzqyah was inspired to writ this prophecy over 600 years
before the Temple was destroyed in 70 C.E. He was inspired to write
for us who live in these days – these troublous days, the same troublous times that the other inspired prophets proclaimed.**

**In these same prophecies, we are also shown a Peaceful Solution
for building The Temple of YAHWEH! What is even more important
is the fact that those same prophecies show us how we, in this generation, can bring peace to Jerusalem and to the world.**

**In Yechetzqyah's prophecies are the complete measurements for
a Temple unlike any other that we have ever built before. Many of
these measurements have never made sense to any other scholar, but
with YAHWEH's inspiration, we have come to see exactly what the
prophet Yechetzqyah saw: The pattern for building the Temple in
these last days.**

**The pattern with all of its measurements exactly fits the area of
land sitting north of The Dome of the Rock Mosque. Yes, the pattern
offers us, the last generation, a peaceful solution to building the Temple, and an end to the troublous times that Jerusalem now faces. All
we now ask is that you study this information carefully. Then contact
The House of YAHWEH if you have any questions."**

Truthfully, the witness is right on point in the Scripture. We were
already instructed a long time ago, for today's answer, if we had any ques-

tions to:

"Ask at Able and that will settle a matter " {Abilene) II Samuyl (Samuel) 20:18.

Allow me just one more quote from the witness magazine, please. Then I will show you for sure our vital part in the equation, African Americans. We hold the Key. On page 18 of the same magazine he gives us a very important truth, by Scripture. He said:

"Many scholars have thought that Yechetzqyah made a mistake as he wrote down some of the measurements; that he was just going by memory, or trying to remember the measurements of Solomon's Temple. They claim his memory failed him, and he wrote the measurements wrong. That is not the case at all! First, we can see from the magnificent prophecy that he wrote, that it was a prophecy destined to take place at a later date. Moreover, those prophecies are for our day!

Yechetzqyah shows us the Temple mount as it appears in this day, not in his day or when he was alive. Yechetzqyah 40:1-5 shows that he was brought to the Temple Mount in our day, in our generation. The Measurements that Yechetzqyah wrote have never been used before, but are to be used now by this generation.

Yechtzqyah (Ezekiel) 40:

3. In the vision of YAHWEH, he brought me into the land of Israyl, and set me upon the great-exalted mountain: and on it, like a building of a city on the South.

5 And behold, there was an adjoining separation; (dividing structure) around a Temple. In the beings hand was a measuring reed six long cubits; about 10 ½ feet – each cubit about 1 ½ feet, with a handbreadth; about 3 inches. So he measured the Separation's width to the structure, one reed; (about 10 ½ feet) and the height; (rise) one reed.

Let us now deal with African American's vital roll in this picture. We do now absolutely hold the other half of the puzzle. It is key to the solution to Peace. The first thing that happened to black people, in this dispensation, upon entering America was the denial of salvation by the Savior because you were never allow to know Him. You were forbidden to learn how to read and write, so that you would not have a chance to read about or even to hear about the Savior. That was forbidden! Some of us have never even heard to this day His name. But we can today! Now!

Roman 10: (The Book of YAHWEH)

12. **For there is no distinction between Yahdai (Jew) and Greek. For the same Father of all is rich to all who call upon him.**
13. **For whosoever calls with the name of YAHWEH will be saved.**
14. **How, then, can they call upon Him in whom they have not believed? And how will they believe in Him of whom they have not heard? And how will they hear without a preacher?**
15. **And how can they preach, unless they are sent? As it is written: How beautiful are the feet of those who preach the message of peace, which bring glad tidings of righteous things.**

Do you see the plot unfolding now? The Savior has been purposely held back from you. You can NOT CALL or BELIEVE in something you have NEVER HEARD about. The devil knows that.

When the enemy starts telling black America about their past slave history and how the old white man in America is the devil and that it was he that kept your ancestors from learning how to read and write. Plus he gave you a false religion, he took advantage of your women folk, he gave you and your ancestors inferior names – Nigger – and on and on and on.

Some of that is going to ring true and stir up a spirit of anger like you have never witnessed before in America. This will be true especially among older Americans, southern blacks, who still remember some portions of those allegations. Those older black Americans who are still alive and do not know the full history of man in other dispensations or the true scripture, are going to be just about broken up from the root. And most furious from these reminders.

Of course, some parts of these stories are true. But what the devil will never tell you is that every single person who had anything or any part in helping with slavery is already dead. Not one single person is alive today. They are all dead! Dead! Dead! And they have all been dead for two hundred years or more.

The enemy's whole thought process is going to be geared toward getting black people to feel the need for and to seek the opportunity for revenge. He will never tell you how many white people died trying to reverse the slavery of black people. He will never mention the thousands of Caucasian descendants that lost their jobs, family, and friends just for standing up for what was just and humanly right, as far as they were concerned. You will never even hear of those most sad and unfortunate stories from the enemy.

She (the devil) at this approaching time will only be painting all of white America as the devil and a natural enemy of all blacks. She (the devil) can only advance in battalion if white America is feeling guilty and on the defense from black America.

She (the devil) will also be trying to keep under wrap, all intelligent and contrary information to what she is saying. And the fact that in every dispensation of time throughout history, there have always been a people that dominated another race. Even African Americans has done this same thing

The one thing you can be sure of is that She (the devil) is never going to bring up is the fact that in one dispensation black people were Kings and Queens and dominated basically all of the earth. However, this generation was so ornery and hateful that they even offended the Creator of the world. They flat refused to allow the Children of Israel, His chosen people; to cross their land to get to the home the Creator had promised them. This information can be found I Numbers chapter 20:-22

These kings just flat refused to help, even though Moseh {Moses} had promised to pay each one of them just to let them cross. If the cattle drank any of the water or they disturbed anything on the land, Moses promised to compensate them. Balak even tried to put a curse on Israel for no reason.

In any event, that refusal to help His people, and that unhelpful attitude angered the Creator of the world. And for that He promised to set civil war in Egypt and Ethiopia forever more. Egypt and Ethiopia, is US! African Americans! (Numbers 20:21:22: Deut.23)

So you see, no nation of people or any individual needs to be harboring thoughts of revenge for each other because of something that may have happened before you were even born. The Savior says we are all guilty,

"For we have all sinned and come short of the glory of YAHWEH."
Rom. 3:23

In any event, American blacks must and can become self sufficient. There is no other way to say it. And lets just stay honest about it. In order for self sufficiency to become a permanent condition, African Americans as a whole must start from where it counts the most.The Ghettos. Yes, black America! If we intend to survive the whole ordeal we face today, we must PLANT A NEW SEED of character in the Ghettos.

There is no other way to put it. We absolutely must get rid of the old slave master's mentality. He is dead! dead! dead! Halleluyah, dead! Any negative qualities we have came from our traditional life style. The slave master's training. We must get rid of it! Then we will help bring peace to all mankind. However, in African America's case, it starts first with our tongue!

CORRUPT COMMUNICATION

The Scripture has reveal to us and warned us all of what the adversary is up to with his constant encouragement of corrupt communication, conversations with foul language, usually of adultry, sex, durgs, killings, revenge, and any pervertness. It was to eventuallly destroy a people and a nation through their bad character, preferablely before they even realized that they had been prompted to destruction using their own tongue. Although the devil knew that it's results would take time, cunning craftiness, and excitement, she knew that the final deadly results would eventually manifest itself.

This action, unaware to most African Americans was originally designed to get one into either a fight or jail, or a hospital, or worse. And it is disguise so cunningly that it's real intended purpose may never be discovered. It would eventually create a climate for a world war using nuclear weapons. Yes, all of this by corrupt communication. It will corrupt and divide.

Its main purpose was to cause lack of trust, division, both from one's own people and with his neighbors, and to ensure lack of cooperation and ignorance. Then,finally, one would find himself hopeless, valueless, and unworthy of receiving even eternal life thorough The Heavenly Father. That was the ultimate goal, even if it took the last days (day) when judgement was measured out. The Scriptures explained this in:

II Timothy 3:
1. **Know this also: That in the last days perilous** (dangerous) **times will come.**
2. **For men will be lovers of themselves, covetous, boasters, proud,blasphemers,disobedient to parents, unholy,**

unthankful,unholy

3. Without natural affection, trucebrakers; false accusers, without self control, brutal, dispisers of those who are righteous

4. Traitors; { betrayers} headstrong, arrogant, lovers of pleasure more than of Yah-weh. {God]

5. Having a form of holiness but denying the authority of it – from such turn away.

Notice how the Savior of all mankind had already pointed out what could cause people or a nation to develop such bad character and manners to such a degree that it would cause trouble,division. Consequently it could cause them to even lose or not receive eternal life with the Heavenly Father.

According to **I Cor. 15:33, "Corrupt Communications corrupts good manners."**

What did the Scripture just say corrupted me, ruined my good character, then condemned me? **"Corrupt conversations ruin good character."**

Yet some people may still tell you,especially in the African American community, "This is the way most of the people I know talk. Every where I go, this is just the way we talk."

And I would have to agree, "I know it is! Most of the people you know are probably basically just like you!. They do not know that they are also destitute of The Savior's wisdom; these may be the only kind of people who are able to bear you, or your language, because they are also acustomed to that kind of corruption. BAD MANNERS!"

Truthfully, you will probable find out, if you don't already know, that not many intelligent people are going to be able to stay around long, one who constantly use corrupt communication to express themselves, no matter how hard they try. It will just not sit well or mix well in their spirit, because it is evil at work. So this alone could make one be precieved as an enemy. Lets just be honest here. It is the enemy's language. Bad language and corrupt communiction is from the devil.

DESTITUTE OF WISDOM

It is times like these that I really do hate. There are some times when you can do absolutely nothing to help a fellow human being; one who may be in terrible danger of total destruction and doesn't even know it. I personally hate not knowing how to help. However, if the Savior of mankind says he cannot help a people right now, you and I certainly cannot. Who are we?

The Heavenly Father said, sometimes a people may be so weak that they become un-learnable and at that point unable to be taught at that time. And they would probably have to get into a deeper state of degradation of their already pathetic live before they would even be strong enough to search him out. Or anybody else out, for help! Wow! Did you know that? Listen to the Scripture explain it to us.

Proverbs 15:
16. **He who has a mind of understanding seeks knowledge, but the mouth of fools eats foolishness**.

Now I had to ask the Savior at that point: why would a man eat foolishness, something that would ultimately destroy him?

Little did I know, He had already instructed Solomon a long time ago to answer that question for mankind. Solomon answered for Him, continuing in the same chapter and said it was because:

21. **Folly** (foolishness) **seems delightful... to him who is "Destitute of wisdom" but a man of understanding** {wisdom} **walks uprightly**.

Do you know what **"Destitute of Wisdom"** means? It means, "**almost plum without,**" not just a little bit slow, but just about, "**plum ignorant**" or you could call it, "**an emergency need**" or "**without any,**" or you could say, **"no wisdom whatsoever,"** or **"desperate for wisdom"** That's what the Scriptures has warned us.

And, unless one turns to the Savior, a person may not even be strong enough to stop the foolishness that got him into trouble and seek help! Because they may be under some kind of illusion that they are alright just as they are. The devil has even told some people in this condition that they are smart. Yet The Scripture says, those that love folly are **"Destitute of Wisdom."**

Do you know how evil and stubborn one will become if one allows sin to continue to sink them this low? Yes, it is sin that does this, mainly a perverse tongue. Sin! Listen to what the Scripture says can happen to one if you continue in perversenesses!

Proverbs 27:22
"Though you grind a fool to powder, in a pestle, you will not separate him from his foolishness.

Have you ever been in a position where you were forced to witness a people who seemed to delight in only folly and perverseness? Nothing else seems to hold their interest except perverseness and folly. According to the Scripture, that can only happen when one is, **"Destitute of Wisdom."** These people simply do not know what folly was designed to bring about. They are desperately in need of rescue by The Savior. Yet do not know it. They are **"destitute."**

When you are without wisdom, it is a natural thing for you to love folly (foolishness). You may not have the slightest idea what folly is trying to do to you. But folly does.

If one ties the Creator's hands by rejecting wisdom, He said He could not help them. And neither can you. Nobody can. Because wisdom is the first thing one must seek. The Scripture said it is first in priority.

Proverbs 4:
6. **Wisdom is the first priority, so get wisdom. And with all you have gotten, get Understanding.**

We are just going to have to stay honest here, my people, and tell it exactly like it is. Did you know that there are just some things that the Savior absolutely hates? He hates this:

Prov.6:

16. These six things does YAHWEH hate, yes seven are an abomination to him.

17. A proud look, a lying tongue, hands that shed innocent blood.

18. A mind that devises wicked imaginations (plans); feet that are swift into running to evil.

19. A false witness that speaketh lies and one who sows discord among brothers.

That is all foolishness there. Folly! Folly was designed to eventually kill us people. No matter how innocent it may seem to start off, its ultimate goals are destruction. The Creator of the world wants us to live. Folly wants us to die. Do not participate in any more folly anymore! Whatever! It kills!

THERE IS SIMPLY NO OTHER WAY TO SAY IT

There is simply no other way, honestly, to help, save, or deliver any people of any kind from crime, poverty, corruption, ignorance, or even drugs. Except be honest. That is the only way, the right knowledge, YAHWEH's knowledge. And it all starts with words.

Prov.15:1
"A soft (gentle) answer turns away wrath, but a cutting retort stirs up more anger."

That is what we are going to try to do here, "Turn away wrath." Corrupt or defiled words defiles a character eventually, and just makes one hard to take in general.

I Cor.15: (KJV) 33.
"Be not deceived: evil communications corrupts good manners."

On the other hand, pleasant words produce good character in a person and can make one's company easy to accept and to be around. Pleasant words will produce and promote an at least tolerable and teachable environment. But corrupt words bring chaos and division.

It is indeed a sad thing to say, but let us just get to the point here. We need to all face this fact, then correct the situation if we ever expect there to be any positive and lasting change in this African American struggle for real dignity, for real. One of the greatest problems is, there is just not nearly enough black politicians, preachers, teachers, businessmen, and just black leaders in general, who are supposed to be our care takers, that are insisting or demanding, aggressively and forcefully enough, on the teaching that the Creator of the Universe said we need to be teaching to African American youth today.

And that is, **CHARACTER EDUCATION.**

Prov. 22: 6
"Train up a child in the way he should go, and when he is old he will not depart from it."

That is The Savior's law for peace. As a matter of fact, most of them are actually overlooking, or at least neglecting, to teach this law and only real solution to the most important problem facing African Americans personally today. This teaching could be called, "**Word communication and character building.**"

Because contrary to getting better, statistics will show that African Americans, especially black youth, did in fact inherit this serious problem of "corrupt communication" and are now progressively being forced deeper and deeper into a situation where it is inevitable that they have to get even worse. And every corruption known to man will more than likely have to flourish in them at the present rate of being imprisoned.

The court system's attitude toward African Americans has demanded that our youth go to jail for basically any and all violations, never even considering an educational training center for treatment of character as an alternative. As a matter of reality, there are no real **Character and Words, Educational Training Centers.**

Black leaders, united and armed with information, unity and strength, simply has not demanded that there be such a thing as a center or institute that teaches on the power of words. Just words! Good or bad character starts with words! Yet, very few people today are teaching this. But the Scripture does say:

Matt. 12:37
"For by your words you will be justified, or by your words you will be condemned."

If we could just start, as African Americans, to stand up and insist that our youth attend training schools or centers for character building rather than going to jail, in most cases we could influence the courts. We must also recognize that you cannot expect good character to come out of corrupt surroundings. According to the Savior:

Corrupt communication ruins good character. I Cor. 15:33)

On the other hand, good communication and surroundings would produce good character. Then the crime rates among blacks would probably drop by half or better. And our youth would become saved and productive and our communities would become united and profitable and safe.

Not only should our youth, as an alternative to going to jail, be sentenced to go into a character and word training center program, but in a lot of cases it might be a good idea if some of the parents were encouraged to go right along with them. You may be very surprised, but no doubt, delighted, to see how everyone would benefit from such an alternative sentence and replacement learning program. This has never been tried but America would definitely prosper as we build strong character and bring it back into our neighborhoods. Survival of America is all about good or bad character NOW! That is just what has developed through allowing the devil to train our people through all these years. Bad Character! Is from the devil!

Let us face it! American black youth have been written off! Replaced! Or, at best, sort of stored out of the way for safekeeping. Intelligent people know this is true and they know the reason why this has happened. It is simply because of the lack of demand on them for education. There just simply has not been a demand for a word and character training programming. How ever, that is the exclusive responsibility of African Americans. Somebody blew it. There is just simply not a real honest demand on them for character change. I'm sorry! But it is mandatory for survival!

This character change must become a demand! Not just a command. And it must come from our black leadership and from our communities. If we say we love, or is even concerned about, our youth, our race, our communities, and even our selves, we must demand this change!

Actually, there is no real way for America as a whole to survive without this change. It is not our color, anymore, that will determine our future or destiny, but rather our character! Can you be trusted to unite with America today, or will you help destroy it? It starts with our tongue!

PLANT A NEW SEED, SURVEY

Let us do a little survey right here, and see if you really agree with this promoting of this particular word or not. Where are you now, Justified or Condemned?

Matt. 12:37
"For by your words you shall be justified or by your words you shall be condemned."
There are some alphabets that were assembled a long time ago, taken from the most negative words that could be found, then a word formed of its own, with its own meaning. This word was formed for a special group of people. This word was created in extreme hostility, and under the strictest discipline; and trained every day to grow. There was a demand for this training and this word to control a special group of people.

First I would like to ask you to listen closely to how this word was created, trained, and administered, and then tell me how much you really like and enjoy this word.

Keep in mind though, above all things, the rules, and laws for everything that grows and how its strength would have to come from The Creator of Heaven and Earth who said:

"Everything on earth that bears fruit, has a spirit, and must produce after its own kind, for its seed is in itself." Gen. 1:11
That principle goes for everything that is created or planted here on earth and trained, good or bad. Keep in mind also, He has explained: **"The words I speak, they are Spirit and Life." John 6:63.**
The Savior said that **words are alive!** And this word that we are going to talk about is no exception and no accident. **It is alive!** Words can form a character in us if used repeatedly enough. This is true whether the words

are good or bad.

First, the slave master, who was the administrator of this word, took some chains and some whips and beat the backs of this people as he forced this people to call themselves this word every day, day after day, repeatedly; or face hanging. Sometimes they would put two people together from the same race or sometimes from even the same family and demand that they fight each other until one of them was dead. Sometime they were forced to fight with pick handles, or axe handles, knives and at other times, with their bear fists. And as they fought each other, the most unforgivable rule was that they must not forget to call each other by this name that the slave master had created for them, until one of them was dead; or both of them would be hung.

The one left standing was expected to beat his chest and proclaim victory by screaming repeatedly as loud as he could that he was the best of the bunch of this thing. All the while, the slave master, the administrator and creator of this word, would rather cover his mouth as he stood there snickering at them. He knew that they had no idea what the word meant and what they were claiming.

Now this group of people, that was being trained by this word to destroy each other by fighting and repeating this word over and over and over until it settled in their spirit and became well with their soul, They were also forbidden, under any circumstances, to learn how to read or write. They were only allowed to learn to make an X for their names. Just the mere suggestion that you wanted to learn to read and write was a hanging offence. But it was mandatory that you learn and claimed this name that was given you and say it loud and clearly with conviction and feeling. Or face disqualification. And if you were disqualified, even for not saying this word loudly enough, you could be hung on the spot.

Also, communication among this people had to be kept to a minimum. If these people just spoke to, or about, anybody that looked like them, they were instructed to identify that person by no other title or name other than the name that had been created just for them. The instruction was, "Just call them and your self by this one name only!" That is, if you two looked alike.

The reward for excellence would normally come after the slave master or someone would put this people and a monkey in a cage or together somewhere to be observed for the final finishing touch or examination.

Then, if the people could act, talk, or scream louder or more ridiculously than the monkey, they earned the right to be called the best. **The Best?**

Ok, you probably want to know what that word is, that we have been talking about, don't you? The word created was **NIGGER!** The best **Nigger!**

Well, how do you like it? How does that word sit with you? Would you like to claim it for yourself? According to the Creator of the world, all words will do exactly what they are supposed to do eventually. It is HIS law. **Matt. 12:37,**

"By your words you will be justified or by your words you will be condemned." They are all alive, the Savior said, **"All the words that I speak, have life in them."**

John 6:63 (The Book of YAHWEH) **"The law that I speak to you, they are Spirit, and they are life everlasting."**

This particular word, Nigger, was designed and created for one purpose and one purpose only! Its intended purpose was the destruction of a race of people; by the old slave master. It was created in extreme hostility to keep one people, a nation, ignorant of their human rights and dignity, making them purposely un-trusting, first of themselves, then each other, and undependable and unstable. The designers of this word knew that the seed would continue to destroy whatever it produced. According to the Scripture, **"Its seed is in itself. (Gen. 1:11)**

So now we ask you, how do you like the word now? According to history it has been the single most effective tool for destruction one could feed his spirit. It has been proven that it works.

Is there any wonder why the devil loves to hear African Americans, or anyone else, call them selves by this foul and potent title? In doing so they are promoting his spirit here on earth. She (the devil) knows that this word has to produce exactly what it was designed, created, and trained to produce, sooner or later. Evil!

With this habit deep in one's heart, the devil knows that you are mouthing exactly what you are supposed to be at this time. His! It is SIN. So, would you tell us now for the survey, how much do you like that word? Oh, by the way,

"And Sin, when it is fully matured, brings forth Death! (James 1:15)

THE HERALD LEADER ON MONDAY
MARCH 25, 2007:

People across the Caribbean bowed their heads for a moment of silence to mark the 200th anniversary of the end of the slave trade in the British Empire. "We unite as a region and a people as we remember one of the greatest tragedies in the history of humanity, which denied over 25 million Africans, for over 400 years, the basic human right of freedom." Said Ralph Gonzales, Prime Minister of St. Vincent and Chairman of the Caribbean Community.

British Prime Minister, Tony Blair expresses the Nation's "deep sorrow and regret." Arch Bishop of York, John Sentamu, a senior Church of England Cleric, said Blair should go further and apologize for Britain's role in the Slave Trade Act of 1807, which did not legislate to emancipate slaves in its territories until 1833.

THE NAME ABOVE ALL NAMES

Acts. 4:

(The Book of YAHWEH)

7. When they had set them in the midst, they asked: By what power (authority)
Or by what name have you done this?

8. Then Kepha (Peter) filled with the Holy Spirit, said to them; Rulers of the
People and Elders of Israel:

9. If today, because of the kindness to a sick man, we are asked by what means he was healed:

10. Let it be know to you all, and to all the people of Isryal (Israel), that in the
Name of YAHSHUA MESSIAH of Nazareth who you nailed on a stake, but whom <u>YAHWEH raise from the dead</u> – by Him does this man stand here before you HEALED:

In this oration, inspired by the Creator of the world, Kepha (Peter), filled with the Holy Spirit, told all humanity in the original text of the Holy Scripture, that if you wanted to know how the helpless man was healed, and who could save you, there is one and only one who can do it. But through one specific NAME. Also:

"Neither is there salvation in any other, for there is NO OTHER name under heaven given, among men by which we must be saved." (Acts 4:12)

Did Peter say, any name you call upon from your heart would be all right, as long as you are serious? Did he say, any name that you are used to calling on and are comfortable with, will be just fine, because you do not live in this country or that country? No! He said, there is NO OTHER name UNDER HEAVEN GIVEN, that we can call, by which we must be saved!but the NAME that was given the MESSIAH of Nazareth, by YAHWEH! Which is YAHSHUA.

Do you believe Peter, or the original Scripture? Hold on now, make sure, because if we believe Peter, then we all probably need to know that one, and only Name given to all mankind under heaven, that has salvation with it, and just plain forget about any other substitute name. Shouldn't we?

Yeremyah (Jeremiah) 23:13
"I have seen folly (offense) **in the Prophets of Samaria – They prophesied by Baal:** (the lord) **and caused my people to err** (Go astray).

25. **I have heard what the prophets say, who prophesy lies in my name, Saying; I have a dream! I have a dream! I have dreamed!**
26. **How long will this be in the hearts of the prophets who prophesy lies? Yes, they are prophets of the deceit of their own minds;**
27. **Who devise;** (plan and scheme) **to cause my people to forget my Name through their dreams, which they tell every man to his neighbor, just as their fathers have forgotten my Name for Baal;** (the Lord)

Forgot your NAME?... for who, Baal?...who is Baal?

Do you really want truth? The word Baal simply means, **"LORD"** as is shown in any Bible Dictionary. Unger's Bible Dictionary, for instance, under the subject **"Lord"** on page 665 says:

"Lord" (Hebrew-Adon) an early word denoting ownership; hence, absolute control. It is not properly a (righteous) title...Master; of kings, as the lord of their subjects"

(4). **"Lord. Master,** (Greek Kurios) supreme..."

(5). Baal (master) (as noted above, it means lord) applied only to heathen deities (gods) or to man as husband, etc."

Unger also tells us, on the same page, "The Jews, out of superstitious reverence for the name YAHWEH, always in reading pronounce "Adonai" where YAHWEH is written." On page 413 of his Bible Dictionary Unger tells us:

"Baal – common Canaanite word for "**master, lord**" was one of the chief male deities of the Canaanite Pantheon, now well known for religious epic literature discovered at Ras Shamra (an Uqarit of the Amarna Letters) from 1921 – 1937.

The 1872 Edition of Smith's Bible Dictionary on pages 195 – 196 states (emphasis ours):

"The substitution of the word Lord is most sad; for while it in no way represents the meaning of the sacred NAME, the mind has constantly to guard against a confusion with its lower use and above all, the direct personal hearing of the NAME on the revelation of YAHWEH…is injuriously out of sight." (explanation taken from The Book of YAHWEH)

I used to say, "Oh, it's alright if I don't know or call Him by His real name. He knows what I mean, he knows my heart, He looks on the heart of men." He most certainly does. As a matter of fact, that is exactly how He is going to Judge us

Proverbs 20:27
"The spirit of man is the lamp of YAHWEH, searching all of his innermost being..."

According to what The Savior sent Yeremyah (Jeremiah) to warn us about, He also knows: **Yeremyah (Jeremiah) 17:9-10**
"The heart is deceitful above all things, and desperately wicked; who can know it? I YHWH search the heart, I test the mind, even to give every man according to his ways, and according to the fruit of his doing."

It sounds as though none of us can fool Him. If one's heart were truly fixed and determined to try and serve or honor HIM the CREATOR, why would we not go by His rules, His laws, His word, and look earnestly for His one and only Holy NAME that He has given for those whose desire is to be saved? Those are the ones who are truly looking for salvation. It is The Creator of the universe's first requirement. before we can even obey the Savior. **Matt. 22:37 "You must love YAHWEH with all your heart and all of your soul."**

This is the Creator of the entire universe's first rule, this was, and still is, his first rule, before any other books, religions, or gods were formed. We cannot get around that this is His law for salvation. Then YAHSHUA his son agrees with Him. He said He didn't come to change His laws, but to make it clearer. Establish it! Matt. 5:17-18

"Do not even think that I have come to destroy the law or the Prophets; I have not come to destroy them, but to establish them. For truly I say: Unless heaven and earth pass away, one yodh – the smallest of the letters – will in no way pass from the law until all things are perfected."

I really don't know how he could make his laws any clearer than that. Still, there are those who will say, "oh, I don't need to worry about all of that proper NAME stuff. He has many NAMES."

That understanding is not according to any of the original writings in the Holy Scripture. And oh, what a serious error! The Scripture plainly states, even the ones that we consider not the best translations, they even plainly say, "There is NO OTHER NAME! NO OTHER NAME that we could call to get to the Creator of the world and be saved by, but the NAME that was given to our MESIAH by YAHWEH, YAHSHUA MESSIAH. The name itself means, MY FATHER IS SALVATION.

Acts 4:12

"Neither is there salvation in any other NAME for there is NO OTHER NAME under heaven given among men by which we must be saved."

Every prophet that He sent to redeem us back, from gods and lords and masters, to himself said the exact same thing. Before he was even born the Malak (Angel) told us why we should call HIM YAHSHUA MESSIAH...

Luke 1:31-33 (The Book of YAHWEH)

"And behold you will conceive in your womb and bring forth a son, and will call his NAME, YAHSHUA. He will be great and will be called the son of YAHWEH; and Father YAHWEH will give him the throne of his father David. And He will reign over the house of Yaaqob (Jacob) forever: and of HIS KINGSHIP there will be no end."

Shaul (Paul) the Apostle also concurs with Kepha (Peter) and the rest of the Scripture by reporting to us, under the unction of the Holy

Spirit, saying: **Philippians 2:9, "Because of this, YAHWEH also has highly exalted HIM and given HIM a NAME which is above EVERY NAME."**

Now wait a minute, did Paul just say this NAME was above some names? Or did he say it was above most names? What I heard the Holy Spirit say was that this NAME was above EVERY NAME! Also,

(10). **That in the NAME of YAHSHUA, every knee in heaven or on earth or under the earth, must bow.**

(11). **And EVERY tongue must confess that YAHSHUA is KING to the glory of YAHWEH the FATHER.**

Mankind has continuously searched and searched and searched for a special religion or that One Special Name, trying to replace the original NAME of the Savior, and a name that could save mankind, but with no success. There are many, many religions, with names, names, names, that each of them will swear they have found the one that can get them to the Creator and save the world. Yet the Holy Scripture will not change. It continues to admonish and warn us, that there is now and never will be NO OTHER NAME. (Acts 4:12)

So isn't it time that we just accept what the Creator of the World has said and be saved? It doesn't look like He is going to change His rules any time soon. He has not done so in over 2000 years. **Yaaqob** (James) **4:12**

"There is one lawgiver, who is able to save and to destroy –YAHWEH – who are you who condemns another?"

WATCH AND WAIT

People, you must watch and wait prayerfully, while you are expecting your salvation or your change, or the Savior to come, or some people will say, more clearly, the new system of things. It would be indeed another terrible error for those who are expecting to be delivered or saved, to enter in without truly watching. Watch! Watch, with the expectation of Him certainly coming back, for He is surely on His way. There are those who would say, "How can we be expecting Him when no man knows the day or the hour?"

That understanding, or misunderstanding, could be the worse misconception of all times. And that may be a disaster for some people who do not know how to truly watch for the Savior of the world. This precept is concerning The Savior Savior. He said in

Luke 12:
**(55). And when you see the wind blows from the South, you say;
there will be heat, and it come to pass.**

**(56). Hypocrites! You can discern the face of the sky and the
earth, but why is it that you do not discern this time?**

The devil would love for you to think that you had all the time in the world to get right with the Savior of the world and use the excuse of "no man can tell the day or the hour." But everyone who has been truly watching for the true Savior of the world, YAHSHUA MESSIAH, like the Scripture instructed, and has not been blinded by the gods of this world, already knows he is at the door. (II Cor.4:3)

"In the same way, when you see all these things, know that His coming and the end of the age is near, at the very door."

He personally warned us of his coming back, and also what would happen to those who would not watch for him, in what He revealed to Yahchanan (John) on the Isle of Patmos. He wants us to know. He said in **Revelation 3:**

(1) "For if you will not watch, I will come on you as a thief, and you WILL NOT KNOW what hour I come upon you."

(2) Be watchful and strengthen the things, which remains that are ready to die; for I have not found your work perfect before YAHWEH.

(3) Remember, therefore how you have received and heard, hold fast, and repent. For if you will NOT watch, I WILL come on you as a thief and you WILL NOT know when I have come on you.

Most of us have listened to vain ministers and false teachers babble on and on and just assumed they were telling the truth based upon the Scriptures for most of our lives. And that is also our fault. We should have gotten in touch with the Spirit of Truth for ourselves. Honestly! However, most of those false prophets will quote I Thess. 5:2 when they are trying to make the point of "**nobody knows the day nor the hour.**" And it will sound correct, if you don't read it all. Especially if you have never studied seriously the end time prophecy where the Savior has said **in Matt. 24:**

(11). And many false prophets will rise and will deceive many.

(12). And because iniquity (the breaking of YAHWEH'S laws) will abound, the love of many will grow cold.

(13). But he who endures until the end, the same will be saved.

(14). And this message of the kingdom will be preached to the whole world, by the one who bears witness to all nations AND THEN THE END WILL COME.

However, it does sound right, if you would just isolate that verse of **Thess. 5:2** because it certainly does say:

"For yourselves know perfectly that the day of YAHWEH so comes as a thief in the night."

That Scripture would certainly be acceptable and clear to say, "**We just cannot tell when he is coming back**" to anyone who read that verse alone, and was in a hurry to get back to his worldly events and then business as usual. It would be perfectly acceptable and clear.

However, that is only part of the precept. That is certainly not watching. But to the ones who has been watching honestly for the Savior's return, examining the whole message, know that we are not in darkness that they should come upon us like a thief. How could it, if you have been watching as he told you to do? And on top of that, he told us to: **Rev.3:3,**

"Remember, therefore, how ye have received and heard, and hold fast and repent. For if you WILL NOT WATCH, I WILL come on you like a thief and you WILL NOT KNOW what hour I come upon you.

Do you see the difference between those who are seriously and honestly searching and waiting for the MESSIAH because he has told them to, and of his return from those who may be just waiting for, who knows? Paul said in:

I Thess. 5:

(1). **But concerning the times and the seasons brother YOU have no need that I should write to you!**

(5). **YOU are all children of the light, and children of the day; we are not of the night, nor of darkness."**

Let us just go all the way back to the 4th verse and read the Scripture in tact, and let the Savior explain clearly to us the same thing He told Paul:

(4). **But you, brothers, are not in darkness, so that this day would overtake you like a thief.**

(5). **You are children of the light, and the children of the day. We are not of the night, nor of darkness.**

(6). **Therefore, let us not sleep as others do; but let us watch and be sober.**

Notice the difference now, in those who will just join some organization or the other for their own personal reasons rather than honestly seeking the kingdom of YAHWEH? As do the children of light. The Savior is not trying to sneak up on anybody. He told us exactly that he is coming and that he is at the door.

THIS IS WHAT FATHER YAHWEH SAYS

"Return" to Me! And I will return to you!" Zec. 1: 3 (The Book of
YAHWEH)"

Yeremyah (Jeremiah) **23:13,**
"I have seen folly (offense) **in the Prophet of Samaria- They
prophesied by Baal** (the lord)**; and caused my people to err (go
astray);"**

Yeah, but the majority of the people say!...........
Did you know that the majority is usually wrong? And that the Holy
Scriptures had already warned us to: **Matt. 7:13,**
    **"Enter in through the narrow gate; for wide is the gate and broad
is the way that leads to destruction, and many are those who go that
way.**
    **(14). Because straight is the gate, and narrow is the way which
leads to life, and few there are who find it."**
    The whole world today, is now starting to look for sure and right direc-
tions. They are looking for leaders who know for sure, right from wrong.
The world is looking for leaders who will act on honest facts, and will give
them the truth as the Creator of the universe gives it. Leaders who will not
be swayed just because of even popular opinions on matters. The world
wants leaders, now days, which will stand up, prove, direct and tell the
truth, the whole truth, and nothing but the truth, from the Savior of the
world's standpoint, no matter what or whom it contradicts?
    Mankind as a whole, has now, just about reached the conclusion that
something that we have been doing is wrong! They may not know exactly

what it is, but the world does know that something is definitely wrong with society's business as usual approach to life. And is it! The truth is, what is wrong with the world is we have all been deceived by the devil, as sad as it is to say. However, this was no surprise to the Creator of the world. And if mankind had seriously humbled themselves, to the true Scripture's warnings, it would not have been a surprise to us either. **Rev.12:9,**

"And the great dragon was cast out, that old Serpent called the Devil and Satan, who deceives the whole world. She was cast out into the earth, and her Angels were cast out with her.

(10). **And I heard a loud voice saying in Heaven: Now is come salvation and strength and knowledge of our Father and the power of Messiah: for the accuser of our brothers is cast down, who accused them before our Father day and night.**

(11). **And they overcame her by the blood of the lamb and by the word of their testimony** (the Law and the Prophets) **and they loved not their lives unto death.**

(12). **Therefore, rejoice you heavens and you who dwell in them! Woe to the inhabitants of the earth and of the sea! For the devil is come down unto you, having great wrath because she knows she has, but a short time."**

Matt. 7:15,

"Beware of the false prophet who come to you in sheep's clothing, but inwardly they are ravening wolves."

One should never depend solely upon what a majority says for any decision concerning righteousness and salvation, but rather, what the Creator of the world has said. We should personally search the Scripture, and depend on the Holy Spirit exclusively, and His admonishments over and above everything and anybody, no matter how many there are that may be saying the same thing, if it is opposite to the Holy Scripture. Actually, the world for the most part, has spent too much time already, listening to teacher and preachers that has mistranslated Bibles, tickling our ears. This is also no surprise to the Savior of mankind. This is what Father YAH-WEH says about it:

"Turn to me, and I will return to you." (Zec. 1:3)

II Tim. 4:3,
"For the time will come when they will not endure sound doctrine; but after their own lust they will heap to themselves teachers who will tickle their ears. (Tell them what they want to hear).

Zecharyah (Zechariah) 1:2

"YAHWEH has been exceedingly angry with your fathers.
(3). Therefore, say to them; this is what YAHWEH of host says! Turn to me, says YAHWEH of host: and I will return to you says YAHWEH of host.

He said this to convince them with YAHWEH's judgments, that they should not provoke him as their fathers had whom YAHWEH grievously punished.

(4). Do not be like your fathers unto whom the former Prophets have cried out saying: This is what YAHWEH of host says! Turn away now from your evil ways, and your evil doings. But they would not listen, nor pay attention to Me, says YAHWEH.

(5). Your fathers, where are they now? And the prophets, do they live forever?

(6). But My words and my laws, which I command through my servants the prophets, did not they overtake your fathers? So they returned and said, just as YAHWEH of host determined to do to us, according to our ways and our doings, so has he dealt with us."

YAHWEH says that these men were astonished by His judgment against them, but they were not moved to true repentance. The world today should be moved by now to true repentance before time runs out, and return to YAHWEH.

GET RIGHT CHURCH AND LET'S GO HOME!

With this admonishment, the Savior of the world and Creator of heaven and earth is asking and warning the Church and the entire world to get right Church and let's go home. No! The Church is not right today! But we all, can now, get right! Today!

We have now, finally, the greatest opportunity in the history of mankind, to make sure, who the Savior of the world is, His name, His laws, and receive the Creator of heaven and earth and get right with Him and all go home. Because this dispensation is just about to close. The Savior Himself made all of this possible; just for the last days on earth, by launching the EPHAH, (the standard of perfection) which was sent by YAHWEH's Law.

Zecharyah (Zechariah) 5:6,

"**And I asked: what is it? And he answered; this is the ephah** (the standard of perfection), **which is sent by YAHWEH's Laws. Then he added; this is honor, knowledge, and understanding throughout the whole earth.**"

The Creator of the world has sent to us, just like He promised He would do, the two witnesses with the Standard of Perfection that will enlighten every man who is interested about His true Scriptures. And they are showing us the deception that was caused by false teachings. He has also warned us of all of the events that was prophesied and must take place in the last days on earth, just before He returns to gather his elect.

Revelation 11:

"**And I will give to my two witnesses to perform their prophetic office, and they will foretell events about the three and one half years,** those cast about with darkness.

(4). These are, as it were the two olive trees, and as it were, the two lamps (of the seven lamp stands) ministering for the Father in the earth.

Isayah (Isaiah) 44:

(1) Yet now hear, O Yaaqob (Jacob) My servant, and Yisrayl (Israel) whom I have chosen;

(2) This is what YAHWEH says, who made you and formed you from the womb, who will help you: Do not be afraid, Yaaqob (Jacob) My servant and Yeshurun (beloved Israel); whom I have appointed.

The heavenly Father has chosen, a long time ago, His two witnesses for the last days to give all mankind one last chance for eternal life, by preaching and teaching the only way to salvation. This message will be preached to all nations, and tribes, and languages, and people right before he comes and sets all things in order. In the eight verse He continues confirming this revelation of exactly who He was talking to and what they were sent to do in the last days of this man's government by man. He specifically says:

"O Yaaqob (Jacob) and Yisrayl (Israel)" two brothers from one womb:

(8). Have not I told you from that time, and have declared it? You are my witness.

Notice the Savior even starts the conversation with, "Hear O Yaaqob My servant and Yisrayl, whom I have chosen! You are my witness."

It was prophesied long, long ago, that again, there would be this powerful Holy Spirit preaching and teaching on the earth, for every one that is looking for the true and only way to eternal life. And they, the two witnesses, are preaching and teaching right now, as we speak, on the earth!

Revelation 14:6-7

(6). And I saw another Malak (Angel) fly in the midst of heaven, having the everlasting message to preach to those who dwell on earth – to every nation, and tribe and language and people

(7) Saying with a loud voice; reverence YAHWEH and give

glory to Him: for the hour of his judgment is come! And worship Him who made heaven and earth, and the sea and the fountains of water.

Isn't it amazing and doesn't it make you curious, that from the beginning of The Book, all the way to the end of The Book, Book 1 and Book 2, that He is so extremely passionate, and keeps on insisting and demanding that HIS NAME, HIS NAME, HIS NAME, not be forgotten but declared on earth? And separated from Baalim! (Acts 12:23/ Romans 9:17) Have you ever had the desire to seriously search out, just who is Baalim? And Elohim (El)? He has warned us that one day,

Hosheyah (Hosea) 2:

(16). And it will be in that day, says YAHWEH: that you will call me Ishi (my husband) **and will no longer call me Baal** (my lord);

(17). For I will take away the names of Baalim (the lords, gods, elohim and goddesses); **out of her mouth, and their names will no longer be called upon!**

(18). And in that day I will establish My Covenant for them with the animals of the field, and with the birds of the sky and with the creeping things on the ground; and I will break the bow (strength) **of the sword, and abolish battle equipment from the earth to make them lie down safely.**

(19). I will betroth you to me forever; yes I will betroth you to me in righteousness, in judgment, in loving kindness and in mercy.

(21). In that day I will respond, says YAHWEH: I will respond to the heavens, and they will respond to the earth;

(20). I will betroth you to me in faithfulness, and you will KNOW YAHWEH...

Did you hear HIS promise? And you may already know that way before men decided to name **THE BOOK** the Bible, it was always simply called **THE BOOK, BOOK 1 & BOOK 2,** or did you? That is all the Messiah preached from. **THE BOOK, BOOK 1:** Let us listen to Luke for a moment: **Luke 4:16,**

Then He went to Nazareth, where He had been brought up; and as His custom was, He went into the Synagogue on the Sabbath Day,

and He stood up in order to read.

(17). And handed Him was THE BOOK of the Prophet Isayah (Isaiah). When He had opened THE BOOK, He found the place where it is written:

(18). The Spirit of YAHWEH is upon me, because He has anointed Me to preach glad tidings to the poor: He has sent Me to heal the broken hearted, to preach deliverance to the captives, and recovering of sight to the blind, and to set at liberty those who are oppressed.

Yeremyah (Jeremiah) 23:13 tells us what YAHWEH said:
"I have seen folly (offense) in the Prophets of Samaria – they prophesied by Baal (the lord): and caused my people to err go astray"

The Creator of the world says, he has seen a lot of foolishness in the land through some of the ministers, preachers, and teachers. They prophesy in the name of the lord, and gods and goddesses and all kinds of man made religious names and caused His people to err. The world has gone astray because of this continuous folly (foolishness). He wants mankind to return to Him, YAHWEH, and be saved. He wants mankind to live by his laws that the preachers are telling us the savior got rid of.

However, His laws are the only way to bring peace to the world. So He is saying, return to YAHWEH. In YAHWEH's Holy Scripture, . He has ordained a law that by the mouth of two or more witnesses, let everything He said be established. He has sent prophet after prophet to remind us of this. (II Cor.13:1, Matt. 18:16, Deut. 17:6 Deut. 19:15)

Shaul (Paul) the Apostle echoed His demand by saying:
"Prove all things; hold on to that which is good!" (I Thess. 5:21).

Then long before Shaul (Paul) YAHWEH has been warning mankind that we have erred in turning to the Canaanite and Phoenigan deities. Yeremyah (Jeremiah) warned us again, of what YAHWEH said:

Yeremyah (Jeremiah) 23:

(25). I have heard what the prophets say; who prophesy lies in my name, saying, I have a dream! I have a dream!

(26). How long will this be in the heart of the prophets who prophesy lies? Yes they are prophets of the deceit of their own minds;

(27). Who devise (plan and scheme); **to cause my people to forget My Name through their dreams, which they tell every man to his neighbor, just as their fathers have forgotten My Name for Baal** (lord);

For hundreds of years, YAHWEH has been telling mankind through the prophets in His Holy Scriptures that we have erred, and have gotten separated from the Savior and His laws, but he wants us to have eternal life by the only way it can be obtained. By returning to Him. **Acts 4:12, "Neither is there salvation in any other, for there is no other Name under heaven given among men by which we must be saved."**

By following the Creator of the universe's rules is the only way to be saved; the same rules that His Son Yahshua (Jesus) Messiah established for us through obedience and death on the cross. Yahshua (Jesus) and his Father YAHWEH are in perfect agreement. Even Yahshua's Name means exactly what his Father is, salvation. It means **"My Father is Salvation."**

Romans 7:
(12). Therefore the law is holy, and the commandments are holy, and just and righteous.

The Scripture has also warned mankind that there would come a time when man would kill other men and think that they are doing their God a favor. And that is true. The problem, though, with being obedient to that thought is, you should first know who their god is; and his requirements, and his end. The truth of the matter is, you really must know what a god (elohim) is, and who Father YAHWEH is, before you can ever be safe from deception. That is a must. Or you could be snared (trapped). (Exodus 23:33)

All of the Apostles and the Prophets has explained this to us explicitly in the original text, way before man ever started using the pagan title of lords and gods (elohim). As a matter of fact, the Creator of the universe admonished the children of Israyl (Israel) upon leaving Egypt to make sure that they did not get involved and mixed up in the worship of lords and gods over in the land that he was giving to them, or they would be snared and turn away from Him. This is the very reason we got separated from the Creator of the world. They started listening to gods, even after Yahweh had warned them against this practice (The Book of YAHWEH) **Exodus 20:**

{1} and YAHWEH spoke all these words, saying:

(2). I am YAHWEH, your Heavenly Father, who brought you out of the Land of Egypt, out of the house of bondage.

(3). You shall have no hinder gods (elohim) at all. They are in opposition against me.

YAHWEH IS NOT A GOD

Another deception Satan spreads among men is that YAHWEH is just another, or one of many, gods. By this false doctrine, Satan has deceived many and equalized herself with YAHWEH in the eyes of the world.

Many people today even believe Satan is mightier than YAHWEH, and openly raise up groups to call upon Satan to help them gain riches. This has been accomplished because deceived man thinks YAHWEH is just a god among many gods:

Exodus 20:3, (KJV) "Thou shalt have no other gods before me.

Exodus 20:3 is part of the first commandment of The Ten Commandments. The word, which has been translated "other" in the King James Version, is the Hebrew word, **"acher"**, and means **"hinder,"** or those left behind.

YAHWEH commanded His people not to worship the gods they left behind in Egypt. The word "**other**" was deliberately placed in the King James Version to deceive man into thinking YAHWEH is just another god.

In the days of Mosheh (Moses) the Egyptians worshipped every god know to man. Jewish writings say the names of the gods were written in a book. Jewish writings also say the Egyptian Priest could not find the Name of YAHWEH in that book.

The word "**el**", which has been translated into English as **God,** was never a title for YAHWEH in the days of Mosheh (Moses).

It was only after the Israylites (Israelites) moved into the land of Canaan that the title, "**El,**" was accepted by the Israylite (Israelites) to identify our Heavenly Father.

In the original and up to the days of Yashua Ben Nun, this title "**El,**" was not applied to YAHWEH by the followers of YAHWEH.

In the days of Mosheh (Moses), YAHWEH was never known nor identified as **El, Elohim, or God**. YAHWEH commanded Mosheh (Moses) in **Exodus 20:3, "You shall have no hinder Gods** (elohim) **at all, in opposition against me.**

YAHWEH brought Israyl (Israel) out of Egypt where all the gods were worshipped and He said to the Children of Israyl (Israel**), "Leave the Gods alone! I am YAHWEH your Heavenly Father, your guide and your protector! I am all you will ever need!"**

The truth is not hidden. All the Apostles and Prophets have explained this clearly, even in mistranslated Bibles. The whole world does worship some god or other. The Apostle Shaul (Paul) explained this reason once that, **"The god of this world has blinded those"**

Those who?

Those who have never, for the most part, heard the true Scripture from the Father of all mankind, and the Father of Heaven and Earth. Those who have not seriously humbled themselves to study and simply do not know how the early translators and scribes manipulated the Holy Scriptures to hide the Creator of Heaven and Earth's Name.

Not only did they change His feast days, changed His laws, but they did the worse things that could ever have happened to separate man from the Creator; Changed His Sabbath Day! In reality, this was done by those who were led by the gods (elohim) of this world; And now deception has effected basically the whole world, according to the Scriptures. **Rev. 12:9.**

II Cor.4:3

"But if our message is hidden, it is hidden to those who are lost. (4). For the gods (elohim) **of this world** (led by Satan) **have blinded the minds of those who do not believe, so that the light of the message of the glory of Messiah, who is the image of YAHWEH** (God) **should not shine unto them.**

The first thing the world needs to search out or ask is, "how did we ever get separated from the Creator of man?" And search it out to your own honest satisfaction. There is a world of difference between Gods (elohim) and The Holy Father of heaven and earth; the Father of light and all creation. Paul explains:

I Cor. 8:5,

"For even though there are many called gods (elohim) whether in heaven or in earth, as there are many gods; (elohim) and many lords (Baalim);

(6). Yet to us there is only one Authority; The Father from whom all things came, and for whom we live. And there is but one King Yahshua Messiah, on whose account are all things, and on whose account we live.

(7). However, not all possess this knowledge, but some throughout all their lives until now, accustomed to the worship of gods (elohim) still eat that which is offered to gods (elohim). And because of this lack of this knowledge, they are defiled.

It is not strange though, people, that the whole world shares in the same belief, same conduct, and the same worship of elohim (gods). Because in reality they are the same; deceived! The world has been deceived. This is also no surprise to the Holy Father of creation, YAHWEH. He warned men of this coming deception long before it happened:

Rev. 12:9,

"And the great dragon was cast out, that old Serpent, called the Devil and Satan who deceives the whole world. She was cast out into the earth and her angels were cast out with her."

The Savior is now and has been trying for decades, to warn mankind, and to turn this god worshipping world back to His laws and to Him, through his Holy Prophets, and His Holy Spirit.

II Cor. 4:

(3). But if our message is hidden, it is hidden to those who are lost.

(4). For the gods (elohim) of this world (led by Satan) have blinded the minds of those who do not believe, so that the light of the message of the glory of Messiah, who is the image of YAHWEH, should not shine unto them.

Even with these great warnings, deceived ministers are still deceiving people that every thing is all right because the Savior got rid of the law. In spite of what the Savior said about all this.

---

(17). Do not even think that I have come to destroy the law or the Prophets; I have not come to destroy them, but to establish them.

(18). For truly I say unto you; unless heaven and earth passes away, one yodh – the smallest of the letters- will in no way pass from he law, until all things are perfected.

The King James Version of the Bible, which is the most trusted of all, by Christians, has added even more confusion to an already chaotic situation, like most other Bibles do, when he added to its many mistranslated verses that the Savior abolished the law. It read in **Ephesians 2:15** (KJV) **"Having abolished in His flesh the enmity, Even the law of commandments contained in ordinance"**

However, that is far from what the Holy Scriptures originally said or meant. The Hebrew Scrolls has never said the law has been done away with. Shaul (Paul) or none of the other Apostles or Prophets has ever said that. If you would ever investigate the true Scripture translations, you would find that what it really said originally before men added to His law was:

Ephesians 2: (The Book of YAHWEH)

(13). But now in Yahshua Messiah, you that were once far off, have been brought near through the blood of Messiah.

(14). For He is our Peace, who has made both one, and has broken down the dividing wall separating us.

(15). Abolishing the enmity: THE HATRED, AND THE OPPOSITION, to the law, the commandments and ordinances, through his own flesh, in order to create in Himself one new man from the two; making peace.

There is a world of difference between abolishing the law and the commandments, and abolishing the enmity and opposition to the law of the commandments. These are just a few of the little trick and mistranslations that the translators tired; sometimes leaving out only one word. Like in this case, "Opposition."

Verse 2:15-16, The Anchor Bible, Volume 34, pages 290-291 shows that Yahshua Messiah, through his sacrifice, did not abolish the law of YAHWEH, but rather he abolished these two things:

1. Any reason man might have to hate the laws of YAHWEH.
2. The hatred of the different races for one another.

Actually, it is a disgusting and shameful thing to see the Scriptures that were designed to bring us salvation being manipulated like that by the translators. And just as disgusting a sight to the true Creator of heaven and earth to witness is people witnessing and worshipping today, and claiming it is by the Holy Spirit, yet call on some god!

Long ago men left YAHWEH for Baal (lords) and changed His feast days, His laws, His Name, and His Sabbath Day. They also changed the way The Savior ordained that they should worship Him. They have even refused to use His Name anymore. And the world, for the most part, in their worship, has not returned to Him. The world much prefers the traditions of men to YAHWEH's rules.

Amosyah (Amos) **5:** brought a message from **YAHWEH. It said:**

(21). I hate; I despise your feast days! I take no delight in your own appointed assemblies!

(22). Though you offer Me burnt offerings and your grain offerings, I will not accept them, nor will I regard the peace offering of your fatted calves.

(23). Remove from me the noise of your songs! I will not listen to the melody of your stringed instruments.

(24). But let justice run down like waters, and righteousness like a mighty stream.

(25). WAS IT TO ME! You brought sacrifices and offering in the wilderness forty years, O house of Israyl (Israel).

(26). Instead you have lifted up the idolatrous temple of Molech; your god (El) and Chiun , your star-god (El); Saturn, the star of your god (El) which you made for yourselves.

Does this sound like he is happy with those gods (elohim) you made for yourselves, which you have lifted up? This is some of the tradition that goes on every Sunday in those buildings and worship services that has nothing to do with Him or His appointed feast days. The world today is just continually following the traditions of men.

He asked a very simple question in the 25th verse of this chapter; He asked, **"Was it me, YAHWEH, you called on?"** He doesn't seem to think it is cute. He said, **"It was your star god you called, that you** made for yourself."

Plus as far as the Savior abolishing the law for worship, Yahshua Messiah (Jesus) said:

Mattithyah (Matthew) **5:**

(17). **Do not even think that I have come to destroy the law or the prophets; I have not come to destroy them, but to establish them.**

(18). **For truly I say to you; unless heaven and earth passes away, not one yodh- the smallest of the letters- will in no way pass from the law until all things are perfected.**

Eph.2:15-16

Verse 2:15-16 – The Anchor Bible, volume 34, pages 290-291 shows that Yahshua Messiah through his sacrifice did not abolish the laws of YAHWEH but rather, he abolished two things:

1. Any reason man might have to hate the laws of YAHWEH
2. The hatred the different races have for one another.

KNOW THIS ALSO

II Tim. 3:

(1). Know this also; that in the last days perilous (dangerous) **times will come.**

(2). For (because) **men will be lovers of themselves, covetous, boaster, proud, blasphemers, disobedient to parents, unthankful, UNHOLY.**

The Creator of the world is Holy, and we must be Holy, if we ever expect to see Him. It is the only way we could ever be accepted into eternal life. According to the Scripture, **"Without holiness we can not see the Creator of the world."** (Heb. 12:14)

There is another very sad misconception in the world today, due to the deliberate mistranslation of the Scriptures. This one could mean the difference between eternal life and condemnation. However, the mistake the world makes today is that it does not know the difference between godliness and holiness. The Savior and Creator of the world has never been godly whatsoever. He has always been Holy. There is a world and an eternal life difference between godliness and Holiness. The King James Version of this oration reads that fifth verse like this: **11 Tim. 3.**

(5). Having a form of godliness but denying the power thereof, from such turn away.

It is explained clearly in the Holy Scriptures that the world does have a form of righteousness, or of being saved, but are not. They are religious (godly) but they are not Holy! Because they deny the only Authority of Holiness and Salvation. To be Holy .one must honor and live by the laws of YAHWEH and not the man made laws of man. It is definitely not godliness that will save the world; for Yahweh is not just another one of the gods. The Holy Scriptures have shown mankind over and over again that it only Holiness that can save you, through the only Creator of heaven and earth, who is also Holy.

"For His Laws are holy just and righteous" {Romans 7:12}

"Without Holiness, you simply cannot see the Savior." Heb.12:14 (The Book of YAHWEH).

I Cor. 8: (The Book of YAHWEH)

(5). For even though there are many called gods (elohim) **whether in heaven or on earth** (as there are many gods and many lords: Baalim).

(6). Yet to us there is only one AUTHORITY, THE FATHER from whom all things came and for whom we live. And there is one KING YAHSHUA MESSIAH on whose account are all things, and on whose account we live. However, not all possess this knowledge. But some throughout all their lives until now, accustomed to the worship of gods (elohim), **still eat that which is offered to gods** (elohim). **And because of this lack of knowledge, they are defiled.**

The worship of any gods (elohim) will defile you; According to the Scriptures and the Holy laws for they are in opposition to Yahweh's laws. It is a law of salvation that you must worship Father YAHWEH and him only. **Deut.10:20**

"You shall revere YAHWEH your Father, and serve Him, hold fast to Him and take your oaths in His Name.

Romans 7:12,

"Therefore the law is holy and the commandments are holy, and just, and righteous.

We can fully depend on YAHWEH who inspired the original Scriptures to bring anyone who obeys His inspired words to eternal life. It is very easy to prove the reliability of the words of our Creator, but what about the changes that have been made in today's translations of the Bible?

What will you do about the mistranslations, additions, and subtractions from the original Holy Scriptures, when the facts of the truth are brought to you? One of the facts of truth is told to us in the story of Yahshua (Jesus) talking to the Samaritan woman:

Yahchanan (John) 4:

(19). The woman said to Him: Man, I see that you are a prophet.

(20). Our fathers worshipped on this mountain, but you Yahdim (Jews) say that in Yerusalem (Jerusalem) is the place where men ought to worship.

(21). Yahshua (Jesus) said to her: Woman, believe me: the hour comes when you will WORSHIP THE FATHER NEITHER ON THIS MOUNTAIN, NOR IN YERUSALEM (Jerusalem).

(22). YOU DO NOT KNOW WHAT YOU WORSHIP; we know what we worship, for salvation is of the Yahdim (Jews).

(23). But the hour comes, and now is , when the TRUE WORSHIPPERS WILL WORSHIP THE FATHER IN SPIRIT AND IN TRUTH: for the FATHER seeks, just such worshippers to worship Him.

(24) YAHWEH is a Spirit, and those who worship him must WORSHIP HIM IN SPIRIT AND IN TRUTH.

(25) The woman said to Him; I know that the Messiah comes, and when He comes, He will tell us all things.

(26). Yahshua (Jesus) said to her: I am He speaking to you.

The fact of the truth is that salvation is for the true worshippers who worship the Father in Spirit and in Truth! Many deceived people say, "It doesn't make any difference just as long as we believe." Many deceived chaplain and preachers have said, "The House of Yahweh is correct in proclaiming that YAHWEH is the Father, but (they say in the same sentence) it is just as good to worship in the Name of the Lord."

DOES IT MAKE ANY DIFFERENCE?

The Samaritan woman Yashua (Jesus) was speaking to was a God worshipper. Yahshua (Jesus) said to that God worshipper, "You know not what you worship." So it definitely does make a difference, if you want eternal life!

Yahchanan (John) 4:10,
"Yashua (Jesus) answered and said to her: If you know the gift of YAHWEH, and who it is that says to you; 'give me a drink,' you would have asked Him instead and HE WOULD HAVE GIVEN YOU LIVING WATER.

If the Samaritan woman had worshipped YAHWEH, He would have given her the way to eternal life, but she could not receive it through her way of worship. Yahshua (Jesus) showed us that this makes an eternal life of difference. The whole world today is like the Samaritan woman. They do not know what they worship because our Heavenly Father's Name has been forgotten.

The whole deceived world worships Gods and Lords. In the majority of the churches, you will hear the phrases, "Praise God, or Praise the Lord." The reason we can safely say they are deceived is because they do not know who these gods and lords are, or they would not be worshipping with those names.

Webster's Dictionary says the word God means, **"Any of various beings, a person or a thing."** If God means various beings, then God can also mean Satan or demons.

DOES CHAGING THE LAWS OF THE HOLY SCRIPTURES GIVE MAN THE MARK OF THE BEAST?

People of America and all over the world, this will help anyone who is not already completely reprobate. And I trust that you are not. You cannot just pick what you want to hear and do, and still go into eternal life with the Savior. Which is, by the way, coming very soon. This is the world's problem. I know that all the major religions want to believe that they are the chosen one of the Creator. But remember the Book of Revelation was written to show YAHWEH's (God) servants and prophets concerning things that must come to pass. History shows us clearly that these religions changed YAHWEH's Sabbaths, His Name and His laws and it was no surprise to Him. You cannot change the Creator of mankind's Name, rules and days and still say you worship the Savior. He is the Savior.

Isayah (Isaiah) 24:
(5). The earth is also defiled under the inhabitants of it, because they have trespassed the law, changed the ordinances, and broken the everlasting Covenant.
(6). Because of this the curse has devoured the earth, and they who dwell therein are desolate; therefore, the inhabitants of the earth are burned and few men left.

There is a book, written by the two messengers (witnesses). Yes, they are on the earth today, right now, and they are preaching and teaching right now from Abilene, Texas in the House of Yahweh. They have made copies of various reference sources and put them in a book called, The Mark of the Beast, volumes 1 & 2. The Sabbath, Every Question Answered. And it is free, from "The House of YAHWEH." It will prove exactly which day is the true Heavenly Father's Sabbath Day to any one who is honest and serious enough to check it out.

The Catholic Church changed YAHWEH's feast and Holy days and they admit it! And the rest of the churches and halls, and congregations go along with this. Everybody knows this, even the lying preachers! Therefore, they are all deceived and have nothing at this time but the mark of the Beast, being rebellious. Basically, the whole world today, all worship and agree with this Beastly System. Wake up! Once you change His Name and His laws, you are not worshipping the Savior. You and Him are not in agreement.

Exodus 31:

(12). **And YAHWEH spoke to Mosheh** (Moses) **saying;**

(13). **Speak to the Children of Israyl** (Israel) **saying; Surely my Sabbaths you shall keep, for they are a Sign** (agreement) **between you and Me throughout your generations, that you may know that I am YAHWEH who sanctifies you, and makes you Holy.**

Can you see it yet? Or do you rather agree with the Beast, 666? The Pope whom the world and all congregations has agreed with, have the Name and Number of the Beast, the lying Whore, written on his Vesture. Some people have never even seen that, but it is not hid. Therefore, here is all you can expect if you rather worship the beast:

Revelation 14:

(10). **The same will drink of the wine of the wrath of YAHWEH, which is poured out without dilution into the cup of his indignation. And he will BE tormented with fire and brim stone in the presence of the Holy Malakim** (angels) **and the presence of the Lamb.**

(11). **And the smoke of their torment ascends up forever and ever. And they have NO SABBATH night and day, who WORSHIP THE BEAST and his likeness, and whoever receives the Mark of his name.**

Exodus 20:
"Remember the Sabbath to keep it Holy."

It is the worse thing you could do and the worse sin you could commit, to take the fourth commandment out and follow the rules of the great whore that sits on seven hills. It is an un-forgivable Sin! If we do not repent

Hebrews 10:

(26). **For if we sin willfully, after we have received the knowledge of the truth, there no longer remains a sacrifice for our sins.**

(27). **But a certain fearful expectation of judgment, and fiery indignation which will devour the adversaries.**

However, we who trust the Savior through the Scriptures will just believe Him rather than our religion; and just enter his rest that He spoke of, on a certain day. (Heb. 4: 1-7)

Hebrews 10:

(21). **And having a High Priest over the House of YAHWEH: Yahshua Messiah {Jesus)**

(16). **This is the Covenant that I will renew with them after those days, says YAHWEH: I will put my laws in their hearts and in their minds and I will write them**

(17). **Then He says: Their sins and iniquities I will remember no more.**

THE TRUE DEFINITION OF A MAN

MEN, LOVE
MEN, ARE STRONG
MEN ARE COMP~SSIONATE
MEN, ARE PATIENT
MEN, ARE FAIR, AND LOOKS FOR JUSTICE AS IN ALL
SITUATIONS MEN, ARE LEADERS
MEN, ARE ORGANIZERS IN RIGHTEOUS
MEN, DON'T GO ALONG WITH WRONG
MEN, WILL STAND ALONE AND SPEAK TRUTH WHEN
IT IS NOT POPULAR IF IT'S TRUTH
MEN, WILL NOT LET WRONG DOMINATE THEM
MEN, ARE CONSIDERATE OF THE WHOLE PICTURE
MEN, LOVE RIGHT
MEN, HATE WRONG
MEN, ARE DEDICATED
MEN, WILL NOT BE A CROSS OUT ARTIST
MEN, WILL BE THE FIRST TO SAY, I MIGHT HAVE MADE
A MISTAKE. MEN, ADD TO THEIR LEARNING DAILY
MEN, WILL BE THE HEAD OF HIS FAMILY
MEN, WILL NOT LEAVE HIS FUTURE AND FAMILY UP
TO CHANCE
MEN, Will assert themselves
MEN, ARE NOT AFRAID TO LOOK FOR TRUTH
MEN, ARE ALL OF THAT AND MORE
MEN, ARE RESPONSIBLE
MEN, WILL INSIST ON QUALIFYING HIMSELF FOR
SOMETHING

MEN, ALL REAL MEN,WILL RESPECT THE CREATOR OF HIM

MEN, GIVE RESPECT AND INSIST ON RESPECT FOR THEMSELVES

MEN, WILL INSIST UPON GETTING UNDERSTANDING BEFORE GOING OFF HALF COCKED.

WHY DID GOD MAKE ME BLACK?

Lord. why, did you make me black? Why did you make me someone the world wants to hold back? Black is the color of dirty clothes... The color of grimy hands and feet... Black is the color of darkness the color of tired beaten streets!

Why did you give me thick lips? a broad nose and kinky hair, Why did you make me someone who receives the hated stare?...Black is the color of bruised eyes, when someone gets hurt Black is the color of soot, black is the color of dirt!

How come my bone structures is so thick? my lips and cheeks so high how come my eyes are brown and not the Color of day sky?

Why do people think I'm useless? how come I feel so .used? why do people see my skin and think I should be abused?

Lord I just don't understand, what it is a bout my skin Why do some people want to hate me, not knowing the person within? Black is what people are listed, when people wants them away, black is the color of shadows east, black is the end of the day

Lord you know my own people mistreat me, and I know this just ain't right, they don't like my hair they say that I'm too dark or too light

Lord don't you think it's time, for you to make a change? Why don't you re-do your creation, and make everyone the same?

THE CREATOR'S ANSWER

Why did I make you black? Why did I make you black? Get off your knees and look around, tell me what you see...I didn't make you in the image of darkness I made you in the image of ME!

I made you the color of coal, which beautiful diamonds are formed, made you the color of oil, the black gold that keeps people warm

I made you from the rich dark earth, that grows the feed you need, your color is the same as the black stallion a majestic animal is he

All the colors of the heavenly rainbow can be found through out the nations, when all these colors were blended, you became my greatest creation

Your hair is the texture of lambs wool, such a humble little creation is he, I am the Shepard who watches them, the one who will watch over thee.

You are the color of midnight sky, I put the star's glitter in your eye, there is a smile hidden behind your pain, that's' why your cheeks are high

You are the color of dark. skies. formed when, I send my strongest weather, I made your lips so full, so when you kiss the one you love they will remember

Your stature is strong your bone structure thick to withstand the burden of time, the reflection you see in the mirror is the reflection of MINE!

One of the things we have always complained and seem to be quite baffled about is, the lack of respect we may not have received from main stream America or from maybe other races. That seems., to be a favorite crutch of ours to acknowledge how the system did' nt let us do this or that. Or how some individual didn't show us the kindness we wanted. They just won't show us no respect. And most times, that is probably true

However, it is high time that we face one definite fact. That is, respect and consideration is really never free or automatic and unconditional. It is usually granted by some action or the other, present or past. Usually the only people that are going to receive respect almost certainly, is the people that act in a manner that it is hard to deny them benevolence

It is just going to be hard for any intelligent person, black or white or what ever color to give a person automatic unwarranted respect when his actions is that of an idiot.

On the other hand, when ones actions. ,. reputation present or past is thought to be one of intelligence, or if one believes you may be a respect deserving being no matter what color you are, any reasonable person is normally reluctant or very hesitant in disrespecting you first. They will probably try and put on their best manners in front of you if 'they think that you are mannerly or obviously deserving of some kind of respect.

So we may need to give up on trying to receive those honors without giving it or earning it first. Through the years human nature just have not bought that idea.